ALI SM

Contemporary Critical Perspectives

Series Editors: Jeannette Baxter, Peter Childs, Sebastian Groes and Sean Matthews

Guides in the *Contemporary Critical Perspectives* series provide companions to reading and studying major contemporary authors. They include new critical essays combining textual readings, cultural analysis and discussion of key critical and theoretical issues in a clear, accessible style. Each guide also includes a preface by a major contemporary writer, a new interview with the author, discussion of film and TV adaptation and guidance on further reading.

Titles in the series include:

J. G. Ballard edited by Jeannette Baxter
Ian McEwan edited by Sebastian Groes
Kazuo Ishiguro edited by Sean Matthews and Sebastian Groes
Julian Barnes edited by Sebastian Groes and Peter Childs
Sarah Waters edited by Kaye Mitchell
Salman Rushdie edited by Robert Eaglestone and Martin McQuillan
Andrea Levy edited by Jeannette Baxter and David James
Ali Smith edited by Monica Germanà and Emily Horton

ALI SMITH

Contemporary Critical Perspectives

Edited by
Monica Germanà and Emily Horton

BLOOMSBURY

LONDON • NEW DELHI • NEW YORK • SYDNEY

Bloomsbury Academic

An imprint of Bloomsbury Publishing Plc

50 Bedford Square	1385 Broadway
London	New York
WC1B 3DP	NY 10018
UK	USA

www.bloomsbury.com

Bloomsbury is a registered trade mark of Bloomsbury Publishing Plc

First published 2013
Reprinted 2013

British Library Cataloguing-in-Publication Data
A catalogue record for this book is available from the British Library.

ISBN: HB:	978-1-4411-5760-7
PB:	978-1-4411-0518-9
ePDF:	978-1-4411-5990-8
ePub:	978-1-4411-8155-8

Library of Congress Cataloging-in-Publication Data
Ali Smith : contemporary critical perspectives / edited by
Monica Germanà and Emily Horton.
pages cm. – (Contemporary Critical Perspectives)
Includes bibliographical references and index.
ISBN 978-1-4411-0518-9 (pbk.) – ISBN 978-1-4411-5760-7 (hardcover) –
ISBN 978-1-4411-5990-8 (pdf) – ISBN 978-1-4411-8155-8 (epub)
1. Smith, Ali, 1962—Criticism and interpretation.   I. Germanà, Monica,
editor of compilation.   II. Horton, Emily, editor of compilation.
PR6069.M4213Z54   2013
823'.914–dc23
2013008915

Typeset by Newgen Imaging Systems Pvt Ltd, Chennai, India
Printed and bound in Great Britain

Contents

Foreword

Marina Warner

Siste viator – Stay a while, wayfarer – used to be incised into tombstones, on the Appian Way in Rome, for instance: the dead were calling out from their burial place to the living, and asked them to pause and listen.

Sometimes the spirit demanding witness was a child, and this haunted imperative, voiced by the spirit of someone long vanished through the stone, and asking for the attention of the casual passer-by, resonates with the idea of literature itself, especially when it is fiction or poetry written in the voice of characters who are given breath, existence, and presence – acoustic vitality above all – by the writer. Such epitaphs speak as if their subject were still alive, while their hauntedness is intensified because their words often remember the circumstances of their death. Like the voices that rise from *Hotel World*, these inscriptions tell a story that can disturb as well as fascinate, and their speakers refuse to be silenced in the grave:

'Stop now, wayfarer, but do not search deeply lest I be the cause of sorrow' warns one young girl, inviting us to want to know more.

The writer as stenographer, as secretary of her characters, as taking dictation from the beings in the book and passing them on down a live wire – these are the roles that Ali Smith takes up in her multi-vocal stories and novels, with marvellously fine-tuned wit, invention and exhilaration.

The classical scholar Florence Dupont, in her book, *The Invention of Literature* (1999), writes that literature was always created to resist death and bring back the dead as if they were still there, able to communicate. Margaret Atwood, who is one of several important figures in Ali Smith's writers' pantheon, puts forward a similar idea in her series of lectures, *Negotiating with the Dead* (2003). There she puts forward the 'hypothesis . . . that not just some, but *all* writing of the narrative kind, and perhaps all writing, is motivated, deep down, by a fear of and a fascination with mortality – by a desire to make the risky trip to the Underworld, and to bring something or someone back from the dead.' This is also the quest for *le temps perdu*, as Marcel Proust put it, which is literature's attempt to reanimate those who have gone before, are absent, or are simply phantoms in the magic lantern of desire.

Fiction is a dance of the dead; but also, in its dance, a conjuration against lifelessness. Before the printing press and mass literacy, texts existed as blueprints for performances, recitals, speeches, songs, and other forms of oral communication. The written down object was an archival tool, a record, a subordinate to the main endeavour, which was to give voice – and with voice, life – to absent friends. This approach isn't culture-bound. In the thrilling ghost story, *Kwaidan*, written after a Japanese folk tale by Lafcadio Hearn, a monk is summoned every night to play and sing to a gathering of ghosts; they flock around him to listen, and he sings to them of their past and their great deeds, just as Homer stages the descent of Odysseus into the Underworld, where he meets Achilles and Agamemnon and other heroes and heroines of his own poem. They meet the possibility of their eternity through the Homeric poems – and it has come about, for they do still live. As does Ovid, who ends his great work, *Metamorphoses,* with the single defiant word, *'vivam',* I shall live. And his stories, the characters in them, do live again in contemporary variations – Ali Smith was inspired by the tale of Iphis from Ovid's book, to write her characteristically irrepressible and incisive love story, *Girl meets boy* (2007).

Alongside poems which were recited aloud, sometimes accompanied by a harp, there were tragedies played by actors on a stage, funeral orations and political diatribes, prayers and incantations, hymns and love ditties, nursery rhymes and ballads, snatches and catches . . . the repertory is rich, it is ancient, and it is also as modern as James Joyce's ventriloquy and Kurt Schwitters' madcap *Ursonate* – and as Ali Smith's kinetic prose. Ali Smith takes what she wants from all these forms, and more – she is a writer who skilfully moves between voices and modes and genres while keeping a picture of the whole story she is telling, and the rich aural fabric of her narratives reminds me of the composers, John Cage and Steve Reich, who listen in to the soundscape of the world out there and carry it home until it becomes, for us, for their audience, a universe inside our minds. The characters in *The Accidental* (2005), *There but for the* (2011) and in any number of the marvellous, inventive short stories, similarly pluck language from the atmosphere of their habitat and circumstances and it becomes transmuted into their personal linguistic, emotional, psychological inscape, the hum of their innermost thoughts. The vitality of her writing quickens the scene, and resists absolutely that condition of literature that conspires with death.

Ali Smith's imagination has inscape rather than landscape, the interior scene flowing from her characters' perceptions outwards onto their surroundings: they transfigure them. Amber, the mysterious radioactive core of *The Accidental*, creates shinings of different colours and brightness to spread around her, while Magnus the brother of Astrid, the child at the heart of the book, sees a darkness closing in like the edges of vision when losing consciousness. The effect is metaphysical, like a seventeenth-century love poem, and the sensuous chromatics are so tightly spun into the physical fabric of the story that certain scenes strike at the reader's body as if the words on the page were material. Love of different kinds and degrees fills the Aliverse; she is brave – and unusually among contemporary writers – in her belief in it, and it beams out to take hold of the reader.

This strong emotional current flows in counterpoint to sharp wit, wordplay and bravura stylistics. The voices she captures are sprightly and melancholy, jagged and mellifluous; she has a devilish ear for cliché conversation, as in the sustained comic horror of the dinner party in *There but for the*. Children young and not so young matter very much to Smith, and she raises them to full consciousness, through patterns of nonsense, riddles, counting out and skipping rhymes. There are layers of lore in the playfulness, sayings and proverbs from her Scottish background, and from her huge, happy appetite for songs and films. In this too, she makes word music. Rarely, too, has a writer shown such ingenuity with pronouns, most especially in relation to their markers of gender. The texture of her erotic world gains richness and pleasure from unsettling premises about the characters' sex; such shape-shifters transfuse the stories and the novels with their unpredictable energy.

But possibly Ali Smith's most particular innovation is the attention she pays to tiny parts of speech, how she presses prepositions and definite articles to reveal their depths: each one a life, each one a loaded gun. Since Virginia Woolf began *A Room of One's Own* (1929) with 'But . . .' there has not been another writer who can make a little do so much.

To leave the emphasis falling on these aspects chiefly of style – interior, private, sensuous, psychological and grammatical – would miss, however, another important dynamic in the fiction: Smith's sense of the present as history in the making, happening now. At the Edinburgh World Writers Conference in 2012, she made a passionate and witty contribution to the debate about 'style vs content?', and declared 'Style is never not content . . . More, style proves not just individual human existence, but communal existence.' Accordingly, she has her ears and her eyes wide open for the larger communal scene in which her stories are taking place. She can give a pyrotechnical retrospective of a certain year or decade – through headlines, film plots, pop songs – but in an era of costume drama and history as re-enactment, it is immensely refreshing to read a writer who is not afraid to take on how people experience contemporary politics, socio-economics and value systems. However, we are always made to see these concerns and to feel them from the inside – from a spare bedroom, from a dumb waiter or through the viewfinder of the video camera that Astrid uses to chronicle her days until Amber throws it off a motorway bridge.

Ali Smith's imaginative fiction gives us all of us hope for literature now, for she remembers what writing can do but is often diverted from doing – by a dozen different contemporary pressures; she is a bold and independent experimentalist and has won a large, loyal and popular following. Her fiction also quests, through the intimate study of her characters and their feelings, to reinvigorate the important things that matter to life, grappling with the meaning of love and loss without shying away.

Series Editors' Preface

The readership for contemporary fiction has never been greater. The explosion of reading groups and literary blogs, of university courses and school curricula, and even the apparent rude health of the literary marketplace, indicate an ever-growing appetite for new work, for writing which responds to the complex, changing and challenging times in which we live. At the same time, readers seem evermore eager to engage in conversations about their reading, to devour the review pages, to pack the sessions at literary festivals and author events. Reading is an increasingly social activity, as we seek to share and refine our experience of the book, to clarify and extend our understanding.

It is this tremendous enthusiasm for contemporary fiction to which the *Contemporary Critical Perspectives* series responds. Our ambition in these volumes is to offer readers of current fiction a comprehensive critical account of each author's work, presenting original, specially commissioned analyses of all aspects of their career, from a variety of different angles and approaches, as well as directions towards further reading and research. Our brief to the contributors was to be scholarly, to draw on the latest thinking about narrative, or philosophy, or psychology, indeed whatever seemed to them most significant in drawing out the meanings and force of the texts in question, but also to focus closely on the words on the page, the stories and scenarios and forms which all of us meet first when we open a book. We insisted that these essays be accessible to that mythical beast, the Common Reader, who might just as readily be spotted at the Lowdham Book Festival as in a college seminar. In this way, we hope to have presented critical assessments of our writers in such a way as to contribute something to both of those environments, and also to have done something to bring together the important qualities of each of them.

Jeannette Baxter, Peter Childs,
Sebastian Groes and Sean Matthews

Acknowledgements

Special thanks are due to Marina Warner, whose Foreword offers a significant fellow author's perspective on the intertextual creativity that is Ali Smith's oeuvre, in particular in relation to her engagement with myth, fantasy and the spectral. We would also like to thank her agent, Cara Jones, at Rogers, Coleridge and White Literary Agency.

Likewise, we would like to offer our thanks to Dame Gillian Beer for agreeing to interview Smith for this collection. We also especially thank Merete Alfsen for offering us her insider's insight on the project of translating Smith's works into Norwegian.

We are grateful to our series editors, Sebastian Groes (Roehampton University), Jeannette Baxter (Anglia Ruskin University) and Sean Matthews (University of Nottingham), and to our consultant series editor, Peter Childs (University of Gloucestershire), for the advice given throughout the development of this collection. We also owe special thanks to Bloomsbury's Senior Commissioning Editor for Literary Studies, David Avital, and Editorial Assistant, Laura Murray, for their continued support and patience with us in the long process of putting together this wonderful collection.

We are indebted to Lucienne Loh (University of Liverpool) and David James (Queen Mary's College, University of London), who were incredibly helpful in offering guidance in bringing together this great ensemble of scholars, and Simon Avery and Alex Warwick (University of Westminster), who deserve special thanks for supporting the development of this book.

Last but not least, we are immensely grateful to Ali Smith for her enthusiastic and continuous support of this project.

MG/EH
Westminster/Brunel, November 2012

Contributors

Merete Alfsen has been a literary translator for 25 years. Her list of about 80 titles include books by Jane Austen, Virginia Woolf, Margaret Atwood, Alice Munro, Eudora Welty, Jeanette Winterson and A. S. Byatt, most recently *The Childrens' Book* and *Ragnarok*. She has translated seven of Ali Smith's books into Norwegian, most recently *There but for the*.

Dame Gillian Beer was the King Edward VII Professor of English Literature at the University of Cambridge. In recent years she has been the Andrew W. Mellon Senior Fellow at the Yale Center for British Art. Among her books are *George Eliot* (1986), *Arguing with the Past* (1988), *Darwin's Plots* (1983, 2000, 2009), *Open Fields: Science in Cultural Encounter* (1996), and *Virginia Woolf: The Common Ground* (1996). She is completing a book provisionally called *Alice in Space* for Chicago University Press and her collected and annotated edition of Lewis Carroll's poems, *Jabberwocky*, came out from Penguin in 2012.

Ian Blyth is a member of the Editorial Board for the Cambridge Edition of the Works of Virginia Woolf, for which he is co-editing *Orlando* (with Suzanne Raitt). His published works include *Hélène Cixous: Live Theory* (Continuum, 2004), and various articles on Woolf and others. He is one of the organizers of StAnza, Scotland's International Poetry Festival.

Mark Currie is Professor of Contemporary Literature at Queen Mary, University of London. He is the author of *The Unexpected: Narrative Temporality and the Philosophy of Surprise* (Edinburgh University Press, 2013) and *About Time: Narrative, Fiction and the Philosophy of Time* (Edinburgh University Press, 2007), both of which explore issues in narrative time. His other publications include *The Invention of Deconstruction* (Palgrave, 2013), *Postmodern Narrative Theory* (Palgrave, 1997 and 2011), *Difference* (Routledge, 2004) and *Metafiction* (Longman, 1995).

Monica Germanà is Senior Lecturer in English Literature and Creative Writing at the University of Westminster. Her research interests and publications concentrate on contemporary British literature, with a specific emphasis on the Gothic, women's writing and Scottish literature. Her first monograph, *Scottish Women's Gothic and Fantastic Writing* was published by Edinburgh University Press in 2010. She has also edited a special issue of *Gothic Studies* (November 2011) on contemporary Scottish Gothic and is currently working on a new book on Bond Girls.

Dominic Head is Professor of Modern English Literature at the University of Nottingham. His books include *The Cambridge Introduction to Modern British Fiction, 1950–2000* (Cambridge, 2002), *Ian McEwan* (Manchester, 2007), *The State of the Novel* (Wiley-Blackwell, 2008) and *The Cambridge Introduction to J. M. Coetzee* (Cambridge, 2009). He edited *The Cambridge Guide to Literature in English*, Third Edition (Cambridge, 2006), and is currently working on a new book entitled *Modernity and the Rural English Novel* (Cambridge, forthcoming).

Emily Horton is a visiting lecturer in English Literature at Brunel University. Her research interests include contemporary British and American fiction, specializing in trauma fiction; contemporary genre and popular fiction; and contemporary explorations of globalization and cosmopolitanism. Her first monograph, *Contemporary Crisis Fictions*, is forthcoming with Palgrave. She is also currently co-editing a volume with Philip Tew and Leigh Wilson on *1980: A Decade in Contemporary Fiction* (Continuum, forthcoming in October 2013).

Stephen Levin is Associate Professor of English at Clark University, where he teaches courses in postcolonial and British literature, social theory and transnational cultural studies. His publications include a book, *The Contemporary Anglophone Travel Novel: The Aesthetics of Self-Fashioning in the Era of Globalization* (Routledge, 2008), and forthcoming articles on the fiction of Amit Chaudhuri, literary aesthetics and the history of the Booker Prize, and figures of everyday life in contemporary global fiction.

Kaye Mitchell teaches modern and contemporary literature at the University of Manchester, where she is Programme Director of the MA Contemporary Literature and Culture. She is the author of two books, *A. L. Kennedy* (Palgrave, 2007) and *Intention and Text: Towards an Intentionality of Literary Form* (Continuum, 2008), and editor of *Sarah Waters: Contemporary Critical Perspectives* (Bloomsbury, 2013). Current projects include a book on literary and theoretical engagements with shame since the 1990s.

Patrick O' Donnell is Professor of English and American Literature at Michigan State University; he is the author and editor of several books on modern and contemporary literature, most recently *The American Novel Now: Reading Contemporary American Fiction Since 1980* (Wiley-Blackwell, 2010). He currently has two books in progress on David Mitchell and on Henry James and contemporary cinema.

Ulrike Tancke has taught at Johannes Gutenberg-Universität Mainz (Germany), Lancaster University (UK) and Universität Trier (Germany), where she was awarded a PhD in English Literature in 2006. She has published a monograph on sixteenth-century women's life writing (*'Bethinke Thy Selfe' in Early Modern England: Writing Women's Identities*, Rodopi, 2010) as well as various articles on early modern literature and contemporary British fiction. In 2010/11 she held a Research Fellowship at the Centre for Contemporary Writing, Brunel University, United Kingdom, funded by DAAD (Deutscher Akademischer Austauschdienst/German Academic Exchange Service) to pursue her current research project, which focuses on violence and trauma in British novels around the Millennium.

Chronology of Ali Smith's Life

1962	Born in Inverness on 24 August to Don and Ann Smith.
1967–1974	Attends primary school at St Joseph's RC School.
1974–1980	Attends secondary school at Inverness High School. Teenage and early jobs: waitress, lettuce-cleaner, sandwich maker and packer, desk assistant in Inverness tourist office, receptionist at BBC Highland, advertising copywriter.
1980–1985	University of Aberdeen.
1982	First in year, joint English Literature and language, University of Aberdeen.
1984	Top first, University of Aberdeen Senior Honours English.
1984	Wins Bobby Aitken Memorial Prize for poetry, University of Aberdeen.
1985–1990	Newnham College, University of Cambridge.
1986	Play *Stalemate* (Trouble and Strife) produced at the Edinburgh Fringe.
1988	Play *The Dance* (Better Half) produced at the Edinburgh Fringe.
1989	Play *Trace of Arc* (Smug Cat) produced at the Edinburgh Fringe.
1990	Plays *Amazons* (Cambridge Footlights) and *Comic* (Smug Cat) produced at the Edinburgh Fringe.
1990–1992	Lectures at University of Strathclyde.
1992–2002	Fiction reviewer for *Scotsman*.
1994	Short story 'Text for the Day' wins Macallan Scotland on Sunday short story prize.
1995	Publication of debut short story collection *Free Love and Other Stories*.
1995	Awarded Saltire First Book of the Year Award for *Free Love and Other Stories*.
1997	Receives Scottish/Canadian exchange fellowship (Scottish Arts Council/Canada Council).
1997	Publication of *Like*.

1998	Receives Junior Creative Writing Fellowship, UEA.
1999	Publication of *Other Stories and Other Stories*.
2000	Publication of *Brilliant Careers: 100 Years of Women's Fiction* (Virago) (co-edited with Sarah Wood and Kasia Boddy).
2000	Editor of *Shorts 3: The Macallan/Scotland on Sunday Short Story Collection*.
2001	Teaches Creative Writing MA, spring semester at UEA.
2001	Publication of *Hotel World*.
2001	Awarded Encore Award, East England Arts Award, and the inaugural Scottish Arts Council Book of the Year Award for *Hotel World*.
2001	*Hotel World* shortlisted for Orange Prize for Fiction and Man Booker Prize for Fiction.
2003	Publication of *The Whole Story and Other Stories*.
2004	Radio play *State of the Art* produced by David Jackson Young.
2005	Publication of *The Accidental*.
2005	*The Accidental* shortlisted for Man Booker Prize, Orange Prize for Fiction, James Tait Black Memorial Prize, Scottish Arts Council Book of the Year.
2005	*The Accidental* winner of the Whitbread Novel of the Year Award.
2005	Radio play *Big Bed* produced by David Jackson Young.
2006	Publication of *The Seer*. Produced by Dogstar; the play premieres at the Inverness Spectrum Centre.
2007	Release of 'Half an Apple', performed by Trashcan Sinatras in the album *Ballads of the Book*.
2007	Publication of *Girl meets boy*.
2007	*Girl meets boy* winner of Sundial Scottish Arts Council Novel of the Year and *Diva* magazine reader's choice Book of the Year.
2007	Elected Fellow of the Royal Society of Literature.
2007	*Hotel World* adapted for the stage by Kidbrooke secondary school and performed at the Greenwich Theatre and the 2007 Edinburgh Fringe Festival.
2008	Radio play *The Switch* produced by David Jackson Young.
2008	Publication of *The Reader*, a collection of extracts from other writers' works.

2008   Publication of *The First Person and Other Stories.*

2011   Publication of *There but for the.*

2012   *There but for the* longlisted for the Orange Prize for Fiction, wins Hawthornden Prize and SMIT Scottish Fiction of the Year Award.

2012   Publication of *Artful*, the series of lectures in Comparative European Literature given in February and March as Weidenfeld Professor, St Anne's, Oxford University.

INTRODUCTION

MONICA GERMANÀ AND EMILY HORTON

In the beginning was the word, and the word was what made the difference between form and formlessness, which isn't to suggest that the relationship between form and formlessness isn't a kind of dialogue too, or that formlessness had no words, just to suggest that this particular word for some reason made a difference between them – one that started things.

(Smith, 2012, pp. 64–5)

[Ali Smith] likes to mess with your head – to jar and disorientate, to twist ideas out of their formal boundaries and make them crash around like irascible poltergeists.

(Myerson, 2012)

As the second epigraph, taken from a review of Ali Smith's latest publication, *Artful* (2012), poignantly puts it, reading Smith's work is an experience that will not leave the reader unchanged. Her idiosyncratic dedication to formal experimentation, captured in the words of her 'ghost-writer' in the above quotation from *Artful*, becomes a haunting addiction to her readers, making her one of the most distinctive contemporary writers. But the appeal of Smith's writing goes beyond the self-reflective language games Smith enjoys playing with her readers: her ethical and political preoccupations offer insightful critiques of the contemporary condition, touching on topics as diverse as globalization and technology, consumerism and gender norms.

Since the publication of her first collection of short stories, *Free Love and Other Stories* (1995), Smith's work has gradually positioned itself at the forefront of the late twentieth- and twenty-first-century British literary scene. Since the publication of *Free Love*, winner of the Scotland on Sunday/Macallan Prize and Saltire First Book Award, among other accolades, Smith has been shortlisted for both Orange and Booker prizes for *Hotel World* (2001), winner of the Whitbread Prize for fiction for *The Accidental* (2005), and shortlisted for the James Tait Black Memorial Prize for *There but for the* (2011); her writing has attracted enthusiastic reviews from authors such as Jeanette Winterson and Kate Atkinson, published internationally and translated into several languages. This collection promises to explore the *jouissance*, ebullience, subversiveness, playfulness, political forcefulness and eloquence which are Smith's writing, and to highlight her invaluable contribution to contemporary literature.

Commenting on Smith's play on the word 'cleverest' ('cleverist') in *There but for the* (2011), *Guardian* reviewer Alex Clarke observed: 'It's a label that can easily be applied to her creator, who has given us, once again, a novel that is playful, humorous, serious, profoundly clever and profoundly affecting' (Clarke, 2011). From the beginning of her writing career, Smith's earlier works (*Free Love*, *Like* (1997), *Other Stories*) emerge as playfully evocative stories of the unsaid, the unexpected, frequently unveiling the 'other' side of human existence and always resisting 'easy' closures. Pivoting on apparently ordinary events are the big issues that haunt postmodernity: the ineffability of language, the blurred boundaries between real and imagined worlds, the non-linearity of time, the instability of the self. Engaging with poststructuralist and postmodernist concerns with spectrality and the hyperreal, Smith's later novels (*Hotel World*, *The Accidental*) explore questions about authenticity, language and desire, displaying a distinctive engagement with such contemporary anxieties. More recently, Smith's work has continued to display preoccupations with the lack of authenticity and the changing values of an increasingly globalized twenty-first-century society (*The Seer* (2001), *There but for the*), while, simultaneously, celebrating the redemptive power of language and self-fashioning (*Girl meets boy* (2007b), *Artful*).

Born in Inverness, Scotland, in 1962, Smith identifies a childhood talent for rhyme as what first attracted her to writing: 'I found this out because we were given something to do at school; I could do it and I enjoyed it. So I wrote a set of little poems and gave them to my sister. That's when it started' (Higginbotham, 2012). More generally, Smith describes her upbringing as 'happy, secure', where despite her working-class background and five siblings, Smith's parents 'were adamant that all their children went to university' (Denes, 2003). Smith also credits these formative years for her flexible outlook on gender:

> With two brothers and two sisters, she almost felt she could choose which sex she wanted to be; she went for boy. On the other hand, she has a natural tendency to want to even things up, or at least to look at life from the opposite perspective. (Denes, 2003)

This latter concern is evident throughout Smith's writing, including her first collection of short stories, *Free Love*, which often creatively manipulates gender pronouns, as well as in *Girl meets boy*, in which she updates Ovid's myth of Iphis for modern times. In both of these works, Smith undermines conventional gender and sexual prejudices, embracing instead a perspective of gender fluidity and sexual open-mindedness.

Later, Smith attended the University of Aberdeen, where she was taught by Bernard MacLaverty, William McIlvanney and Iain Crichton Smith, and where the latter encouraged her to turn her attention to prose, explaining that this was where her real talent lay (see Smith's interview with Gillian Beer in this book). However, before beginning her professional career in writing, Smith followed a different path, embarking on a PhD at Cambridge University, in which she explored the works of James Joyce, Wallace Stevens and William Carlos Williams, and where she also met her long-term partner, Sarah Wood. The doctoral thesis fell through, due partly to the enormity of the task Smith had set herself; as she admits, 'modernism and joy in Irish and American literature' was just too big a subject (Denes, 2003). Following this, Smith turned her attention to university lecturing, at the University of Strathclyde, only then to leave this too, due to falling ill to chronic fatigue syndrome. She explains, 'I hated my job so much, when I was ill and came out of it and decided to leave, a lot of things got off my back. It took a long time of lying on my back for that to happen' (Gapper, 2003). In this way, illness appears to have helped Smith to begin her career in writing.

Saying this, Smith herself has always been wary of biographical readings of her work, and has explicitly resisted categorical pigeonholing as an inevitably reductive reading of writers and their works: 'I don't find labels at all helpful', she claimed in an early interview with Caroline Gonda, 'Where do you start and where do you stop? Scottish, lesbian, right-handed, Catholic, Invernesian . . . everything is relevant and none more relevant than the other' (Gonda, 1995, p. 5). Two aspects of Smith's background, in particular, exemplify the complex ways in which an author's 'real' experiences may be creatively negotiated in their writing: her Scottish heritage, especially in terms of her literary influences, and her lesbian sexuality, which despite reductively categorizing her texts as 'lesbian fiction', is also thematically important. Thus, on the one hand, Smith herself, and many of her readers, have often positioned her work in a tradition of Scottish (Gothic) writing, including such figures as James Hogg, Robert Louis Stevenson and Muriel Spark (Denes, 2003; Gapper, 2003; Germanà, 2010), which manipulates aspects of the uncanny, supernatural, and the spectral in order to disrupt, dismantle and overturn established approaches to the 'real'. On the other hand, this fascination with liminality, and the unstable boundaries of self, reflects Smith's wider preoccupations with desire, love and commitment as functioning outside accepted heteronormative structures of contemporary society, in ways which often astonish and confound those involved. Sara Wilby's mesmeric surprise on falling in love with the girl at the watch shop in *Hotel World* speaks to this, where the broken watch she has brought to be fixed reflects her own unexpectedly frozen experience of time. Likewise, in *The Accidental*, Amber's hairy

legs and unembarrassed sexuality disturb the repressed, bourgeois outlook of the Smarts, confronting them with their own unacknowledged
and hidden desires and fantasies. In this way, realist and non-realist
narrative conventions are combined to produce a larger nonconformist
vision to make apparent the ultimately multiple and often mysterious
dimensions of desire, and the nature of identity not as fixed but fluid
and unstable.

All of these concerns would appear to link Smith's work to the formal
and political preoccupations of postmodernism, and certainly her work
can be and has been read in this way. Emma Higginbotham describes
her novels as 'deliciously quirky postmodern' (Higginbotham, 2012)
and Nina Sankovitch calls *There but for the* 'a kind of postmodern ode
to life' (Sankovitch, 2011). More negatively, Raoul Eshelman identifies
Hotel World as a novel perhaps too dependent on postmodern tropes and
devices: '[T]he radical undecidability of the spatial, temporal and causal
relations, the author's superior, infinitely receding play with figures of
lack – these are all typical, well-established procedures of postmodernism' (Eshelman, 2004/2005). These readings, in different ways, highlight
Smith's questioning of overarching meta-narratives, her awareness to
language's fluidity and heterogeneous meaning, and her fascination
with liminal boundaries between reality and fiction, truth and lies.
Nevertheless, these readings depend of course on a certain idea of what
constitutes postmodernism, one associated generally with theorists
such as Lyotard, Lacan, Kristeva and Derrida, as well as writers such as
Italo Calvino, Angela Carter, Margaret Atwood, and Christine Brooke-
Rose, many of whom Smith herself has cited as influences (Denes, 2003).
Smith also invokes, at times, a Jamesonian or Baudrillardian element in
her work. Thus, while calling attention to the way in which '[l]anguage
and fiction give us how we could be, how we can be, it there's a realisa-
tion of other words, voices, structures' (C. Smith, 2007, p. 78), she also
admits to a certain political despondency, particularly in relation to the
disaffected, apathetic responses generated by the politics and aesthetics
of twenty-first-century media. When asked to comment on the 'inter-
face' between the fictional world of the characters in *The Accidental* and
the real world of readers, she notes:

> The interface notion is interesting because all of those characters have
> something between them and the world and questioning if that's a good
> thing or whether you should see, whether you actually see anything. When
> we look at a TV screen, do we actually see anything any more? (C. Smith,
> 2007, p. 78)

That Smith's view of the contemporary is informed by scepticism regarding global media culture is also equally visible in the surveillance architecture of the 'Global Hotel' in *Hotel World* and in the repeated forms of
hyperspace and non-place which run through her short stories. In this

sense, Smith's political and ethical engagement displays ambivalence towards the simulacral order of postmodern culture.

At other times, Smith's work reflects a Modernist sensibility, particularly in its concern for formal consciousness and experiment. In addition to her thesis on Joyce, Stevens, and Williams, Smith has also recognized the influence of W. B. Yeats, Virginia Woolf and Katherine Mansfield in her work (Denes, 2003; Marr, 2012). Thus, commenting on Woolf's influence in writing *Artful*, she explains, 'art is always about life-force and mortality', and in trying to get this message across through a set of lectures, it is Woolf's writing, as she 'stood up in Girton and Newnham in Cambridge in the late twenties and talked about *A Room of One's Own*, which has inspired her' (Marr, 2012). Likewise, Smith also speaks with passion about how Modernism 'broke everything up and everything could start all over again. So you could understand both reality and books from a new angle, a renewed angle' (Gapper, 2003). In this sense, in her view, Modernism defies the popular conformity in the contemporary: 'Though it's been canonized, it's never going to be main-stream' (Marr, 2012).

This Modernist influence, of course, also figures in Smith's short story writing. In an article on Katherine Mansfield, she writes:

> A brief glance at literary modernism and its aftermath reveals just some of the force of both her presence, and her importance . . . She wrote nearly 100 [stories], the strongest of which challenged and altered much in the nature and form of literary fiction of the modernist period and beyond. (Smith, 2007a)

Clearly Smith's own writing is indebted to Mansfield, in so far as she too has worked to promote and to reshape the short story tradition, adding to this her own brand of satire, experiment and wit. And Mansfield is one of the literary revenants that frequently return to haunt Smith's writing, as she does in *Artful*, the uncategorizable collection of creative critical essays on time, form, edge and 'on offer and reflection', which, while offering Smith's own insights into key ideas and figures from a wide spectrum of literary sources, in turn reflects on Smith's own practice. In the section on time, for instance, Mansfield stands, once again, to represent the short story, here defined by its strange relationship with time:

> The difference between the short story form and the novel form is to do, not with length, but with time. The short story will always be about brevity, '"The shortness of life! The shortness of life!"' (as one of Mansfield's characters in her story At the Bay can't help but exclaim). Because of this, the short story can do anything it likes with notions of time; it moves and works spatially regardless of whether it adheres to chronology or conventional plot. It is an elastic form; it can be as imagistic and achronological as it likes

and it will still hold its form. In this it emphasizes the momentousness of the moment. At the same time it deals in, and doesn't compromise on, the purely momentary nature of everything, both timeless *and* transient. (Smith, 2012, p. 29)

This tension between Modernist and postmodernist influences and identifications throughout Smith's work constitutes a central strand of discussion in this book, as contributors take their own views on what best describes Smith's expansive literary heritage. Repeatedly, contributors call attention to postmodern motifs, structures and influences in Smith's work, in particular in relation to linguistic self-consciousness, generic experiment, representations of time and subjectivity and narrative construction. Nevertheless, on the whole, these collected essays tend to challenge Smith's postmodern designation, highlighting her concern with ethics and notions of authenticity and materiality as extending her work beyond the dominant scepticism in the postmodern era, and positioning it in some ways as an extension of Modernism.

Focussing on the politics of space in Smith's short stories, Emily Horton's contribution interrogates postmodern or 'supermodern' interpretations of the author's work with regard to the alienating spaces of late capitalism: referring to Marc Augé's notions of 'supermodernity' and 'non-space', the chapter throws light on Smith's engagement with these concepts, while registering possibilities for individual agency displayed in the short stories.

The ambiguous politics of language, as detailed in the work of Hélène Cixous on a 'nonappropriating' affirmative economy, inform Ian Blyth's argument in the second chapter, which focuses on Smith's debut novel, *Like*. Here Smith's self-reflective concerns with language and wordplay highlight the novel's preoccupations with 'like', exploring the ways in which language can be used to elide or obscure actuality.

Blurring the boundaries of visible and invisible, Levin's chapter offers an insightful reading of the political function of spectrality in Smith's *Hotel World* and *The Accidental*. Placing particular emphasis on the subversive role of the spectre in two of Smith's major works, the chapter explicitly links the spectral motif in Smith's fiction with a mode of subaltern critique.

Continuing the exploration of Smith's *Hotel World* in a comparative analysis with her latest novel, *There but for the*, Mark Currie's chapter draws attention to the movement between philosophy and grammar in Smith's writing: as Smith's self-reflective deployment of linguistic metaphors casts light on both the philosophy of grammar and the grammar of philosophy, Currie argues that it also helps to define the method of a fictional enquiry into the comprehension of time.

The language of gender underpins Kaye Mitchell's essay on Smith's rewriting of Ovid's *Metamorphoses*, *Girl meets boy*: the chapter reads Smith's transposition of the myth of Iphis and Ianthe cogently arguing that the uses and the notion of metamorphosis, simultaneously pointing to the pivotal concepts of continuity and change, support a reading of Smith's work within the framework of post-identity politics.

In a comparative critical reading of a recurrent trope in Smith's fiction, Ulrike Tancke's contribution focuses on the disrupting arrival of an intruder in *The Accidental* and *There but for the*. The chapter reads Smith's resistance to closure in relation to what it reveals about readers' expectations, making apparent our refusal to acknowledge the uncomfortable realities of violence and desire concealed in human actions.

In a different mode, Patrick O'Donnell's chapter revisits the concept of the stranger in *Hotel World* and *The Accidental*, using Julia Kristeva's work to evaluate the representation of the foreign other in Smith's works. As O'Donnell would argue, what the cosmopolitan fabric of these novels points to is the way in which otherness is both disruptive and conducive to the construction of post-global identities.

Assessing the position of Smith's oeuvre in relation to the problematic context of prize culture and the notion of canonicity with regard to contemporary writing, Dominic Head's chapter reads Smith's major novels, *Hotel World, The Accidental, and There but for the*, pointing to her oblique use of satire to highlight a critique of vested interest. Such critique, Head suggests, implicitly identifies the dichotomy about value at the heart of the critique of the contemporary as, in some senses, Smith's central topic.

Concluding the critical overview of Smith's work, Germanà's chapter considers the intersections of language and desire in her analysis of Smith's *The Seer*. The play's self-reflective commentary on language exposes its ambiguity: language can manipulate people and their desire, but it can also, in its poetic function, fill the social vacuum left open by the postmodern condition, reasserting the importance of community and communication.

Complementing this collection of critical essays, the final sections in the book offer additional material to the scholars of contemporary fiction and, specifically, Smith's work. The reflective essay by Smith's Norwegian translator, Merete Alfsen, provides particular insight into the mechanics of Smith's use of language, highlighting the challenges it poses to the translator and her attempt to do justice to Smith's experimentalism and formal playfulness. Finally, Gillian Beer's interview with the author, while raising fresh ideas about Smith's works of fiction, also considers Smith's concerns with meaning, place, memory and time, as recently explored in *Artful*, which, Smith suggests, is framed by the paradoxes implicit in meaninglessness:

> The thing about meaninglessness is that it never stays meaninglessness for long, because we will make meaning of it. I mean, we will translate our meaninglessness. We are human beings; it's what we do. The character in *Artful* is . . . it's a great liberation for him or her to think there's no

meaning in the words. But even seeming meaninglessness is meaningful. (See INTERVIEW in this book, p. 150)

While seeking to engage with the complex meanings of Smith's fiction, we are confident that this pioneering collection of essays on Smith's work does not attempt to anchor the author's work to a singular mode of writing or literary tradition. Conversely, we hope that scholars approaching Smith's texts will find in this an invitation to explore her oeuvre further beyond the boundaries of this book.

CHAPTER ONE

Contemporary Space and Affective Ethics in Ali Smith's Short Stories

EMILY HORTON

Chapter Summary: This chapter explores the representation of space in Ali Smith's short story writing in relation to notions of spatial affect, phantasmagoria and affective ethics explored by such theorists as Steve Pile, Nigel Thrift, Gilles Deleuze and Felix Guattari. More generally, my aim in positioning Smith in this way is to challenge postmodern or 'supermodern' readings of her work in relation to a socially estranged and defunct late capitalist space. Against these readings, I highlight how her work instead confronts this very dilemma of a restrictive consumer and technological space by bringing into play 'supermodern' understandings of space reflective of Marc Augé's 'non-space', only then to disrupt this theoretical perspective by registering possibilities for agency and connectivity dismissed by Augé but made possible precisely through an affective reading of space.

Key words: affect, ethics, short story, space, supermodern

Even before her first novel, *Like* (1997), Ali Smith's debut short story collection *Free Love and Other Stories* (1995) won two literary prizes: the Saltire Society Scottish First Book of the Year Award and a Scottish Arts Council Award, thus making her well known as a short story writer. Subsequent collections: *Other Stories and Other Stories* (1999); *The Whole Story and Other Stories* (2003); and *First Person and Other Stories* (2008) have also drawn widespread attention both from academic and popular readers, winning her the Arts Foundation Award for short story writing in 2001, as well as largely positive reviews from such presses as *The Times Literary Supplement*, *The London Review of Books*, *The New York Times Book Review*, *The Guardian*, *The Scotsman*, and the *Atlantic Monthly*. Moreover, Smith has also edited collections and written introductions for other short story writers, including Katherine Mansfield, Margaret Tate and Tove Jansson, in this way making herself known as a spokeswoman for the genre. More generally her view of the short story sees this not as secondary to the novel but rather as a different but equally exciting genre, whose 'brevity [. . .] challenges aliveness with the certainty of mortality, and vice versa too', so that one of its most engaging features entails the celebration of its own form as 'a force and source of life' (Smith, 2009a).

In this chapter, I explore this life-enthusing dynamic of short stories in Smith's own writing, in relation to her short story representations of contemporary urban space. Thus, calling to attention contemporary society's consumer capitalist and global technology, in ways which at once elicit and qualify 'supermodern' readings of space, Smith stories, I argue, invoke simultaneously a critique and celebration of contemporary urban space, in such a way as to challenge the dominant theoretical pessimism regarding late capitalist relations. In other words, against the 'supermodern' idea of space as necessarily restrictive and disempowering – as contractualized by the consumer structures of late capitalist experience – Smith instead calls up the hidden psychic and affective possibilities latent within urban spaces, in this way making evident an alternative notion of immanent spatial becoming. This latter concept comes from Gilles Deleuze, in his spatial reading of postmodernism, and importantly it allows Smith an ethical outlook on space, an idea of community and situational awareness within supermodernity, which implicitly challenges the hegemony of critical cynicism.

To explain this, I want to look first at one postmodern theoretical account of space, put forward by Marc Augé, which I believe at once introduces but also ultimately contrasts Smith's vision. In his seminal work, *Non-Places: Introduction to an Anthropology of Supermodernity* (1995), Augé introduces space within contemporary culture as dominated by 'non-places' – supermarkets, highways, airports, malls, theme parks, heritage sites – which, by contrast to 'anthropological places', are not there to be lived in but rather 'passed through', experienced transitionally, as if 'measured in units of time' rather than space:

> Everything proceeds as if space had been trapped by time, as if there were no history other than the last forty-eight hours of news, as if each individual history were drawing its motives, its words and images, from the inexhaustible stock of an unending history in the present. (Augé, 2006, p. 105)

In other words, 'non-place', for Augé, is a code word for contemporary urbanity's rootlessness, which offers, in place of residence or respite, a spectacle of newness, anonymity and incessant passage. For Augé, this proffers a new understanding of identity within the present, as individuals become contractualized within the codes of everyday 'supermodernity':

> The passenger through non-place retrieves his identity only at Customs, at the tollbooth, at the check-out counter. Meanwhile, he obeys the same code

as others, receives the same messages, responds to the same entreaties. The space of non-place creates neither singular identity nor relations; only solitude, and similitude. (Augé, 2006, p. 103)

In effect, for Augé, supermodern 'non-place' introduces a paradox within contemporary identity, wherein despite the apparent ubiquity of individualized experience – 'at Customs, at the tollbooth, at the check-out counter' – selfhood remains preset, restricted to a limited body of social clichés. As Scott Barnett writes, 'non-place manages relations by constraining rhetorical agency and agent functions to largely uniform expressions, constituting transhistorical consumer subjects with ideological discourses expressive of late capitalism' (Barnett, 2005, p. 46).

In relation to Smith's short stories, this offers a useful starting point for analysis, where these too are concerned with the spaces of 'supermodern' culture and the forms of identity, responsibility and obligation that emerge from these. Indeed, identity in Smith's stories is often defined in relation to job title, as well as to the roles that characters play as consumers, clients, citizens or family members, often in direct connection to spaces that Augé calls 'non-places'. Thus, for example, Smith's short story 'Paradise' (*The Whole Story and Other Stories*, 2003) introduces characters conceived in terms of their employment: as night-shift manager at a fast-food restaurant and cruise assistant on a tourist boat. Likewise in 'Gothic' (*Whole Story*) the protagonist is a bookshop cashier; in 'No Exit' (*First Person and Other Stories*, 2008), a customer at the cinema; in 'The Definite Article' (2009), a corporate office worker; in 'The Child' (*First Person*), a shopper at Waitrose; in 'Present' (*First Person*), a customer at a pub; and in 'Being Quick' (*Whole Story*) and 'Okay So Far' (*Other Stories and Other Stories*, 1999), passengers on trains. These identities come accompanied by civic obligations, of employment, civility, or consumption, as I shall explore below. Even so, it is questionable in many cases how fitting Augé's reading of space is in relation to character identity or how relevant his purview of homogenization results. Thus, Smith's short stories, I argue, challenge Augé's 'supermodern' conception, disclosing a complex urbanity beyond 'non-place'.

Indeed, what is compelling in these stories in relation to Augé's argument is the primary importance they ascribe to space as a source of agency, a category which Augé finally dismisses as unavailable. Thus, Smith's short stories see agency as always *already* available, functioning not *despite* prevailing urban designators and obligations but to the contrary precisely because of these. Thus, in accordance with Steve Pile's vision of the contemporary city as alive with unactualized potential, which needs only to be activated and lived order to be made 'real' (Pile, 2005, p. 3), Smith remodels Augé's 'supermodern' conception in favour of a more fluid spatial vision, which recognizes the city's affective and utopic dimensions.

This can be seen initially in 'Gothic' (*Whole Story*), which crystallizes the affective territory explored by Smith in terms of space. Here, the narrator is initially 'cowed' by her employment in a bookshop, where her manager scolds her for 'not wearing the right kinds of clothes' and where her fellow employees resent her privilege in being given money to buy clothes (Smith, 2003, p. 16). From the start this situation affects her with a sense of boredom with her workplace and a feeling of estrangement from what she deems 'real life':

> People had died in the bookshop . . . My blouse was too tight under my arms . . . I'd been wondering again about leaving bookselling . . . I stood and wondered if there was anywhere in this city I would work where I wouldn't feel that while I was doing it life, real life, was happening more crucially, less sordidly, somewhere else. (Smith, 2003, pp. 17–19)

In fact, this concern with estrangement from 'real life' is common for many of Smith's characters, who often feel their employment denies them social authenticity. Thus, in 'Paradise' (*Whole Story*), for example, one character, a fast-food employee, reflects on how

> she wants a holiday. She wants some time in the sun . . . She wants to not to have to know that there are bits of food going round and round in the air-conditioning. She wants the last four years back. (Smith, 2003, p. 86)

Similarly, in 'The Art of Elsewhere' (2010), the narrator comments, 'I've been trying to go elsewhere all my life', and then proceeds to list the places that she has visited while 'still trying to get elsewhere'. Likewise, in 'The Unthinkable Happens to People Every Day' (*Free Love*, 1995), the plot turns on a journey of escape, in which a television employee (on a show which sensationalises 'everyday' trauma) leaves his employment to embark on a cross-UK road trip. Here, following an unexpected encounter with a young girl he meets on the trip, everyday life is transformed into narrative potential, as the protagonist comes to appreciate alternative possibilities offered by space. In this case, the girl invites him to sit on her parent's restaurant roof with her, so that they might throw rocks at the restaurant sign – a hobby of hers. His rock misses the sign, but it hits the nearby lake, provoking a response of glee from the girl: 'Yes! You did it! Nobody's ever done that before!' (Smith, 1995, p. 138). In this way, a simple encounter with a child and an unusual perspective on a familiar setting remodels the everyday into unimagined achievement.

In 'Gothic', the solution to this problem of estrangement emerges from another unexpected encounter, a situation of crisis which compels both reassessment and renewed agency. The story recalls the appearance, in a bookshop, of an anti-Semitic bookseller, whom the narrator, a cashier, identifies as a 'bigot' (Smith, 2003, p. 23), but whom she fails to expel from her bookshop on account of her timidity. In fact, the narrator stands paralysed as the anti-Semite recounts his Nazi conspiracy theory, unable to provoke herself to renounce his racist insinuations. Finally, the appearance of a fellow employee saves her, as the latter immediately ejects the man from the shop. However, the response of another customer, known as 'Toxic' (Smith, 2003, p. 18), indicates her failure of professional responsibility, where her timidity constitutes a form of ethical madness – 'Mad, he said. She's mad, man' (Smith, 2003, p. 24). In this way, the story considers the paradox of unrealized potential in an event in which, despite the narrator's position of power as an employee, she fails to see responsibility as other than conventional: a matter of rule following and obedience to norms. In contrast, the ending revises this outlook, affirming the narrator's engagement as a form of self-enablement. She reflects, 'I tell you. I'm ready. I stand at the counter behind the computers and I'm waiting' (pp. 25–6).

Thus, while Augé understands space as a rigid contractual framework, in which the individual is 'trapped' in a web of texts and images (Augé, 2006, p. 104), the narrator of 'Gothic' instead learns to appreciate spatial opportunities, coming to terms with the bookshop's latent agentive potential. In other words, she initially dismisses the possibility of change at the bookshop, seeing choice as restricted to obligation, and deriding the customers for their eccentric habits. Nevertheless, following this encounter with 'Toxic', she finally reassesses her situation and comes to see agency not as passive but rather active. She reflects, 'That was the day I decided to make No Smoking signs and stick them round the yellow walls. It almost caused an all-out war' (Smith, 2003, p. 25). More generally her shift in spatial perspective enables a change of agentive relations in which she comes to grips with her own capacity for assertive involvement. In this way, her move to the 'New Town', where she becomes ground-floor manager at another bookshop (Smith, 2003. p. 25), encapsulates a spatial epiphany, in which she is made aware of unrecognized prospects for agentive becoming.

One way of conceptualizing this can be taken from Steve Pile's psychoanalytic writing, which manipulates a concept of 'phantasmagoria' as a mode of spatial analysis.[1] Thus, for Pile, the city lends itself immediately to psychoanalytic reading, in so far as it presents itself as having 'a personality . . . a particular mood or sentiment' and also 'privileg[es] certain attitudes and forms of sociation [sic]' (Pile, 2005, p. 2). Pile continues:

> [P]hantasmagoria implies a particular mix of spaces and times: the ghost-like or dream-like procession of things in cities not only comes from all over the place (even from places that do not or will never exist), but it also evokes very different times (be they past, present, or future; be they remembered or imagined). (Pile, 2005, p. 3)

In other words, cities, for Pile, have the capacity to manipulate active agencies, whether of circulation or procession, working through (Pile,

2005, p. 21), or condensation and displacement (Pile, 2005: p. 27), which simulate the unconscious processes of urban inhabitants. Pile explores the city's own psychic potentials – its capacity for 'dream-work' (Pile, 2005, p. 21), a concept which he borrows from Benjamin, but updates to the contemporary (see Benjamin, 1999, pp. 388–404; Pile, 2005, pp. 50–8). Thus, 'dream-work', for Pile, encodes the city's latent psychic energies, which allow the city space to be feared, loved and awed, rather than merely inhabited, in this way contesting Augé's 'supermodern' idea of space as basically contractual. As Ayo Mansaray explains: 'In the same way that the psychoanalyst has to decode latent meanings of dreams through their manifest content and read beyond the surface, so too must the urban theorist' (Mansaray, 2007, p. 1). In this way, 'dream-work' offers Pile and, as I see it, Smith, also a tool for interrogating spatial agencies and contemplating how 'urbanites are as much dreamt by their cities as they dream within them' (Pile, 2005, p. 29).

In 'Gothic', this connects to the narrator's depressed view of her surroundings, where as I have argued, the bookshop initially simulates a form of deathtrap. Likewise, in 'No Exit' (*First Person*), affect underpins the narrative trajectory, where a 'locked room crisis' in a cinema motivates a re-examination of space and the fantastic/affective scenarios implicit within this. In this case, this concerns the narrator's shock in visiting the cinema, where she witnesses a woman exit through a fire door which she knows has no way out. The subsequent panic that ensues as she fails to act on this knowledge, and then returns home to agonize over her indecision all night, issues a distress in relation to agency. It is as if responsibility is (again) inaccessible, and even the awareness of personal obligation proves insufficient. In this way, Smith signals the possible breakdown of contemporary moral systems and the uncomfortable knowledge that spatial agency may be conscribed within late capitalism: the narrator sleeplessly frets that 'still' the woman may be in there without 'any lights on' (Smith, 2008, p. 111).

Even so, this story moves beyond a comment on bystander ethics in relation to the trapped woman, and in the second half changes direction to consider more fully the space of agency. Thus, what begins with a narrative of entrapment ends with a story of liberation, as the narrator's partner (or former partner) recounts to her a builder's escape from behind a wall of soundproofing. Here the narrative structure encodes the same 'locked room horror' as earlier and again the mode of suspense turns on catastrophe: the builder 'realises he is trapped between the two walls' and cannot escape (Smith, 2008, p. 117). Nevertheless, rather than accept this claustrophobic ending in passive concession to horror fatality and fall prey to the generic anxiety of spatial entrapment (encoded by a sly reference to 'film cliché' [Smith, 2008: p. 110]), the narrator instead invokes the builder's yet unactualized potential, in the form of an escape narrative that effectuates affective strength. Thus, the text reflects, 'he turns to the new wall and kicks it. It doesn't give. He kicks it. He kicks it and punches and throws himself against it until it makes a hole in the plasterboard. Then he rips his way out' (Smith, 2008, p. 117). Here, the builder's intensity of response (also evident in a similar scenario in 'I know something you don't know' [*First Person*]), encodes his spatial liberation; he is able to break down the walls because, simply, he recognizes an opportunity to demonstrate his own affective might.

In relation to the larger narrative, the narrator's reaction to this story reflects her own spatial empowerment, as she vows to 'call that cinema and threaten to report them if they haven't made that fire exit a real exit with a proper, easy, simple, push-down-bar way out' (Smith, 2008, p. 116). In this way the structure of the text reflects a process of personal discovery, as the narrator responds to and awakens to existing affective coordinates. Indeed, the order of the ending, where Smith positions the story *after* the narrator's pronouncement, as a reflection for the reader (Smith, 2008, p. 115), reiterates this sense of weightiness regarding affect. The text, in effect, elevates affect's importance as a mode of reading, in this way challenging the received assessment of spatial fixity.

In the writing of Deleuze and Guattari, this idea of affect as a mode of reading underpins a larger philosophy of reflexive ethics. As Guattari writes:

> [T]here is an ethical choice in favour of the richness of the possible, an ethics and politics of the virtual that decorporealises and deterritorializes contingency, linear causality and the pressure of circumstances and significations which besiege it . . . On a small scale, this redeployment can turn itself into a mode of entrapment, of impoverishment, indeed of catastrophe in neurosis . . . But it can also make use of other procedures that are more collective, more social, more political. (Guattari, 1995, p. 94; qtd. in Thrift, 2004, p. 68)

Smith's writing similarly introduces the importance of affect in *spatializing* ethics. Thus, if on the one hand, affect functions as a way of reading space in fiction and of recognizing a host of unregistered narrative possibilities, on the other hand, it also concerns the choices and actions of individual and collective agents who, without exhausting affect, answer to respective understandings of community involvement. As Deleuze and Guattari explain: 'Affects . . . go beyond the strength of those who undergo them': they enliven reality beyond the personal and entwine human and non-human agents collectively (Deleuze and Guattari, 1994, p. 164). The stories explored thus far already reveal this dynamic, as Smith's characters challenge uncivil and passive behaviours which threaten the community, including racism, indoctrination, apathy and uncritical thinking.

In 'Present' (*First Person*) and 'Being Quick' (*Whole Story*) likewise, collectivity is at the heart of both of these stories, where the spaces of contemporary technology threaten to obstruct caring. Indeed, these narratives arguably go beyond those we have explored thus far, depicting community as a necessary feature of utopic society. Thus, despite their focus on solitude as a fundamental aspect of contemporary experience, where again (as for Augé) agency is curtailed by consumer capitalism, community in these stories takes on a key role in shaping meaning, as it awakens the narrators to the importance of social involvement.

In 'Present', set in a small-town pub, the narrator is distracted by a nearby conversation in which a local resident (a stranger to her), unsuccessfully woos the barmaid:

> Have you seen them, covered in all the frost? the man was saying to the barmaid. Don't they look just like magic roofs, don't they look like winter always looked when you were a little child?
>
> The barmaid ignored him. She held the glass up to the light to see if it was clean. She polished it some more. She held it up again . . .
>
> You don't half talk a load of wank, the woman behind the bar said. (Smith, 2008, p. 39)

Here the narrative scenario hinges on a relationship of affect, in which the stranger's nostalgic wonder at a snowy November contrasts the barmaid's cynicism, an opposition further heightened by the weighty atmosphere of the near-empty pub. The conversation takes on a performative quality, as if staged for the enjoyment of the narrator: 'He said it all very loudly, as if he was saying it not really to me but for the barmaid back behind the bar to hear' (Smith, 2008, p. 45). In contrast, the narrator herself self-consciously resents her part in the conversation, begrudging the unwanted intrusion into her alone time:

> I had driven into the car park of this pub tonight precisely because I believed there would be nobody here I knew, nobody here who would bother me, nobody here who would ask anything of me, nobody here who would want to speak to me about anything, anything at all. (Smith, 2008, p. 46)

In this scene, the narrator's refusal of involvement conjures a ghostly spatial scenario, in which imagined absence takes the place of actual presence: 'nobody . . . nobody . . . nobody'. This culminates in the narrator escaping to the solitude of her car, where she reflects on the vehicle's comfort and designer amenities: 'Cars were great. They were full of things that simply, mechanically met people's needs. Inside seat-heating. Adjustable seat levers. Little vanity mirrors in the windscreen shades' (Smith, 2008, p. 47). In this way, technology offers a solace from obligation, a kind of escape zone in which independence is wilfully maintained.

Nevertheless, just as Deleuze and Guattari challenge the subject's prioritization within enlightenment philosophy and re-conceive ethics in virtual, affective terms – as *process* rather than fixity (Deleuze, 1988, p. 127–8; Thrift, 2004, pp. 63, 68) – so the narrator's reflection prompts a reassessment of emotional relations, reminding the narrator of her connections to other people and places. Thus, sitting in her car, she recalls the memory of a childhood winter, in which she and a group of hikers were trapped in a mountain snowstorm. What is important about this memory is not only the content of the narrative but also its conveyance, in so far as it is told in the form of an imagined dialogue which promotes togetherness. The narrator reflects: 'Imagine if we had all been friends in that bar, had been people who really had something to say, had wanted to talk to each other' (Smith, 2008, p. 48). In this way affective belonging takes the place in her reflections of solitary identity.

The story the narrator remembers, of the snowstorm, echoes this verdict, recalling the mysterious disappearance of the narrator's childhood heroes, the Fenimores, whose own narrative, it would appear, remains incomplete: 'Where were those people, the hopeful man and his sad helpful love; where were the Fenimores tonight, nearly thirty years later?' (Smith, 2008, p. 53). This narrative query spurs the narrator's further reflection, prompting her to imagine latent possibilities present in her own situation:

> But if I went back inside, I could eat. And if I went back inside, if I was simply there, those two people would speak to each other again, they'd be able to, even if I was just sitting reading my paper or eating my supper ignoring them. (Smith, 2008, p. 54)

In this way, the story's conditional mode invokes a renewed community encounter, which might be produced through an acknowledgement of personal interrelation and mutual responsibility. As Rosi Braidotti reflects, 'The ethics of affirmation [proposed by Deleuze] is about suspending the quest for both claims and compensations.' Rather, 'it is the force that aims at fulfilling the subject's capacity for interaction and freedom' by recognizing how subjects exist within 'a community or collectivity' (Braidotti, 2006, p. 11).

In 'Being Quick' (*Whole Story*) likewise, affect is central to the narrative progression, as a mode of engagement which again functions to introduce community. Here, the story begins with the narrator walking through King's Cross train station and the fantastic scenario that, while she is talking on her mobile phone, 'Death nearly walked into me' (Smith, 2003, p. 27). The Gothic mode of this scene – again, with phantasmagoric implications – echoes Pile's notion of psychic 'reality': where space takes the form of a spectral encounter. Pile comments:

> Ghosts . . . possess places, often taking possession of domestic spaces, such as, famously, the haunted house. Such stories will expose both the heterogeneous temporalities that comprise places, but also illuminate what it means to possess, or haunt, a place. (Smith, 2003, p. 143)

In this case, this 'haunting' relates to the anxiety produced by technology, where the sense of community impelled by the train's intimacy is poignantly missing. As the narrator reflects, 'I hadn't ever cared at any point in my life about anything other than myself and [. . .] I had no idea how to change this or make it any different' (Smith, 2003, p. 32). Here, 'Death', in the form of spectrality, augers crisis.

The train setting of this scene is especially significant, not only for its connection to Augé, as it invokes transitional space, but also for its psychoanalytic connotations, building on Freud's idea of the train journey as a source of an *uncanny* encounter. Thus, as Laura Marcus explains, train travel for Freud 'produces the chance encounter with one's own image. This is another version of railway "shock", in which a "more than usually violent jolt" results in the appearance of the other, the "double"' (Marcus, 2007, p. 174). Likewise, Smith here depicts the train as haunted by an experience of solitude, where spaces exist as surface encounters, or reflections, and where the individual remains atomized despite the presence of others. The text's vision of the passengers, as they pass through a tunnel, 'shouting their hellos forlornly' into the air (Smith, 2003, p. 31), speaks to this, creating a comedy of Gothic estrangement: 'the stray hellos reached nobody' but rather 'hung unanswered above our heads . . . and cancelled out everybody they weren't for' (Smith, 2003, p. 31). Thus, the supposed community of the train space better resembles an opera of ghosts, as each voice calls out but never receives an answer. Smith herself directly remarks on this experience:

> We live in a culture where we are so fixated on surfaces. The fastness that we now think life is about, that we think of as our due, cover this great absence. And maybe so-called extrasensory perceptions are the echo of what's there. (Denes, 2003)

In this way, Smith's engagement with the spectral responds to contemporary urbanity, with its fixation on surfaces which covers over community dysfunction.

Indeed, the train hampers relations between individuals but also ethical commitment more generally. Thus, agency within the story becomes disembodied from social experience, as relations are detached from any notion of civic responsibility. As one man remarks 'out loud to himself': 'Nobody takes responsibility . . . Nobody's responsible. Nobody does anything about it. Nobody's in charge. Who's to blame? Nobody' (Smith, 2003, p. 37). In this way, as in 'Present', a ghostly absence in the text offers a comment on de-socialized ethics, where 'nobody' represents a ubiquitous denial of involvement within modern life.

Nevertheless, the second half of the story redirects this Gothic narrative, such that, following a rail suspension at an unnamed station, the narrator walks home rather than wait, a decision which opens the way for a host of new sensory experiences. The narrator reflects, 'I could smell it all, I had cold air in my nose and at the back of my mouth and it tasted of diesel or petrol and behind that it tasted of stripling wood, grass and earth' (Smith, 2003, p. 40). Here, Michel de Certeau's reading of space as obliging an insurrectional activity, which happens below the regulatory vision of 'panopticonic administration' (de Certeau, 1984, p. 96), comes to mind, as the narrator appropriates unconventional 'tactics' of walking to reframe the city (de Certeau, 1984, pp. xviii–xix). More generally, the 'immanence' of the world which Deleuze and Guattari locate as at the heart of spatial ethics and which they describe as enabled through an engagement with physical community (Deleuze and Guattari, 1987, p. 411; 1994: p. 59) is revived through walking, inciting an insurgent celebration of pedestrian experience, in particular in relation to the periphery space of train track urbanity.

Indeed, the second half of the narrative reintroduces not only spatial connection but also communication, as the narrative voice transitions to the narrator's partner, who has been waiting all night for her to come home, and who speaks to her again when the narrator calls her. Here, the phone conversation brings to attention an imagined spatial experience (conjured by the partner), which is characterized by catastrophe: 'You are somewhere I can't reach or hear you and you are in pain . . . You are somewhere you don't want me to know about, with someone you don't want me to know about' (Smith, 2003, p. 49). Thus, the journey provokes anxiety in the partner, and the possibilities for space that she imagines are nothing like the actual. Indeed, she remains hampered by a sense of mechanical estrangement produced by the phone call: 'It was the fact that it was just your first name; something about it by itself in all that machinery was making something inside me actually hurt' (Smith, 2003, p. 41). Even so, the first narrator's positive response to her surroundings distinguishes a new network of connections underpinning urbanity:

> While we're usually asleep someone somewhere is cutting open great big boxes of stuff and arranging them, or cutting bales of new newspapers open for newsagents in supermarkets and shops, and we never even think about it when we buy a paper or whatever. (Smith, 2003, p. 42)

In this way, the invisible connectivity of experience which the narrator had longed for on the train is re-established on her walk home; the world appears integrated, a network of multiple, often invisible, interwoven relations made accessible through affect. (Note also that a similar scenario emerges in *Hotel World*, where in the final chapter the narrator recognizes the invisible links that exist between strangers and random encounters in contemporary Britain [Smith, 2001, pp. 225–36].)

These later two stories, 'Present' and 'Being Quick', exemplify Smith's concern for social community, even as they also recognize the important component of personal (individual) involvement. As Braidotti writes, in relation to Luce Irigaray and Judith Butler, '[t]hey stress that

moral reasoning locates the constitution of subjectivity in the interrelation to others, as a form of exposure, availability, and vulnerability'
(Braidotti, 2006, p. 5). Likewise, Smith's stories emphasize how the self
relies on multiple connections: 'True to oneself. Which self?' she quotes
Katherine Mansfield as saying (*First Person*, epigraph).

Nevertheless, at the heart of the stories explored here, including these
latter, is a concern for affective *becoming* which underpins this vision.
Thus, following Deleuze and Guattari, Smith spatializes human agency
and embeds it within a framework of *transhuman* relations. Thus, as
Deleuze and Guattari write, affects are 'the nonhuman becomings of
man' which circumvent any notion of agency as purely intentional
(Deleuze and Guattari 1994, p. 169). Likewise, for Smith, spatialized
existence extends the meaning of the human, characterizing an immanent body of relations existing alongside and in connection with human
individuals. In other words, what is integral to Smith's vision of space
is an idea of spatial interconnectedness, such that *both* the individual
and the community are tied into a network of invisible affective bonds,
which may or may not finally be realized. As Claire Colebrook explains,
'life [for Deleuze] is a plane of potentialities or tendencies that may be
actualised in certain relations but that could also produce other relations, other worlds' (Colebrook, 2004, p. 9). Similarly, Smith understands
space as a complex network of possibilities, which await realization
depending on the moment.

One last story which helps clarify this is 'The Definite Article' (2009).
Here, the setting of Regent's Park introduces a contrast to corporate
London life, but one which remains bound up with the immanent intensity of urban space. The story begins with a declarative pronouncement:
'I stepped out of the city and into the park. It was as simple as that'
(Smith, 2009, p. 5), in this way establishing a clear opposition between
two worlds. Nevertheless, as the story unfolds, what emerges concerns
not contrast so much as connectivity, as the setting awakens the narrator to the beauty and interrelatedness of life around her. The framework
for this encounter concerns again the experience of urban walking, as
the narrator commences her regular trajectory to an office meeting. Her
flustered outlook is evident in her language, which is dominated by a
vocabulary of corporatism:

> I had come the whole way underground saying over and over in my head,
> urgent, ensure, feasibility, margin, assessment, management, rationalisation,
> development strategy . . . I went up the stairs repeating to myself the phrase
> not a problem not a problem not a problem, then stopped for a moment at
> the Tube exit because (ow) my eye was really hurting, out of nowhere I'd got
> something in my eye. (Smith, 2009, p. 5)

Here, the collision of an insect with the narrator's eye disrupts the rhetoric of corporatism, provoking a change of thought and subject matter,

just as the word 'ow' disrupts the sentence itself, reframing its focus. The narrator declares: 'Then I saw myself pressing the button on the pedestrian crossing. Then I was crossing the road anyway, between the fast-coming cars, before I changed my mind' (Smith, 2009, p. 6). In this way, the moment of engagement invokes action without hesitation, as the narrator responds before she can register her own conscious doubts.

As in 'Being Quick', de Certeau's insurrectional take on walking is relevant here, recalling how 'the city is left prey to contradictory movements that counterbalance and combine themselves outside the reach of panoptic power' (de Certeau, 1984, p. 95). The digressiveness of the narrator's passage echoes this: each new movement she makes distracts her and reorients her trajectory. Nevertheless, while de Certeau understands this project largely in terms of human control, such that the subject *appropriates* 'the topographical system' in subversive ways (de Certeau, 1984, p. 97), Smith instead invokes a larger affective network, in which space unfolds around and encompasses the subject dynamically.[2] Thus, the associations spurred by the park create a system of spatial pleasures for the narrator, which enliven her to the multiplicity of life around her:

> Everything I touch and everything that touches me is so complex that all my senses flare . . . Then you take the blindfold off me.
> It's light, colour, it's the top of the hill. It's the city itself I see under the huge sky. (Smith, 2009, pp. 6–7)

In other words, the narrator experiences a moment of inspiration as she celebrates the city's vibrant urban encounter, which emerges not as ambition, finance or power, but rather an immanent unfolding of spatial relations. As Jack Katz writes, '[a] kind of metamorphosis occurs [in emotion] in which the self goes into a new container or takes on a temporary flesh for the passage to an altered state of being' (Katz 1999, p. 343; qtd. in Thrift, 2004, pp. 60–1). Similarly, in 'The Definite Article', Smith explores the transformative experience of urban life, as the self takes leave of itself – 'I stepped out of myself' (Smith, 2009, p. 12) – and becomes connected to the world around it. The narrative focus on spatial agency reaffirms this: 'The city gathered round the park and rose out of itself as usual. I saw it all over again, as if for the first time' (Smith, 2009, p. 13). Here, a change of perspective provoked by a new view of the city intones a new awareness of the dynamicity of urban life.

Looking back to my introduction, Augé's supermodern perspective remains present in this ending, in the recognition of everyday experiences of spatial estrangement. The bookshop in 'Gothic'; the cinema in 'No Exit'; the car in 'Present'; the train in 'Being Quick'; the corporate meeting in 'The Definite Article' – all encode an awareness of 'supermodern' loneliness, estrangement and disillusionment. Indeed, these spaces reflect the threatening temporality of their encounters, where in each case, as Augé puts it, 'everything proceeds as if space had been trapped by time [. . .] from the inexhaustible stock of an unending history in the present' (Augé, 1995, pp. 104–5). Nevertheless, despite this 'supermodern' apprehension, Smith challenges Augé's pessimism, recognizing a potential for freedom and community within urban space, and also a new opportunity for personal and social affective engagement. In this way, her short stories redeem 'supermodern' space by acknowledging affective ethics and the possibility for involvement and compassion which emerges with an awareness of immanent becoming.

CHAPTER TWO

Simile and Similarity in Ali Smith's *Like*

IAN BLYTH

Chapter Summary: This chapter explores the uses and significances of the word 'like' in Ali Smith's first novel. Looking in close detail at a number of key passages and narrative threads in *Like* (1997), and with reference to the work of Hélène Cixous on a 'nonappropriating' affirmative economy, it contends that this novel outlines various concerns about 'like', not least concerning the way in which it can be used to elide or obscure actuality. Amy and Ash, the two main protagonists in *Like*, each come to regard comparison and simile with a degree of suspicion, and develop a more direct approach to reality, one based upon affirmation rather than analogy (what someone or something 'is', rather than what they or it are 'like'). Through this, and in its creative use of word play and syntax, *Like* can be seen as a significant text in the development of Smith's fiction.

Keywords: Cixous, difference, fiction, mimesis, simile

'Like' and 'like' and 'like'– but what is the thing that lies beneath the semblance of the thing?

(Woolf, 1931, p. 176)

Like is an ill mark. Sae ill indeed, that I wad hardly swear to ony thing.

(Hogg, 2002, p. 47)

It is perhaps no great exaggeration to say that Ali Smith's first novel, *Like* (1997), takes its title very seriously indeed. 'Like' can be a troublesome word. Rhoda, in Woolf's *The Waves* (1931), objects to the slipperiness of similes, to the manner in which they can potentially form an endless chain of analogies (something not unlike Derrida's notion of *différance*, in which meaning is held back in a state of deferred difference). For Bell Calvert's maid, Bessy, in Hogg's *Private Memoirs and Confessions of a*

Justified Sinner (1824), 'like' cannot be relied upon as a measure of truth: saying that something is 'like' something else does not necessarily mean that it actuality is – indeed, it can often mean that it isn't. Amy, Ash and others in Smith's *Like* regularly use the word to avoid speaking of things directly, or make it the focus of their concerns when they attempt to question what it is 'that lies beneath'. One of the central mysteries of *Like*, for example, the truth behind Amy's maternal relationship with Kate, is only gradually revealed via a series of 'cryptic' hints and clues which shift from analogy to affirmation and whose full significance is often only registered upon rereading. The creative potential of word play, form, syntax and so on is a thread that runs throughout Smith's fiction: think of the way in which *Hotel World* (2001) is narrated via grammatically themed sections entitled 'past', 'present historic', 'future conditional', 'perfect', 'future in the past' and 'present', for instance, or the main three parts of *The Accidental* (2005), 'The beginning', 'The middle' and 'The end', whose titles also act as the first words of each of the respective subsections. *Like* is a significant text in the development of this distinctive style. As what follows shows, what emerges from a close reading of Smith's first novel (and through reference to the work of Hélène Cixous on an 'affirmative' economy) is the suggestion that beneath the story of Ash and Amy (and Amy and Kate) there is a sense in which *Like* can be read as somehow or other 'about' this word.

Like is a novel which seemingly invites us to make comparisons, to consider questions of similarity and difference, preference and affection, fiction and reality, truth and lies. This is in part achieved through the novel's structure: the narrative is split into two not quite equal halves, 'Amy' and 'Ash', the former taking place at some unspecified point of time (months? years?) after the latter. We see Amy gradually recovering her memories, her ability to read, her sense of self; we know that Ash is trying to forget, or to remember differently, and that at some point she is going to disappear (although the when, where and why of this is left hanging in the air). Amy and Ash appear at times to be conspiratorially close – as if they are, or have been, lovers, for instance (another detail on which the novel is pointedly ambiguous). At other times they could not be more distant, could not be more unlike each other. They share an intimacy and a strangeness that sets them apart, and as Justine Jordan has noted, 'the two women's narratives mirror each other in language and style: Ash's sensuality exists only in relation to Amy's asceticism, Amy's coolness is defined through Ash's ardour' (Jordan, 1999, p. 33). One can also see a certain degree of mirroring if Ash is compared with Kate. Ash's full name, for example, is Aisling: pronounced *'ashling'*, Amy reminds her, as in *'a young ash sapling or tree'*, but also meaning *'a vision, dream poem'* (Smith, 1997, p. 224). One of Amy's first actions in the narrative is to dub Kate 'Kathleen the Hooligan' (Smith, 1997, p. 4), an early indication that there is more to Amy's inability to read than might at first appear – especially if we recall that Yeats told Lady Gregory that the inspiration for his 1902 play, 'Cathleen ni Hoolihan', was 'a dream he had "almost as distinct as a vision"' (Yeats, 1966, p. 273). A coincidence? Probably so, but the cumulative weight of things in the narrative that are somehow curiously alike starts to tell. The same could be said for the various uses to which the word 'like' is put. So much so that each successive time 'like' is encountered in the text it starts to be accompanied by the niggling sense that it must have some special signification – as if 'like' were not simply just another word.

'I had always known that I liked girls', Ash reports early on in her diary. 'I liked boys too, but I certainly liked girls more' (Smith, 1997, p. 160). The problem, of course, is that this was not the sort of thing that one could be open about in Inverness, 'the decent, upright capital of the Highlands' (Smith, 1997, p. 158). 'Imagine the scandal', she writes, the stories which would have spread about her being 'you know, a bit funny, *like that*' (Smith, 1997, p. 159). Ash negotiates her way through this intolerance by exploiting the potential for words to carry more than one meaning, relying on the fact that different people in different contexts can interpret the same word in different ways. An example of this can be seen in the innocently suggestive way Amy introduces Ash to Donna: 'that one over there, Ash, she likes you', Amy tells her after she has been watching Donna, who is behind the cafeteria counter at the Loch Ness visitors' centre (Smith, 1997, p. 193). Ash and Donna's affair progresses in steps from the status of 'friends' to 'edging closer and closer to each other' to 'fumbling at each other' to making 'our fevered first love' (Smith, 1997, pp. 193–4). But just as it began with words, with 'like', so does it end this way. One day at school, Ash's fellow prefect Shona sees (in her words) a 'disgusting' story in a newspaper – 'one of the most revolting things I've ever read', she says – concerning two female tennis players at Wimbledon: 'they're poofs, well, you know, queer', she explains (Smith, 1997, pp. 215–16). There are noises of repulsion and disgust from many of the others in the room. Ash stares at her book, feels her ears 'burning', and then a familiar word surfaces, and we are told that 'a small voice from somewhere inside my throat before I could stop it was saying, well, maybe, maybe they like each other' (Smith, 1997, pp. 216–17). Ash's voice carries on: 'It's perfectly okay for people to like whoever they want to like' (Smith, 1997, p. 217), a remark which, first of all, elicits an embarrassed silence, and then further exclamations of 'disgusting' and 'unnatural' – including (most tellingly) from Donna – but which also draws overt gestures of support and expressions of like-mindedness from two of the girls in the room, Jenny and Ruth (see Smith, 1997, pp. 217–20). Ash's moment of crisis becomes also her moment of triumph or release. The following day, she commences upon what she refers to as her 'next adventure' (Smith, 1997, p. 221) – that is, her summer affair with the home economics teacher, Miss Carroll – which in turn leads on (possibly via an affair with Ruth) to her 'adventures' in Cambridge with Carmen, Simone and Amy. Perhaps it would be pushing things a little too far to describe the second half of *Like* as a form of 'coming out' narrative, but as the above shows, this does not mean that the novel does not engage with such themes.

We might also usefully compare this scene in *Like* with the passage in Woolf's *A Room of One's Own* (1929) where the narrator (while reading *Life's Adventure* by Mary Carmichael) comes across the words 'Chloe liked Olivia'; 'Do not start', she continues,

> Do not blush. Let us admit in the privacy of our own society that these things sometimes happen. Sometimes women do like women.
>
> 'Chloe liked Olivia,' I read. And then it struck me how immense a change was there. Chloe liked Olivia for perhaps the first time in literature. (Woolf, 1929, p. 123)

Woolf's narrator is deliberately vague here about the meaning of 'like' and 'liked', as she is a little further on when she speaks of 'relationships between women' (Woolf, 1929, pp. 123–4), although the suggestion is clearly there that she has something more than mere friendship(s) in mind.[1] The same can be said for Ash's use of the word 'like', both in the example above and in *Like*'s closing pages when she listens to the sound of Amy's heart:

> What does it say? she said.
>
> It's like, like – I said, and I stopped, I couldn't think what it was like, it was Amy's heart, it wasn't like anything else. But she misunderstood me; that's good, she said, like, that's a good word, and she looked so pleased I didn't want to spoil it so I didn't. (Smith, 1997, p. 342)

This is, ostensibly, a stumble over words. But 'like, like' is also an expression that is rich with possible interpretations, including those of same-sex desire (like liking like, in other words) – which may explain why Amy is 'so pleased' to hear Ash say it. However, in the context of the critique of comparison that is developed in the novel, a notion such as 'same-sex' is not as straightforward as it might appear. When paired with the term 'heterosexual', 'same-sex' can be seen as a part of what Cixous refers to as a 'hierarchical opposition' (Cixous, 1986, p. 64). Whether we are conscious of it or not, she argues, contained within this opposition is the idea of 'Superior/Inferior' (Cixous, 1986, p. 64), a mechanism through which one term is seen to have greater authority or legitimacy than the other, and in which the supposedly 'inferior' term can only be understood in relation to the 'superior' one. The result, Cixous notes, is the perpetuation of what she calls 'the Empire of the Selfsame', a process of negation whereby '[the] same masters dominate history from the beginning, inscribing it with the marks of their appropriating economy [. . .]. Always the same, with other clothes' (Cixous, 1986, p. 79). By stressing the 'same' in 'same-sex', so the argument goes, what gets lost is what is 'unique' or 'different' about a particular relationship. Hence, Cixous's preference for *'qualifiers* of sexual difference' in order to avoid falling prey to the belief in 'a "natural," anatomical determination of sexual difference-opposition' (Cixous, 1986, p. 81), which might in turn suggest that there is more than one way of reading Ash's remark that she has been 'misunderstood' by Amy.

The not always welcome facility in words to exceed their supposed meaning(s), the potential difference between sound, sight and sense, is one of the underlying themes of Amy's half of the narrative. Word play is often an important factor in this. On the second page of the novel we are told that Kate reads Amy's signature ('the only words Kate has ever seen Amy write') as 'Amy Shore', which she finds 'very funny now that they live right next to the sea' (Smith, 1997, p. 4). 'Kate likes being called Shone', she adds, 'Kate Shone is like the words of a story', she explains to Amy (Smith, 1997, p. 4). Kate launches into a fantasy about herself shining in glamorous locations, which Amy briefly interrupts in order to correct her use of 'they' as a singular possessive: 'he or she', Amy tells her – another early hint at the hidden identity of Dr Amy Shone – 'Not that it really matters, she adds. It doesn't matter at all, really' (Smith, 1997, p. 5). These words seem to linger in Kate's mind, and are reshaped 20 pages later when she sees a photograph of a famous Swiss mountain and renames it 'The it doesn't Matterhorn' (Smith, 1997, p. 26) – a joke which Kate likes so much she repeats it on several subsequent occasions. Kate is learning to separate language from reality, to create something new within words, and it is soon after this that she reflects on Amy's inability to read, and Amy's comment that 'you can carry more things in your head than you could ever hope to carry on your back' (Smith, 1997, p. 28). The contrast in this particular instance is between memory and the written word, but in expressing a preference for the artificiality (and artifice) of language and speech acts over the actuality of things, Amy is also reflecting on the inconsistency between how words appear and what they represent or stand in for. Kate, on her part, is presumably unaware of the allusion Amy is making to the scholars in the Grand Academy of Lagado in Swift's *Gulliver's Travels* (1726, part III, chapter V), who seek to do away with language altogether and replace it with physical objects.[2] She is, however, aware of the unreliability of words, and (like Ash and Amy) of how to exploit their arbitrary and sometimes contradictory nature: 'Sitting still. Still moving', she notes at one stage, 'She wants to ask Amy about the word and how it can mean both things' (Smith, 1997, p. 43). Kate's inquisitive and playful approach to language shows that she is (up to a point) her mother's daughter. Amy's lecture, 'The Body of the Text III' (Smith, 1997, p. 268), for example, seeks to demystify language and to assert the power of creative interpretation over that of literal meaning. Ash remembers Amy saying that 'words were just random noises', that 'language was all an act', and that 'words could never express anything but the ghost of truth': *'language not real'* is the summary one of Amy's students takes away with her at the end (Smith, 1997, p. 269). All of which should suggest that Amy is a practised manipulator of language, someone who is used to being in control. But when Amy recovers her ability to read again, after almost eight years of 'puzzling at the lost shapes of words' (Smith, 1997, p. 44), her feelings are less euphoric than they might have been expected to be. There is 'excitement', yes, but there is also 'numb fear' (Smith, 1997, p. 44).

One possible reason for Amy's fear is that as her ability to read comes back to her, so do her memories. The refrain from 'Always something there to remind me' goes 'round and round' like a 'needle stuck in her head' (Smith, 1997, pp. 12–13). What it is, this thing that she is being reminded of, is something that is only gradually teased out. She dreams, for example, of opening 'the door into a place that has been scorched black', but 'can't think where she is', cannot comprehend 'what it can mean' (Smith, 1997: p. 34). The full story, or at least one version of the story (we only have Ash's word that this is the 'true' account of events), is not revealed until near the end of Ash's narrative when we see Ash stealing Amy's diaries, Ash not finding herself in them, Ash getting petrol and matches, piling books in the middle of Amy's college room, and shutting the window behind her as 'the night exploded into light' (see Smith, 1997, pp. 303–5). Before this, however, motifs of ash and burning have been threaded throughout the novel. They are there in the story of the phoenix rising from its own ashes, for instance, which Ash includes in her list of 'Things Amy Told Me at One Time Or Another' (Smith, 1997, pp. 170–1). They are also in the letter that prompts Ash to leave home and join Amy (unannounced) in Cambridge (see Smith, 1997, pp. 223–4). Near the end of her narrative it is Amy who burns her now-returned diaries, and the circle seems to be complete; although it is not clearly stated whether or not she also destroys that 'other, different book' Kate asks about (Smith, 1997, p. 151) – that is, Ash's diary. This lack of certainty about the fate of Ash's diary continues until the final words of Amy's narrative: 'Soon, Amy thinks, there will be nothing left of it. Ash, that's all. Nothing else' (Smith, 1997, p. 152). Because the word 'Ash' is placed at the start of a sentence, the distinction between its lower-case and capitalized forms is erased, an effect that is enhanced when we consider that on the facing page across from this there is a single word, 'Ash' (Smith, 1997, p. 153), which stands there as both the title of the second half of the novel, and also, surely, something much more than this.

A sense of uncertainty, an excess or overabundance of meaning, also makes itself felt when it comes to the parts of Amy's narrative concerning Kate, and the question of who Kate is, who she is like. As with the ash/burning motifs, the significances of which are often only noticed when we reread Amy's narrative having read Ash's, the first references to Kate's identity seem to be innocent enough – or they would be, were it not for the presence of a particular word. The remark by one of Kate's classmates' mothers that Kate 'gets more like her mother every day'

(Smith, 1997, p. 14) draws what is in hindsight a curious response from Amy: 'She does, she thought. It still took her unawares, was always a surprise' (Smith, 1997, p. 15). All seemingly innocent and ordinary enough – and yet. Likewise, when Amy and Kate are travelling to England on the train, and Kate sees a baby and asks about her own birth, there is something not quite straightforward in the way in which Amy weaves a familiar thread of tales featuring 'a gooseberry bush', 'the bottom of [her] bed', 'a loch' and, when Kate asks for 'the real truth', the claim that she was delivered to her by a stork (Smith, 1997, p. 53). It is at this point that Kate loses interest in the subject (it is night, and she goes to one of the train doors and attempts to see out of the window), and Amy at last reveals the real 'real truth':

> I went into the big white room where you were with all the other new babies. [. . .] I just picked you up and you came home with me.
>   Kate's name around her ankle and the card at the end of her perspex cot. The last written words to mean anything. (Smith, 1997, p. 53)

Amy has a moment of panic after this, 'unsure' as to whether or not she has spoken these words 'out loud' (Smith, 1997, p. 53). If she has done so, Kate appears not to have heard her. But from the point of view of the reader, Amy's stories start to take on a whole new, and not entirely comfortable, resonance. 'Say you took a small child' begins the next section (Smith, 1997, p. 55), and while the repetition of the word 'say' in this passage is operating in the sense of a supposition, a near equivalent to another of the senses of 'like', as readers we now know (or at least suspect) that there is a second declarative sense lurking beneath this. Kate asks if Amy's mother is her 'granny': 'If you like' is Amy's cryptic and perhaps not entirely truthful response (Smith, 1997, p. 77). 'I think you're meant to be my grandfather', Kate says to Amy's father soon afterwards, in another revealing turn of phrase (Smith, 1997, p. 88). Amy's ambiguous expression, 'Say you took a child', is repeated again at the start of the account of her and Kate's holiday in Naples, and then again in the next sentence: 'Say you just took a child' (Smith, 1997, p. 95). But by now it seems less like an invitation to speculate and more like an imperative to confess: 'Go on. Say it', the narrative continues (Smith, 1997, p. 95).

As truth and fiction begin to intermingle, it is Kate who takes the first and most direct approach to resolving matters. On the journey to England Amy tells her that they are travelling on 'a ghost train', and that the other passengers she sees around her are 'nothing but air' (Smith, 1997, p. 46). Kate realizes this is not true, that 'it's one of Amy's stories' intended to distract and entertain her, but her interest is raised all the same (Smith, 1997, p. 46). She considers the woman sitting across from her reading a newspaper, and when Kate looks down 'she can see legs with thick tights on and feet in shoes' (Smith, 1997, p. 47). Kate then reasserts reality by 'stamp[ing] down hard on the shoes' (Smith,

1997, p. 47), much to the (very real and not at all ghostly) woman's surprise and consternation, an act which Amy is initially minded to treat
'sternly' but which soon has her convulsed in 'silent laughter' (Smith,
1997, p. 48). We might say that Amy here is acting as the Boswell to
Kate's Johnson, as Kate unwittingly echoes the actions of an incident
that took place in 1763:

> After we came out of the church, we stood talking for some time together of
> Bishop Berkeley's ingenious sophistry to prove the non-existence of matter,
> and that every thing in the universe is merely ideal. I observed, that though
> we are satisfied his doctrine is not true, it is impossible to refute it. I shall
> never forget the alacrity with which Johnson answered, striking his foot
> with mighty force against a large stone, till he rebounded from it,—'I refute
> it *thus.*' (Boswell, 1949, vol. 1, p. 292)

The parallels between the false unreality of the passengers on the train
and the unreal and ghostlike nature of language in Amy's lecture appear
to be inescapable. When Kate refutes one of these arguments, does she
also refute the other? The real also makes its presence felt when Kate is
exploring Amy's childhood room and, among the images of birds, flowers, women, girls, angels and stills from *The Wizard of Oz*, she sees 'one
picture that is actually a real photograph, of two girls under a statue';
looking more closely Kate concludes that one of the girls 'looks a bit like
Amy' (Smith, 1997, p. 80). All Amy will tell Kate about the image is that
it is 'a photo of your mother and her friend' (Smith, 1997, p. 81), but Kate's
description is enough to identify the setting as 'the greeny bronze statue
of Flora MacDonald' which Ash takes Amy and her parents to see in the
grounds of Inverness Castle (Smith, 1997, p. 183). Ash might not be in
Amy's diary, but she is on Amy's wall (she might also be the 'beautiful
shining girl' in the story Amy tells Kate supposedly instead of the story
of the statue – see Smith, 1997, pp. 82–3). The word 'like' here then (even
when qualified by 'a bit') comes to signify something that is indisput-
ably real – undermining, in a sense, the other meanings which Amy has
been using to mask the truth about herself, and about Kate.

The cumulative effect becomes increasingly stronger, and likeness
and reality converge even more when Amy and Kate visit Pompeii.
After throwing away a set of postcards given to them by a tour guide,
Amy retrieves one from the bin and tears out a section featuring some
'small deer' for Kate (Smith, 1997, p. 114). She then sees a small 'fragment'
of the torn card on the ground. It depicts a sandalled foot: 'It is very like
a real foot', so much so 'that Amy is shocked' (Smith, 1997, p. 115). The
foot is part of an image which Amy (from her past life) knows very well,
but she has never before 'seen it like this', and she cannot recall having
previously noticed 'how painfully like a foot the painter has taken the
care to make it' (Smith, 1997, p. 115). The shock of the real marks a turning point for Amy, and she begins to become more interested in the

actuality of things. In the museum on Capri, for instance, she calls Kate to come back and re-examine a butterfly's wings: 'look properly, Amy says. Look really closely. If you do, you can see where the colours come from' (Smith, 1997, p. 121). By this stage of the narrative, it is not just Kate who is being encouraged to look closely at things in the expectation of seeing them as they really are. Amy's prompting also draws in the reader, so much so that comparisons are seen as at best ways of delaying meaning, and at worst deliberately obscuring it.

Cixous comments on the perils of using similes when she takes issue with the nineteenth-century novelist Gustave Flaubert for being, as she puts it, 'tempered by *comme* (like)', and overly reliant on 'analogy' (Cixous, 1990, p. 54). Remarking that Flaubert's approach is one which 'could be called an absolute masculinity' (Cixous, 1990, p. 53) – that is, one in which '"difference" is always perceived and carried out as an opposition' (Cixous, 1986, pp. 78–80) – Cixous (in what is admittedly an ironic manoeuvre) offers in contrast to Flaubert the 'absolute femininity' of the Brazilian writer Clarice Lispector (Cixous, 1990, pp. 53–4). Picking up on a sentence from Lispector's *The Steam of Life* (1973), 'I just wanted to look' (Lispector, 1989, p. 52), Cixous suggests: 'That is Clarice's motto. To look absolutely is not to look at anyone or at anything, but to look purely' (Cixous, 1990, p. 54). Lispector's approach can be seen an example of a 'nonappropriating look' (Cixous, 1990, p. 55), and the point Cixous is seeking to make about this is that 'opposition does not need to be made to mark difference' – there is instead, she contends, 'a capacity to make a nonviolent, nonexclusive difference', a 'pure, internal difference [expressed] through affirmation' (Cixous, 1990, p. 78). Difference, in the sense Cixous is using it here, can be thought of as the unique identifiers of a person or thing: not the things that make them like somebody or something else, that is, but the things that make them what they are (that is, 'similarity' and 'difference' are still interlinked – there can be no meaningful 'relation' between two subjects without some common ground – but what Cixous is arguing for is a change in where the emphasis is placed). Being content to leave what is specific or even strange about the other in place, she would observe, is what enables the other to retain its or their otherness – affirmation not analogy. What is required is an approach that steps away from the need to understand, to codify, and instead develops an economy in which one accepts the other *as* other:

> Philosophy has always wanted to think its other, to interiorize, incorporate it. From the moment it thinks its other, the other is no longer other but becomes the same. It enters into the space of what can be thought, it loses its strangeness. (Cixous, 1991, p. 90)

As has been noted, there is a growing recognition of the importance of such an approach to identity and reality in the latter parts of Amy's narrative. Questions of analogy and comparison, difference and uniqueness, also come to occupy a central role in the second half of *Like*. Indeed, Ash's diary, or her 'liary' as she describes it at one point (Smith, 1997, p. 169), documents a variety of ways in which comparisons or likenesses break down when faced with actuality. That is, as Cixous would put it, they reveal more about the person making the comparison, rather than the person or thing which the comparison is supposed to be describing.

As an actor, the profession from which we derive the word mimesis, Ash is all too aware that it is not just 'self-indulgent' diaries which are full of 'lies' when it comes to their presentation of reality (Smith, 1997, p. 157). Any form of narrative act is guilty of moulding, discovering or even inventing a 'shape' for an event, 'like it's just a story, like it didn't even have to have happened' (Smith, 1997, p. 169). Ash's father is amused to find her reading Defoe's *Journal of the Plague Year* (1722) which, he remarks, presents itself as 'a documentary' so that 'you think what you're reading is real, then you find out afterwards it's all, you know, fiction' (Smith, 1997, p. 201). The point Ash's father is trying to make is that Defoe's narrative is 'real enough, but he made it up' (Smith, 1997, p. 201). That this is the way the stories we tell about the 'real' work, seems to be the implication. This is the way such stories need to work. Ash in turn finds herself regularly puncturing misapprehensions and assumptions about the world around her. Melanie, for example, who comes to Ash's house to play their piano (like so much else in the novel, Ash's father's reasons for this arrangement are not explained), thinks that Ash has been living in Oxford. On being told that 'it was the other place', Melanie still asks her if Cambridge was 'like on *Brideshead Revisited*' (Smith, 1997, p. 240) – which is to say, Oxford as it was portrayed in the 1981 ITV adaptation of Waugh's 1945 novel. 'No, not really, not usually', Ash responds (Smith, 1997, p. 240), before telling a series of stories which lead Melanie to reflect that Cambridge, or at least Cambridge University Library, is in fact not all that different from the Inverness branch of B&Q (see Smith, 1997, pp. 240–2). Ash is also not above revising her own ideas, albeit not always on a wholly conscious level. At one point she even hears Amy's voice 'inside [her] head', rebuking her: 'I think you know I'm less of a cliché than you're inferring, Ash', she is told (Smith, 1997, p. 263). As Ash's diary heads towards the key event in its narrative, the bonfire of books in Amy's college room, it is telling that one of its main concerns becomes the difference between dreams and reality, fantasy and actuality. In a passage that appears to look back to the Berkeleyan idealism refuted by Kate (see above), Amy questions Ash about whether 'our thoughts are the only things that are truly real', whether or not the only way to 'make things real, make them happen, [is] by thinking about them' (Smith, 1997, p. 266). Ash's attempts to reassure Amy that this isn't so cannot stop the chills she feels 'creeping up the back of [her] neck', nor can it halt the dawning realization that she 'had been relegated to random, the wrong person one more time' (Smith, 1997, p. 266). Just who is making up things about whom is explored (exposed?) in greater detail in the Janus-like narrative that describes Ash's final encounter with Amy. First we have the dream version of events, an erotic fantasy seemingly prompted when one of Ash's downstairs neighbours had shouted up to her to 'go fuck [her]self': 'So I do', is her response (Smith, 1997, p. 297). Ash goes round to see Amy and they fall upon each other for the inevitable 'sex scene', 'the moment we've been waiting for', as Ash calls it (Smith, 1997, p. 298). The scene is described in exuberant detail. Doubt only creeps back in at its culmination: 'Didn't we', Ash states, 'Wasn't it' (Smith, 1997, p. 300). 'No', she admits at the start of the next chapter, 'Not how it happened, not what it was like' (Smith, 1997, p. 301). They didn't, it wasn't. The second, real 'version of things', she remarks, 'is simpler, sadder, shameful' (Smith, 1997, p. 301).

We might say that one reason for the initial fantasy version of events is that, like Amy, Ash reaches the point at which, as Eliot puts it in the first section of 'Burnt Norton', she '[c]annot bear very much reality' (Eliot, 1959, p. 14, line 43). However, in the final pages of Ash's diary it soon becomes clear that there is no getting away from reality. It is, on the contrary, an excess of comparison, of like, which cannot be borne. Earlier on, we had seen Ash's sceptical reaction to Donna's fascination with Patrick and James. Donna had 'never seen identical twins so close up before', something which 'she found [. . .] deeply exciting' (Smith, 1997, p. 203). For Ash, on the other hand, her brothers are always 'different' from each other: 'Even if they're just standing there not doing anything it's obvious' (Smith, 1997, pp. 203–4). In the closing pages, comparison and analogy are again brought into focus, questioned, and shown to be wanting. Lying down upon the grave of 'Margaret Ethel Inkster' at the top of the hill in Tomnahurich Cemetery (Smith, 1997, p. 328), Ash begins a litany of 'Like [. . .] Like [. . .] Like [. . .] Like [. . .]' (Smith, 1997, pp. 331–5). As more and more of these comparisons are piled up upon on one and other, the less (individually and collectively) they come to mean. 'Like the time when. Like the time. Like. There was no stopping it', Ash complains, 'You say something's like something else, and all you've really said is that actually, because it's only like it, it's different' (Smith, 1997, p. 335). The actual or real asserts itself fairly swiftly after this: Ash gets home to find a note from her father with a recipe and a prayer; she receives several phone calls from America concerning a part in a film; she thinks of her brothers; she thinks of Amy. As the novel closes Ash is ready to put aside speculation and story-telling, her liary-diary, the territory of things that are like. She hears her 'father coming in the back door'; 'Maybe he caught something', she wonders, 'I'll maybe just go down and see' (Smith, 1997, p. 343).

Ultimately, although it might be tempting to find parallels here with Amy's experiences in Pompeii, to do so by this stage of the narrative would surely not seem right. As with so much else in the novel, the two halves of *Like*, while initially appearing to be set up to facilitate such comparisons, take shape instead as independent versions of a not quite fully explained story – each secure in their own unique 'strangeness', as Cixous would put it. And indeed, by way of concluding this chapter, it may be worth drawing attention to the fact that 'like' continues to be a troublesome word in Smith's fiction. In *The Accidental*, for example, Michael is struck by a feeling of 'glorious renewal': 'Like new. No, not just like new but really new, actually new. Metaphor not simile. No *like* between him and the word new' (Smith, 2005, p. 57). In the short story 'The Second Person' (2008), the two protagonists playfully dispute each other's assertions: 'This is the kind of thing you do', 'That's what you're like' and so on (Smith, 2008, pp. 121, 123). In 'May' (2003), another short story and another text which is split into two seemingly mirrored halves, the first narrator struggles to describe the tree she has fallen in love with:

> The buds were like the pointed hooves of a herd of tiny deer. The blossom was like – no, it was like nothing but blossom. The leaves, when they came, would be like nothing but leaves. I had never seen a tree more like a tree. It was a relief. (Smith, 2003, p. 57)

The second narrator tries to understand, to find the right words: 'Like in the myth? [. . .] It's not a myth, you say. What myth? It's really real' (Smith, 2003, p. 62). 'Don't what kind of tree me', she is told soon after this, 'I've told you, it's irrelevant [. . .] people are far too hung up on categorization' (Smith, 2003, pp. 64–5). In the end, she comes to accept that the tree is simply a tree, and the situation is simply what it is.

CHAPTER THREE

Narrating Remainders: Spectral Presences in Ali Smith's Fictions[1]

STEPHEN M. LEVIN

Chapter Summary: Frequently in Smith's fictions, the arrival of a spectral 'other' throws a scene of everyday life out of balance, thereby exposing the contingency of individual identities and social forms. Drawing mainly on two of her novels, *The Accidental* (2005) and *Hotel World* (2001), this chapter argues that figures of spectrality serve to make manifest the heterogeneous temporalities of late capitalism. Although the appearance of the 'spectre' may prove to be unsettling, or even catastrophic, the chapter associates spectrality with a mode of subaltern critique. Understood as an ethical imperative that can yield new ways of seeing and new modes of social attachments, the 'spectre' calls into question the boundaries of narrative form itself, and compels us to conclude that the perceptible reality of any object owes its materiality to unseen, and often suppressed, historical agencies. This 'revisioning' of the world, made possible by the spectre, calls into question the identification of Smith as a postmodern writer.

Keywords: Global Culture, postmodernism, reparation, spectrality, subalternity

It is a well-recognized irony that Scottish literature, emanating from an important historical epicentre of the European Enlightenment, has produced some of the most visionary critiques of the Enlightenment tradition. Colm Toíbín contrasts the 'wildness' of contemporary Scottish writing with the 'calmness' of contemporary Irish writing: '[I]n the writings of James Kelman, Alasdair Gray, Irvine Welsh, Janice Galloway and Alan Warner there is political anger, stylistic experiment and formal trickery' (Toíbín, 2001, p. xxxii). Ali Smith should surely be added to Toíbín's list, and arguably in her work the amalgamation of these particular qualities – anger, experimentation and trickery – attains its most radical expression. In the move from Adam Smith to Ali Smith, we witness a dismantling of one of the most cherished fantasies of Enlightenment thinking – that of the fully constituted and intentional self.

Indeed, we may extend this logic even further, leading us to see in Smith's work a focussed indictment of the legacy of *The Wealth of Nations* (1776) and an exploration of both the economic and the epistemic cruelty of late capitalism. Since this focus remains a somewhat latent theme in Smith's fictions, my aim in this chapter will be to render that thematic more manifest, with the hope of demonstrating that Smith invents a narrative form that emerges decidedly from the era of globalization. More specifically, I want to propose that this formal innovation may be understood specifically in terms of a structure of *spectrality* that runs through Smith's novels and short stories, which I examine here by drawing mainly on two of her novels, *The Accidental* (2005) and *Hotel World* (2001).[2] Shadowing this discussion, it must be acknowledged at the outset, is Jacques Derrida's *Specters of Marx* (1994), where the 'spectre' is offered as a figure that calls into question the boundaries of form itself, and that compels us to conclude that the perceptible reality of any object owes its materiality to unseen, and often suppressed, historical agencies.

Ghosts in the Hotel: Spectral Presences in Contemporary Culture

In Smith's fictions, there is a pervasive sense that our lives do not entirely belong to us. Subjects are lost in webs of intersubjectivity and caught in invisible links to an array of social determinants, a state that we might begin to understand by turning briefly to some of our great theorists of social displacement. In his *New Introductory Lectures on Psycho-Analysis* (1932), for instance, Freud famously describes a form of narcissistic injury in which modern subjects no longer operate as masters of their own houses. To Freud, the centre of the rational consciousness, the ego, struggles against what are often far more powerful influences, such as libidinal impulses and the injunctions of external social authorities: the 'poor ego', he writes, 'serves three severe masters and does what it can to bring their claims and demands into harmony with one another. These claims are always divergent and often seem incompatible' (Freud, 1933, pp. 96–7). An unlikely resonance to this sentiment by Freud appears in a well-known statement by Marx, where the dislocations experienced by the modern subject are framed explicitly in terms of a sundered connection to the dead:

> Men make their own history, but they do not make it as they please; they do not make it under circumstances chosen by themselves, but under

circumstances directly found, given, and transmitted from the past. The tradition of all the dead generations weighs like a nightmare on the brains of the living. (Marx, 1972, p. 595)

It is precisely this interest in the otherness of the present – the sense that temporality always references a charged absence – that leads Derrida to return to Marx and to concentrate his attention on the figure of the spectre. For the spectre offers Derrida another means of thinking through the aspect of the non-identical that inhabits any identity, of dead generations haunting the living. In one of the 'Envois,' for instance, Derrida writes:

> [Y]ou will never be your name, you never have been, even when, and especially when you have answered to it. The name is made to do without the life of the bearer, and is therefore always somewhat the name of someone dead. (Derrida, 1987, p. 39)

Although they share an interest in thinking through the relationship of the living present with the dead, Freud, Marx and Derrida envision disparate strategies of narrating, or 'conjuring', these spectral presences. Marx frequently regards the spectre as something to be exorcised in order to usher in a radically new future, while Derrida wishes to correct this eschatological dimension of Marx's thinking, insisting that the spectre is a perdurable force to be actively heard and addressed. These tensions invade the fictions of Smith, in which the ghostly linkage between the self and the remote dead surfaces as a persistent theme. Defying any easy equation between narrative experimentation and postmodernism, Smith invokes spectrality as a means of disclosing the multiple temporalities that constitute the present (recalling Derrida's critique of ontological certainty), and of rendering new modes of redemptive attachment and idioms of love (recalling Marx's interest in futurity and redemption).[3]

The Accidental: Spectral Temporalities and the Domestic Scene

As Fredric Jameson has written, spectrality for Derrida entails not so much a belief that ghosts exist, as a sense that 'the living present is scarcely as self-sufficient as it claims to be'. Spectrality alerts us to the possibility, Jameson continues, that the living present 'might under exceptional circumstances betray us' (Jameson, 2008, p. 39). In The Accidental, Smith foregrounds this thematic of betrayal, and yet the exceptional circumstances behind the 'ordinariness' of the living present occupy only a spectral presence in the narrative, a point to which Smith alludes in her curious observation that the text should be read as a war novel (France,

2005, p. 15). Indeed, war occupies only a spectral presence in the narrative, as the action is organized around the Smart family's domestic drama and the mysterious arrival of a stranger to their holiday rental in Norfolk, with only sporadic, ghostly reference to the war in Iraq. It is this suppression of the 'real' fact of the war dead that constitutes the main concern of the novel. Smith figures the intrusion of the spectre as Amber, a young stranger who enters and upends the order of the Smart household and disrupts the ontological constancy of the domestic space. This process of 'disadjustment', to use a Derridean term (1994, p. 1), proves to be both dismantling and euphoric, as the confrontation with the real opens the horizon of the present to radical growth and transformation even as it dissolves the bourgeois fantasies that sustain an *imago* of the self. As is often the case in Smith's writings, the spectre intrudes upon the tradition-steeped living, creating significant struggles that nonetheless hold the potential to restore life to the living.

Before Amber's arrival, the temporal orientation of the narrative is in the synchronic, with the Smarts locked in a homogenized and static present largely shaped by their careers. Eve writes commercially successful pseudo-biographies that resurrect and fictionalize the lives of individuals who died in the Second World War, and Michael works as an accomplished academic who has thrived despite repeated dalliances with students. Yet we find that the imaginary domain of selfhood, the *Bildung* of their identities, is quite fragile and vulnerable to the intrusion of the real. Rather than *choices*, these 'presentations' of selfhood appear more as bourgeois dream-states that keep at bay the messy politics of the external world and sustain illusions of coherence and immutability. The Smarts' children, Astrid and Magnus, remain somewhat less comfortably ensconced in such illusions. Astrid obsessively videotapes every moment of her life and is prone to paralysing bouts of self-consciousness, and Magnus is debilitated by guilt after a high school prank leads, at least as he imagines it, to the suicide of a classmate. Less entrenched in the comforting veneer of the 'everyday', the children more readily embrace the spectral character of time – the sense that temporality is structured not by regularly ticking seconds, but by memory and fantasy. And yet the spectre, in the guise of Amber, manages to 'seduce' each member of the Smart family by opening the present to its many contingencies, a process that has the capacity both to liberate oneself from the deadness of the synchronic and to disclose the 'horror' of the real. The arrival of the spectre, in other words, undoes the Hegelian scene of the novel's opening – the sense of an 'end of history' represented as the culmination of a domestic fantasy – and reveals that the structure of the present is heterochronic, as Derrida suggests, and not entirely self-sufficient.

As with much of her work, Smith evokes the intrusion of a spectral presence by breaking the continuity of narrative form, as registered, for instance, in jarring shifts in point of view, the fusion of genres, and typographical heterogeneity. This heterogeneity of form acts decidedly to frustrate expectations for narrative consistency and closure. Ghosts do not return merely to produce testimony that is, as Shoshana Felman and Dori Laub put it, 'simply relayed, repeated or reported' (Felman and Laub, 1992, p. 3). For Smith, rather, spectrality – the arrival of the 'other' – produces a breakdown of the referential narrative that compels one not simply to 'know' the real that structures the domestic fantasy, but to 'experience' it. With the war in Iraq shadowing the narrative, Smith suggests that such fantasies of omnipotence in fact perpetuate, in a particular moment of globalization, a condition of 'not knowing'. At the same time, the fragmentation of narrative form, hypostatized in the many images of protagonists who imagine themselves to be breaking or smashed into bits, suggests the promise of renewal and rebirth. One of the most striking reflections on the 'brokenness' of the Smart family appears in a chapter narrated from the point of view of Magnus: 'His mother = broken.' To Magnus,

> Everybody at this table is in broken pieces which won't go together, pieces which are nothing to do with each other, like they all come from different jigsaws, all muddled together into the one box by some assistant who couldn't care less in a charity shop or wherever the place is that old jigsaws go to die. (Smith, 2005, p. 138)

As one confronts the loss of the legible unity of forms and begins to recognize their discontinuous and 'unreadable' structure, then one becomes open to what Derrida imagines as the 'arrival' of the other.

A profound illustration of the ways in which Amber's effect on the Smarts proves both catastrophic and emancipatory takes place toward the end of the novel, in a chapter narrated from Eve's point of view, where Smith portrays the mounting tension, and eventual confrontation, between Eve and Amber. After Amber tells Eve that she's 'an excellent fake', Eve examines a photograph that shows 'the idyllic summerhouse of the holiday home of Eve and her husband' (Smith, 2005, p. 183). The photograph both creates an idealized image – of Eve's domestic fulfilment and her success as a writer and artist – and exposes that image as not only fanciful, but also arbitrary. That is, Eve focuses on that which makes the image appeal to the imagination and the coincidence that produced it; she reflects upon the 'the accidental fall of the light through the summerhouse window that day' that produces this particular photographic snapshot (Smith, 2005, p. 183). Instead of representing the *real* Smart family, the photograph seems to confirm Amber's assessment, as it comes to be read as a performance of an imaginary order: 'A family, all of them, smiling. Who were they smiling for? Was it for themselves, somewhere in the future? Was it for the photographer? Who took the photograph? What did it show?' (Smith, 2005, p. 183).[4] The 'ultraviolet' character of the spectrally unspoken utterances that give the image its ocular coherence, until now invisible, enter the spectrum of visible light:

> Did it show that Michael had come home smelling, yet again, of someone else? Did it show that Magnus was a boy so like his father that Eve almost couldn't bear to sit in the same room with him? Did it show that Astrid was infuriating to Eve, that she deserved to have no father, just as Eve had done most of her life, and was lucky still to have a mother at all? (Smith, 2005, pp. 183–4)

Critically in terms of Smith's fictional preferences, these hidden utterances are not symbolized in the photograph, but their spectral presence opens the image to new readings. A similar idea regarding the 'performativity' of photographs surfaces in *Hotel World*, when Sara Wilby's ghost imagines unfreezing the static time of the image and inserting herself into a scene in which the actors have been reanimated (Smith, 2001, pp. 12–13). Recalling Derrida's description of the moment at which circumstances might bring about a betrayal of the living present, Eve realizes that she 'could be something other than what she seemed' (Smith, 2005, p. 184). That kind of moment, emerging out of the tensions between the synchronic and heterochronic, is also strikingly figured in the erotic encounter of one of the novel's culminating scenes, when Amber kisses Eve and Eve then expels her from the house. Even as Amber tells Eve that she's a 'dead person', Eve is 'moved beyond belief by the kiss' and finds that she is 'gifted with a new kind of vision' (Smith, 2005, p. 202).

In this portrayal of the disruption of Eve's quotidian comforts and the exposure of these comforts as a referential illusion, Smith departs from the new historicist 'desire to speak with the dead' (Greenblatt, 1988, p. 1). Rather, she takes up a concern more resonant with trauma theorists, such as Felman and Laub, who seek to understand how past events – more precisely, how other temporalities – become part of the experience of one's living present. In such a framework, any hope of 'speaking with' the ghosts of the past proves untenable because the past, as Walter Benjamin has put it, cannot be *archived* (see Benjamin, 2003). Instead, the past can only be resignified retrospectively as a result of new possibilities for narrativization that emerge in the present, a phenomenon that Freud referred to as *Nachträglichkeit*. And yet, while it may be impossible to speak with the dead – to represent them and make them fully legible – the encounter with these spectral traces may cause a profound breakdown in one's present reality, to the degree that language itself fragments and becomes a source of alienation.

Such breakdowns in signification indeed take place in *The Accidental*. As Amber's influence on the family intensifies, boundaries between past and present become more permeable, and selves become more vulnerable to dislocation. Eve dreams that she sees her dead mother on the edge of the bed and is unable to distinguish dream from reality (Smith,

2005, p. 187). Likewise, as exemplified in meta-literary terms, the erosion of Michael's idealized self is figured literally as the devolution of language into shards of verse, which are then reconstituted in a sonnet sequence. At the end of this process, he reflects on Amber's transformative impact on him: 'The pretty young woman has broken him open while he slept, put her hand in and thieved the heart out of him' (Smith, 2005, p. 270). Like the tesserae referenced in one of the poems, Michael's imaginary ideal of himself is shattered and he is left in a paradoxical state that is both plenitude and absence: a piece of tile, ornamental in its own right, but without the referent of the larger mosaic.[5] He becomes 'a splintery self, a remainder of a' – the naming of the object deferred (Smith, 2005, p. 169). So too, Magnus, the seventeen-year-old son who previously attempts to understand the world in terms of its mathematical simplicity, begins, after his sexual encounters with Amber, to ruminate on the coordinating conjunction 'and' along with its connotations of an interminable additive logic. Magnus repeats the melancholic mantra that everyone around him is 'broken', but then comes to the realization that wholeness – the state opposed to being broken – derives only from a state of non-knowledge: 'Is it innocent, as in a state of goodness or whatever, if you simply don't know about all those people in the Holocaust? Or is it just naïve, stupid? What use is that kind of innocence anyway?' (Smith, 2005, p. 152). In the awareness of his own brokenness – a recognition that he himself is only a partial fragment to which elements can be added with the repetition of 'and' – Magnus becomes open to his own development: 'Amber=everything he didn't even know he imagined possible for himself' (Smith, 2005, p. 153).

The meta-literary, as represented most obviously through both Eve and Michael, underscores Smith's recent proclamation that all of her books have been about writing (see France, 2005). Indeed, the novel's division into three sections – 'beginning', 'middle' and 'end' – parodies the expectation for conventional plot development and the inclination to regard narratives as a closed totality. More subtly, Amber's homelessness and disruptive force suggest that she herself embodies a principle of narration – specifically, the capacity of narrative simultaneously to orient and disorient the emplotment of the self within a particular subject position. Responding, then, to the clichéd structures that pervade narratives produced for mass consumption, Smith challenges the transparent referentiality of language, which allows, for instance, for the arrival of endings to be easily anticipated: a film 'is almost over now because everything is adding up in it' (Smith, 2005, p. 247). In the portrayal of Amber as a figure for narration, Smith highlights the disorienting effects of spectral temporalities. The presence of the real – whether a distant war, a husband's infidelity, or a reminder of the thin line that separates art from commodity – may render one estranged within one's own home. Thus it is fitting that when Eve orders Amber to leave the Norfolk house, Amber reminds her that the house is only a rental.

The startling conclusion of the novel, in which Eve appears to take on Amber's role of saboteur by entering a random house during her travels in the United States, suggests that Smith regards this function of narration as an ethical imperative. To be a writer, and not a purveyor of formulaic biographies, Eve must become a dangerous infiltrator in the reassuring domestic narrative of an 'other'.

From *The Accidental* to *Hotel World*: Spectrality and Subalternity in Global Culture

The reading of Amber as an 'avatar' of spectral time – as the other that intervenes in the narration of imagined selves – gains support in the short chapters centred on the Alhambra Picture House, the place, Amber tells us, of her 'conception' in 1968 (Smith, 2005, pp. 1, 211). She is introduced as a dangerous, even seditious, agency (from her mother, she inherits the ability 'to get what I want'; from her father, 'how to disappear, how to not exist,' p. 3) who seems to embody the social turbulence, political violence, and creative vitality of late 1960s Britain; she says, 'I was formed and made in the Saigon days, the Rhodesian days, the days of the rivers of blood' (Smith, 2005, pp. 103–4). As suggested above, Smith creates a sense that narrative itself wields the capacity to function as a spectral presence: to loosen convention and to produce radical adjustments in the social order. And yet this vitalizing potential of narrative appears to recede in the novel's last ominous scenes, in which the cinema loses its capacity to disrupt and becomes a place where 'a roomful of society people breathe a sleeping gas pumped through the ventilation system' (Smith, 2005, p. 210).

With the proliferation of such images, Smith anticipates the emergence of a new order in which media spectacles collude with global violence. In addition to lulling to sleep, this new mode of spectatorship sexualizes instruments of war, as portrayed, for example, in a passage describing bombs that 'curve at their heavy ends like the naked breasts of women' (Smith, 2005, p. 210). By framing the narrative around Amber's birth in a cinema in 1968, Smith suggests that the spectral return of a political agency from an earlier era may counter this atrophying of global media. Such a possibility is affirmed in a striking image in the Alhambra, in which the dead on the battlefields rise up and walk through the streets to stare through the windows of the living. In the frenzied collision of temporalities represented in the Alhambra sections of the novel, Smith alludes to divergent orientations to spectrality – one that concludes with the banishment of the dead in a Hegelian moment of closure, and another that rouses the living from an intransigent daydream. At one point, the narrator appears to exhort the reader to acknowledge the spectacular novelty of the medium: 'The past appears right there in the room, the woodland glade, the dead person right there in the room'

(Smith, 2005, pp. 207–8). As the Alhambra, and the many cinemas like it, begin to close down, however, the voice warns that we ignore these phantasmatic projections at our own peril: 'Careful. I'm everything you ever dreamed' (Smith, 2005, p. 306). The admonition suggests that the exorcism of the dead made possible by the cinematic sensualization of violence or the production of devitalizing entertainments – may prove misguided. In other words, ignoring the spectral mode of narration may make it possible to displace the war from consciousness, but such phantasms always carry the prospect of a 'real' return.

Like *The Accidental*, Smith's 2001 novel *Hotel World* depicts this return as a kind of 'performance' – figured as the 'arrival' of the other – with the potential to disrupt the dominant narratives of globalization. In both novels, this disruption manifests in the dissolution of language itself, and, subsequently, to a period of mourning when confronted with this loss. The focus of *Hotel World*, however, centres more on subjects marginalized within the field of global culture, thereby associating more directly spectral modes of counter-narration with the condition of subalternity. Despite the stylistic flourishes evident in these works, this dimension of subaltern critique, whether figured as the return of a spectral presence from the late 1960s or as the ghostly labourers and homeless persons 'haunting' an emblematic 'non-place' of global capital, calls into question any easy categorisztion of Smith as a postmodern writer (see Augé, 1995, p. 109).

As in *The Accidental*, the narration of *Hotel World* alternates points of view among protagonists, each of whom suffers from a kind of aphasia. The opening chapter begins with the ghost of Sara Wilby, a young girl who climbs into the shaft of a hotel dumb waiter and falls to her death when the cable snaps. Wilby's ghost remains lost in a purgatorial space between worlds, quite literally fading in and out of language: 'I am hanging falling breaking between this word and the next' (Smith, 2001, p. 31). And yet this breakdown of the rules of grammar and fading into partial significations offers, like narrative dissonance in *The Accidental*, the possibility for new significations and, eventually, the potential for new modes of individual and cultural expressivity. In this incantatory passage, for instance, signification remains partly deferred and unfinished, and yet the injunction to 'remember' gestures toward new instantiations of the subject:

> Remember you must live.
> Remember you most love.
> Remember you mist leaf.

> (I will mist mist. I will mist leaf. I will miss the, the. What's the word? Lost, I've, the word. The word for. You know. I don't mean a house. I don't mean a room. I mean the way of the . Dead to the . Out of this . Word. [. . .]) (Smith, 2001, pp. 30–1)

Evoking a sense of dislocation associated with subalternity, these semantic fragments suggest that to slip outside the domain of the patriarchal 'word' also entails assuming a marginal position in relation to the 'world'. The two signifiers – 'word' and 'world' – occupy a position of proximity, but, as is underscored by the omission of 'world', they are also separated by an irreducible gap. As language disintegrates and the lacunae in the narration become dominant, the 'world' loses its ontological clarity and the subject takes on a ghostly relationship to the social structure. Such spectralizing of the subject produces a decidedly ambivalent state. The loss of referentiality is something to be mourned, even if that guarantee of linguistic transparency derives, as portrayed in the novel, from the highly rationalized and homogenizing rhetoric of the transnational 'Global Hotels' chain. Yet the subsequent transmutations of form – for instance, to the opacity of 'remember you mist leaf' – link the creative inversion of language to a poetics of expression that defies the logocentrism or ideological framework of a bland globalism. At such moments, where spectral narration induces states of mourning or yields new imperatives for living, Smith alludes to a critical practice that moves beyond postmodern pastiche.

The focus of the next chapter of *Hotel World* is Else, a homeless woman, who lives in the margins of the urban streetscape: 'People go past. They don't see Else, or decide not to' (Smith 2001, p. 39). Indeed, her very name, Else, marks her as a partial presence, which Smith clearly underscores by linking Else's relationship to language to a traumatic history of childhood sexual abuse. As with the marginalization of the Iraq war in *The Accidental*, Else's invisibility indicates a suppression of temporality, which, in the context of globalization, creates the false impression that 'actual history is gone' (Smith, 2001, p. 45). In such a global setting, the city has become an object of tourist fantasy, just a place for 'tourists to bring their traveller's cheques to in the summer' (Smith, 2001, p. 45). To this dreamworld, Else appears as a splintered-off bit of excess, a remainder, intruding in language that draws on existing structures and destabilizes them at the same time. Her mantra of '(Spr sm chn?)' persistently interrupts the otherwise totalizing flow of the narrative. Like Amber's destabilizing presence in *The Accidental*, Else gives literal form to a principle of linguistic homelessness; she prevents textual form from being *placed*.

The hotel's 'solid' form – opposed to the partial or 'ghostly' presences of Else and Sara Wilby – reflects a rigidified approach to language that communicates in coercive injunctions and demands discursive uniformity. For instance, attendance at Sara's funeral is 'compulsory,' and the procession becomes an opportunity for a reiteration of institutional power (Smith, 2001, p. 109). Yet the many transient and invisible inhabitants around the hotel, like Else, enter the narrative as 'supplements' to this monolithic discourse, so that the injunctions issued at the hotel become merely one presence in a narrative shaped by multivalent points of view.

The importance of this opposition becomes clearer in the next section, which focuses on a hotel receptionist, Lise, who covertly invites Else to make use of an unoccupied room, an 'intrusion' that mirrors Amber's arrival to the Smarts' holiday rental. In this subversive act, Lise herself underscores the association between spectral and subaltern modes of counter-narration. Having distanced herself from the symbolic order of the hotel, Lise, consigned to a hospital bed, loses altogether her facility with language. In this near-catatonic state, she thinks back on her days behind the receptionist desk, 'her subtly made-up face above her Name Badge, sleek and smiling, emptied of self, very good at what she does' (Smith, 2001, p. 112). Before this sickness, Lise had decided to break the enforced order of the institution by inviting Else to covertly take a room at the hotel. After this transgressive act, language loses its constative function and becomes *merely* performative; even the letters on her hospital questionnaire take on a glyphic character and no longer generate meaningful significations.

Locked in the structure of hotel time, Lise struggles to link signifiers in a way that provides her with some sense of orientation – that permits her to go 'home'. Smith portrays this transition – from the 'langue' of fixed and frozen meanings to the 'parole' of performative enunciation – as a process of mourning. Working through her catastrophic alienation from language – her spectral orientation to 'word' and 'world' – Lise engages in a form of what Theodor Adorno described as 'micrological thinking'.[6] She finds herself ruminating on specific signifiers: 'Shelfily. Was that a real word?' or 'Well: a word that was bottomless' (Smith, 2001, p. 83). Slowly, she begins to supplement her narration with reference to her own associations and affects. The simple exposition of '[s]he straightens her uniform' leads to a recognition of subjective presence: 'Lise has momentarily forgotten that the surveillance cameras are off and that the straightness or otherwise of her uniform will not tonight be reported to or recorded by any authority' (Smith, 2001, p. 107). In this depiction of Lise's modest recovery, Smith links spectrality to a deeply *political* process of mourning that entails both freeing oneself from the 'gaze' of ideology and recognizing the performative and 'ghostly' character of language.

Because this process of mourning in fact carries the prospect of renewed vitality, the spectral outsider becomes a seductive figure for bourgeois subjects whose own orientation remains fixed within the 'world' of the hotel. Just as the Smarts are compelled to Amber, so, too, in *Hotel World*, a spectral seduction throws into disarray, albeit briefly, the comforting fantasies of bourgeois professionalism and privilege. In both novels, this dynamic unfolds primarily in the portrayal of a writer who specializes in prose designed to provide some redemptive consolation for the ravages of historical time. Where Eve crafts narratives that envision surmounting the 'actual' death of war, Penny churns out 'meaningless copy' for the 'style pages' of a newspaper (Smith, 2001, p. 143). Smith shows that the production of these fantasies involves the suppression of death in the portrayal of Penny's tormented daydreams in her hotel room. Having just viewed a television show in which a host claims to commune with the dead, Penny imagines that 'all the people who have ever died' are 'standing behind their invisible wall and beating it with their fists and all of them soundlessly shouting it, *We're* not dead! Don't call *us* dead!' (Smith, 2001, pp. 127–8). This 'terrible endless noise', as she visualizes it, is quieted only by the recollection of comforting bourgeois platitudes: she begins to laugh as she realizes that 'remember you must die' can easily metamorphose to 'remember you must diet' (Smith, 2001, pp. 129, 169). Unlike Eve, Penny refuses to commune with ghosts. She shows that the ontological stability of the bourgeois subject can only be sustained through a disavowal of spectrality.

Gifts of Hospitality: Toward Acts of Reparation and Love

What I have attempted to show in this chapter is that the refusal to recognize the spectral character of narrative necessarily entails an abolition of both the multiplex temporalities of history and the semantic generativity of language. In my concluding remarks, I want to suggest that Smith depicts the arrival of the spectre as an occasion to meet the other with a stance of radical hospitality, as an 'event' that creates the conditions for new modes of attachment and love. In his later writings exploring the subject of cosmopolitanism, Derrida describes hospitality as an example of an aporia. True hospitality, he says, requires an altruistic act of the host, a willingness to meet the other entirely on its own terms, and a cessation of power relations; and yet the very notion of hospitality implies the presence of an asymmetrical relationship between 'host' and 'guest'. Hospitality, then, represents an unattainable ideal:

> Pure and unconditional hospitality, hospitality itself, opens or is in advance open to someone who is neither expected nor invited, to whomever arrives as an absolutely foreign visitor, as a new arrival, nonindentifiable and unforeseeable, in short, wholly, other. (Derrida, quoted in Borradori, 2003, pp. 128–9)

While Smith does not resolve the aporia that Derrida describes, she does represent a response to the arrival of the 'visitor' that departs from her Scottish compatriot Adam Smith, who incorporates the messianic into a narrative of progress; for Adam Smith, the visitor remains entrapped within a singular historical temporality and cannot be embraced on its own terms. In the novels of Ali Smith, however, and elsewhere in her work,[7] the arrival of the 'guest' precipitates a loss of mastery that can, through gestures of radical love and empathy, reconfigure social norms and intersubjective bonds.

This dynamic of loss and recovery is represented in the last section of *Hotel World* with the repetition of the word 'morning', itself evoking the spectre of 'mourning'. In this coda to the novel, the temporal divide between dead and living has been breached:

> Already some of the ghosts are out and about as the day begins, a population that includes thousands of middle-aged ladies at Marks & Spencer, merchants, Princess Diana, and an Elizabethan child actor. These apparitions intermingle in the spaces around *Global Hotel* with café owners and passers-by queuing at *Boots* pharmacy. (Smith, 2001, pp. 225–6)

Against the backdrop of these spectral returns, when temporality is clearly rendered 'out of joint',[8] a final act of reparation and mourning takes place: the young woman who works in the watch shop, the object of Sara Wilby's affection before her death, imagines a visitation from Sara that allows her to return Sara's repaired watch to her at no charge. The novel thus closes with a repetition of an earlier semantic transmutation – 'remember you must live. remember you most love. remember you mist leaf' (Smith, 2001, p. 237) – that underscores the fructifying entrance of 'otherness' into any chain of signification.

Two points, to conclude, must be stressed: first, that this act of reparation takes place decidedly within the cultural framework of globalization; and second, that this production of a 'spectral counternarrative of the global' (Baucom, 2001, p. 162) originates with a writer of Scottish background. These two points bear an important reciprocal connection. From the vantage point of the early nineteenth century, Walter Scott was among the keenest observers of the effects of Scotland's rapid economic development, which split the nation into two incongruous temporalities and created the uncanny effect of 'zones of the noncontemporary in the chart of the contemporaneous' (Baucom, 2001, p. 161). If Scottish writing indeed constitutes a 'point of origin' for postmodern fiction, as Matt McGuire argues (McGuire, 2009, p. 151), that distinction should be understood in terms of its insistence on a return to this originary theme, and not strictly by experiments in narrative form. In the case of Smith, this return assumes the form of a spectral critique, whereby an unexpected visitation unravels the synchronic time of globalization and, at least potentially, 're-worlds' the global through acts of hospitality and love.

CHAPTER FOUR

Ali Smith and the Philosophy of Grammar

MARK CURRIE

Chapter Summary: This chapter focuses on the crossing between sentence structure and narrative structure as a way of exploring Ali Smith's unique mode of enquiry into the relationship between language and time. The analogy between sentence structure and narrative structure is a significant tenet of what is now referred to as classical narratology, which was particularly fond of borrowing analytical resources from the grammar of the verb. This is also a preoccupation of Smith's fiction, in *There but for the* and most notably in *Hotel World*, where sections of the narrative are named after grammatical categories of verbal tense and mood. This chapter argues that the movement between philosophy and grammar in Smith's writing makes metaphors out of linguistic categories that present insights into both the philosophy of grammar and the grammar of philosophy, and helps to define the method of a fictional enquiry into the comprehension of time.

Keywords: grammar, narratology, philosophy, time

Metaphors for the Future

In *There but for the* the future is a foreign country. This statement, which is Anna's modification of the first line of L. P. Hartley's *The Go-Between* in the novel's opening section, is also an announcement of one of Ali Smith's own central themes – the strangeness of the future. Awkward as it is to begin, as I have just done, with a sentence that repeats the 'the', it is an awkwardness that also announces something, because this title is a beginning that leaves its future blank. Embedded in a sentence, it will always produce grammatical infelicity, when the words that follow from it fill in the blanks produced by the incompletion of its grammatical form. These two things, the strangeness of the future and the future as blankness in writing are repeatedly connected in Smith's writing, and this chapter explores the nature of this connection.

On the subject of the 'the', it helps a little that in writing we can mark the difference between the title and the surrounding words, yet in the novel itself that difference between what can be seen and what can be heard, the graphic and the phonetic, is joyfully wrecked. In the 'The' section of the novel, Brooke foreshadows this observation about the 'the', because she has a list of notes that she is trying to incorporate into her History Moleskin notebook, which she calls the 'The fact is' notes. 'The The fact is notes will all go here' she says, counting the blank pages in the notebook. The double capitalization of 'The The' at first marks, like italics, the difference between the 'the' of the sentence and the 'the' of the title, but vanishes as the phonetic overwhelms sense: 'the the the the – !' says Brooke 'so many the's all said together sounds like a car that won't start' (Smith, 2011, p. 334).

The question of a title and the thematics of opening or starting are never far apart, and 'there but for the' is also something of a stuttering start. The titles of these 'The fact is' notes are, like the novel's title, incomplete forms that leave their future blank. They begin from 'the' and point to a blank, as yet unwritten future. There are two things that we can observe here. The first is that incompletion, in literary form in general, has this effect, of pointing to the unwritten; and the second is that the as yet unwritten is a well-established metaphor for the future, drawing on the broad conceptual metaphor that understands and expresses human temporal experience in terms of a written sequence. These are two basic components of Smith's metaphorical system, but there are two further dimensions that need to be acknowledged that relate to these ideas of written incompletion and futurity. The first is a certain kind of crossing that takes place between graphic levels, or more specifically that blurs the boundary between a title and what follows. Any reader of Smith's fiction will have noticed the recurrent game she plays with chapter titles that are both on the outside (as names) and the inside (as beginnings) of sections. These boundaries are more visible in writing than speech: they can be marked in writing but sound threatens to overwhelm and wreck the distinctions that writing marks. The second further dimension is exactly this question of visibility, of what we can see and what we can hear. In the discussion that follows, I would like to explore the interaction of these topics of incompletion, blankness and invisibility. My argument is that these are topics that work together, associatively, suggestively, metaphorically, as part of a philosophical enquiry into questions about the future, but also that this is an enquiry that never breaks off into abstract reasoning, but remains embedded at all times in questions about writing and fiction. I will try to show that these issues of blankness, incompletion, invisibility and unforeseeability oscillate between philosophical questions about time and questions about writing, and that sometimes this oscillation seems to suggest that time and writing are conceptually inseparable. Beyond that, I want to propose that the enquiry into time is in fact also an exploration of a core paradox in the temporality of reading and writing, between the already complete nature of written sequences and their temporal unfolding to a reader, or what I shall call the 'always already' and the 'not yet' which are always involved in a dynamic interaction when we read a written text.

A metaphor, Brooke tells us, is just a way of saying something that is difficult to say, and metaphors abound in this final section of *There but for the* as Brooke, sitting beside the Greenwich observatory, fills in the remaining blank pages of her notebook. It is difficult to know if Brooke is inside the metaphor or outside it: so unusually attentive is she to the metaphoricity of words that her position is that of participant and commentator. The same can be said of the discourse on the subject of 'the', which Brooke is internal to and yet which she also seems to be conducting, and we know that this positioning, this outside which is inside, is part of the novel's enquiry into words. The title which is not external is, as I have said, a recurring trope in Smith's corpus, most notably in *The Accidental*, where the 'The beginning', The middle' and 'The end' function to name but also to begin the novel's sections. In both novels what can be seen about these titles cannot be heard, in the sense that, if we read the novel aloud, nothing will mark the title off from the text itself, and the visible, graphic difference is therefore lost. In *There but for the* we can also see what is graphically marked, four isolated words as names (there, but, for, the), but can hear only their grammatical cooperation with other words in a sequence: 'There was once' (Smith, 2011, pp. 2–3); 'But would a man' (Smith, 2011, pp. 84–5); 'For there was no more talking out loud now' (Smith, 2011, pp. 200–1); 'The fact is, London might not always be here' (Smith, 2011, pp. 278–9). That these words are inside and outside is a condition that is effectively doubled by the fact that the isolation of words, the contemplation of their hidden metaphoricity, and the relationship between their written and spoken forms are the imaginative games that Brooke likes to play with words, so that she is in the metaphor and outside it, whether as its maker or its most imaginative commentator. Even without her commentary it would be hard to miss her own metaphorical resonances. As Brooke, she is a little river, and rivers are obtrusive in the novel, as they always have been in philosophy, as metaphors for time, the flow of time and the direction of time. She is a river herself, but she is also someone highly alert to the metaphorical, and even the literal ways in which rivers can represent time: 'That makes the British Museum kind of like a sort or river too, full of things that have been found like that in, say, real rivers' (Smith, 2011, p. 326). If these are the components of a metaphorical system, the purpose of the assemblage is to say something that is difficult to say otherwise about time, and Brooke's position both within and on the outside of the metaphor is a way of connecting her internality as a character, as an invented person with philosophical and metaphorical interests, with her external predicament as an entity that exists only as writing, with the physical properties of writing and of the book as an object.

It would be wrong to think of this metaphorical framework simply as an affirmation of literary language, or its suitability to a difficult topic like the future. There is always a sense that the novel is showing us the philosophical importance of metaphor, and the importance of metaphor in philosophy, and the question of the visibility of the future is one area of demonstration. The connection between these things – philosophy, metaphor, the future and visibility – can be made explicit in the form of a proposition to which this discussion is addressed: in philosophy, the idea of seeing the future is a metaphor, in the sense that we do not actually see anything, but conceptualize the future as what is up ahead, before the eye, on the horizon, approaching etc. Brooke links all of these things together. She wanders around the department of philosophy at the University of Greenwich, asks what her parents tell her are philo- sophical questions about the relation between past, present and future, aims to study philosophy in the future, if she doesn't do something else, and declares that philosophy is 'actually quite easy'. One of the many places that this relationship between futurity and vision, metaphor and philosophical concept is pointed out is at the observatory, standing on the Meridian, at the place that, more obviously than most, combines time with vision, the telescope with the clock:

> The photo queue out in the Observatory yard, for people who want a picture of themselves standing on the Prime Meridian, is pretty long today. Is the Prime in Prime Meridian the same Prime as the Prime in Prime Minister? The election of the new government is next month so all the news and papers are about who looks best on TV. All the candidates say that they are the man who will win. Even so, nobody knows who will win. The future can't be seen, not even at an Observatory. Observe a Tory! Joke. (Smith, 2011, p. 307)

'Telescopus: far looker' is for Brooke a constant source of associative connection between time and vision, and yet, as here, the future is invisibility itself, and no matter how much paraphernalia of vision surrounds the topic – the line that represents the basis of time, the photographs of people on that line, the election as a measure of who looks best on TV, the observatory – the future is the thing that is not available to the eye. The fact is (Brooke's notes tell us) that 'the Hubble Ultra Deep Field telescope can reveal stars in a sky when it looks to the Naked Eye like there are no stars in it' (Smith, 2011, p. 305), but the fact is that this power to render what cannot be seen visible does not extend to the future.

In terms of theme, the connection of futurity and vision has an estab- lished context in the notion of blindness, and this is drawn upon for comic effect throughout the discussion of telescopes, as in this passage about Nelson:

> I SEE NO SHIPS. That was what Admiral Nelson apparently is reputed to have said historically when he put the telescope to his blind eye and because he did the English won the battle. That was shortly before Nelson died on the deck of the ship and said Kiss Me Hardy to Thomas Hardy the famous author. (Smith, 2011, p. 311)

Brooke's unreliability with history is part of the question that the telescope presents about the relation between what can and cannot be seen from the present, and these moments of comic misunderstanding point in both directions, to the opacity of the future as vision, and the vision of the past as error. So, for example, we see the same kind of unreliability turned on the subject of foresight when Brooke misquotes the traditional Scottish folk song 'I know where I'm going'[1] to produce one of the more bizarre facts in her list: 'The fact is, deer know about weddings and about who you will marry' (Smith, 2011, p. 339). The unreliability of this fact about knowing the future, of course, derives from a certain tension between sight and sound, the written and the spoken word, to which Brooke constantly returns, one emblem of which is Greenwich's talking telescope, which immediately precedes the passage on Nelson's. But whereas Nelson puts a working telescope up to his blind eye, Brooke puts her working eye up to a blind telescope – 'the dark little circle which only lights up if you put in the money' (Smith, 2011, p. 311). What is being said here about time with the help of the talking telescope is either something very difficult indeed, something full of tensions between sight and sound as well as aporetic mixtures of the true and the false, or it is just a childish jumble. I would like to propose that, though the mode here is far from allegory, there is an enquiry into ideas being conducted in this complicated associative universe, and that the principal interest lies in the relationship between writing, as visible language, and futurity as the as yet unwritten.

I have said that the novel's title evokes blanks, or silences, through incompletion, but by the time we reach its end, we do not seem much closer to a complete grammatical sentence. The implied remainder ('grace of god go I') has flickered before the eyes[2] in sections of the novel, but in the closing pages, the figure of incompletion, and of beginnings of untold stories, remains prominent. In Brooke's encounter with Miles, in particular, the blank pages that are left in the Moleskin notebook become an issue about just how much of the story remains to be told:

> And then that will be the end of this history, at least the bit that actually has Mr Garth in it. Though it might be a good idea to leave some pages blank at the end in case there is anything else that happens, in case the history isn't over. (Smith, 2011, p. 335)

The remainder is, at this stage, still blank, and what is to come then becomes the subject of a game that Brooke plays with Miles, where they each write the opening of a story on blank sheets of A4 to be completed by the other, a game inspired by the phonetic equivalent of blankness – the silence of books on a shelf:

> Think how quiet a book is on a shelf, he said, just sitting there, unopened. Then think what happens when you open it. Yes, but what *exactly* happens? Brooke said. I have an idea, he said, I'll tell you the very beginning of a story that's not been written yet, and then you write the story for me, and we can see what happens in the process. (Smith, 2011, pp. 345–6)

Two different kinds of start are involved in this game. The first is the start of reading, of opening a book and hearing it speak in the act of reading, but in order to investigate this, Brooke and Miles begin a different kind of process, which is the act of writing a story. One concerns the silence of books that are complete and on the shelf, and which the reading process brings into the realm of sound, while the other concerns the act of writing, and inventing, on the blank sheet. This is, I am going to argue, the point of this book: to stage the process of reading against the process of writing. This is the core paradox of all written stories that I referred to earlier between the complete temporal sequence that a book represents and the unfolding of that sequence in the process of reading. This dynamic of the 'always already' of writing and the 'not yet' of reading seems to me to lie at the heart of Smith's exploration of both reading in particular and time in general.

I have argued that *There but for the* shows an interest in the physical forms of futurity, finding metaphors for the invisibility of the future in the blank page and in its phonetic equivalent, silence. I have also argued that the novel is preoccupied with boundaries, some of which are those that bound the storyworld itself, such as the line between a title and what follows from it; others are concerned with thresholds that distinguish the present from the past and future. In both cases, these abstract borderlines are given physical existence within the story world, like the descriptions of Brooke's blank sheets of paper, on which stories are yet to be written, or the Meridian line that she jumps over in Greenwich. In this way the physical conditions of writing are constantly reproduced at the level of the book's content. Perhaps the most obvious instance of this internalization, or thematization of writing is the figure of Miles Garth himself, who is the silent and invisible centre of the novel's action, and reproduces on the inside the silence and blankness of its physical predicament as a book. He is, of course, also behind a threshold, the locked door of the bedroom into which he retreats, invisible and silent, like the future to come. The door, much knocked on, much discussed, highlighted by dozens of *knock knock* jokes, might be thought of as the threshold of fiction itself. What the room contains is silent, invisible, and

enigmatic. It resonates, like Miles himself, with the themes of fiction
and writing more generally, almost as if the novel is finding a metaphor for itself and placing it at its centre. If these are physical renditions,
embodiments of themes, we have to remember that they have their only
real physicality in the visibility of writing, and this is why the novel also
repeatedly draws on the graphic sign and on the novel form itself as
topics, and not only in Brooke's metaphorical whimsy. Anna's connection with Miles is a conjunction between the written and the future, in
the sense that they met on a bus tour, a competition prize for 50 writers
and their visions of the future: stories about Britain in the year 2000,
written in 1980. We know only the beginning of Anna's story – 'The
future's a foreign country. They do things differently there' (Smith, 2011,
p. 40) – but we are given a summary of its development, which begins
as follows:

> It's about this girl who wakes up in the year 2000 after being asleep for
> twenty years, Anna says. And the catch is: in the year 2000 pretty much
> everything's exactly like now, except this. When the girl tries to read words
> it's like they're all printed upside down. (Smith, 2011, p. 41)

What then can we make of a future in which writing is upside down?
As for any story within a story there is a dimension of self-commentary
involved in this one, and in this case a close correspondence between
inner and outer themes, of the future, and of the most graphic aspects
of writing. This is, to borrow some words from Derrida, an 'internal
pocket larger than the whole',[3] in the sense that, though it is internally
bounded, what it contains are abstract, perhaps exaggerated versions of
the issues that surround the novel itself, so that what is inside the novel
is also something that the novel is within. As for any story within a story,
this one repeats on the inside the boundary between what is real and
what is imagined that also bounds the novel itself, so that it dramatizes
internally its own relationship with the reality it is within. It functions
in the same way, then, as the room in which Miles encloses himself, in
the novel's centre, as a reproduction of the boundaries that create the
space of fiction more generally, or as the threshold that we cross when
we begin to read. We cross this threshold when we read the first words
of any book, and when we read the first words of this one, the boundary
between what is real and what is imagined is already repeated in the
conjunction of facts and imagination: 'The fact is, imagine a man sitting
on an exercise bike in a spare room' (Smith, 2011, prelims, line 1). We
jump across this threshold whenever there is metaphor, in the way that
Brooke jumps back and forth across the Meridian line, because metaphor, according to Brooke's mother, is 'the only way to describe what's
real' because 'sometimes what's real is very difficult to put into words'
(Smith, 2011, p. 314). If upside-down writing is a metaphor of this kind,
what is it a metaphor *for*?

I think there are two plausible answers to this question, and again, we might use Brooke's mother as a guide on the subject of interpreting a metaphor: 'To describe something indescribable you sometimes translate it directly into something else, or join it with something else so the two things become a new thing' (Smith, 2011, p. 313). I remarked earlier that I thought the mode of writing in the novel was far from that of allegory, and therefore the direct translation does not seem the right account here; the second of these alternatives seems more profitable, especially for the notion that the internal pocket of Anna's story is somehow a commentary on the story world she is in. Writing is upside down here because there is something inverted about any imagined universe, and the new thing that comes about from the conjunction of writing and inversion is a kind of inversion of the relation between what is literal and what is metaphorical. The upside-down-ness of metaphorical writing is literalized here into writing that is actually, as Brooke would say, upside down, so that something metaphorical is rendered as concrete and factual in a way that could only happen in an imagined world.

The second answer introduces something very complex into the picture, because literal does not only mean concrete or non-metaphorical. It also means 'pertaining to letters' or to writing. This is, it might be said, the literal meaning of 'literal' – to do with letters. If my first answer to the question of upside-down letters is offered in the name of literalization (literal upside-down-ness), my second is a double-literalization (a literalization of literalization), since the alterity of the future, its difference from the present, is actually being rendered as a difference in letters, words and writing as marks on the page. It seems clear to me that the literal meaning of 'literal' is at the forefront of Smith's intention here, and indeed that it is one of her favourite subjects throughout her fiction. Apart from the writing on her cornflakes packet, in the newspaper and on the bus, the inversion is focused on the novel whose first sentence she has inverted, *The Go-Between* (1953) by J. R. Hartley, turning the past into the future as the 'there' where they do things differently, so that the first thematic inversion of Bradley is quite literally literalized by the representation of his upside-down book.

Perhaps the most surprising thing about this vision of the future is that apart from this strange literal difference, everything is the same. Not only that. Anna's story is about a girl who wakes up after 20 years of sleep, but the astounding example of what has changed – that writing is upside down – only astounds for a few hours, and quickly becomes invisible again. By lunchtime this girl is 'used to the words being the wrong way up. Her brain just processed it. And by the end of the story, she isn't even noticing they're upside down any more.' (Smith, 2011, p. 42). The surprising thing, that writing is upside down, first reveals the ordinariness and sameness of everything else, and then becomes ordinary itself, like the passing of metaphor into dead metaphor: it is the ordinariness at the heart of surprise and the surprise at the heart of ordinariness. I would argue again here that the novel is finding, in Anna's story, a metaphor for itself, and that this logic, that conflates the ordinary with the surprising, is also the logic that governs the novel's central aesthetic choice. It focuses on a stranger who has barricaded himself in a family home, because this too creates an emblem of something surprising (the arrival of a stranger) and something ordinary (the domestic routine), as if Miles himself embodies something of the logic of the becoming dead of metaphor.

The Grammar of Completion and Incompletion

Many of these preoccupations, with punning, blank pages, internal texts that are larger than the whole, the past and the future in the present, the physicality of writing, and the tension between complete and incomplete sequences are also prominent in Smith's *Hotel World* (2001). I am going to take an excursion into that work, taking the last of these topics – the complete and the incomplete – as a guide into its only slightly different metaphorical world. The complete and the incomplete have grammatical forms which we know as the aspectual distinction between the perfective and the imperfective.[4] The *perfectus* of classical grammar is a kind of viewpoint from which a situation is viewed, from the outside, as if whole and complete, as opposed to the many imperfective grammatical forms which view situations from within, as ongoing and incomplete sequences. I want to develop the idea that these viewpoints are particularly relevant to the physical conditions of writing in which a reader progresses through a sequence of letters, words and sentences, or to the events to which those sentences refer, and yet at the same time knows that the sequence as a whole is already complete, written and unalterable. In writing the future is already there and this seems to present an unassailable opposition to any notion that writing can model temporal experience in general for a reader. At the same time, we all know that it can, and Smith's fiction seems more than normally focused on the interplay between the completed whole and the ongoing sequence,[5] as well as that between the impossible and the possible. *Hotel World* names its parts after grammatical tenses – past, present historic, future conditional, perfect, future in the past and present – and one effect of this is, I would suggest, a strange feeling of intrusion of a descriptive analytical vocabulary into the world of words that it presumes to describe. It is as if the analysis has been appropriated in advance by the object of analysis, which therefore seems to know itself, in quite technical terms, from the start. The fact that these section titles also indicate properties of language such as tense, aspect and mood gives this analytical foreknowledge an atmosphere of temporal self-analysis: the performance is preceded by the grammatical description of the performance, as if it were already complete, even before it has taken place.

The notions of the perfective and the perfect seem to have a special relevance for the idea of a story, and the 'perfect' chapter of *Hotel World* explores this by focusing on the character of Penny, a journalist, for whom everything is a potential story. As a result she translates everything that takes place, and even things that might occur, into something that has already happened:

> And if I help that girl, Penny thought as she skipped from stair to stair, that girl will always remember me as the nice person who helped her the night she was, was, doing whatever it is she's doing. And I will always remember it too, and look back on it many years from now as that night I helped the remarkable teenage chambermaid take the screws out of the wall in that hotel. (Smith, 2001, pp. 138–9)

Something which is only a prospect is being tested here in retrospect, as a memory and a story, to be told many years from now, and what is actually happening in the present seems to fall into the space between. The notion that the anticipation of memory and completion might be the thief of presence, and perhaps also the purveyor of presence, is one of the novel's favourite subjects, and one of its formulations comes from the citation of Muriel Spark at the novel's opening, and which becomes a kind of refrain: 'Remember you must die'. This memory of what is to come is closely linked to the notion of a story throughout *Hotel World*, which is more explicit than *There but for the* in its construction of an analogy between living and reading, or between death and the blank page. The grammatical perfective is one of the ways that presence is contorted into something that will be complete in the future, and this *will have been* is the tense that most clearly links the verbal world to the story world. We know that future tenses in particular are at the centre if only because the central character, Sara Wilby, who is already dead from the novel's beginning, is named after the *will be* of the future tense.[6] But the tense that encapsulates this interplay between what is to come and what has already taken place, the tense that refers to a future event that is already in the past is the future perfect, or the future anterior.[7] In the section that follows 'perfect', Clare Wilby's narrative bearing the title 'future in the past', Smith has rejected both of these names in favour of a more explicit description, rendering more visible the hint of the impossible that inheres in a past future.

There are many senses in which the future is in the past in Clare's heartbreaking, sleepless expression of grief, and none of them linked to any actual occurrence of the future perfect as a tense form. This is important for the way that it transforms the grammatical into something more metaphorical and leads us away from its dreary analytical project into something more poetic. The 'future in the past' is close to being a periphrasis for *death*, and it is this sense of Sara's future as a thing of the past that drives Clare's grief, as she makes lists of all the things her sister could have been and no longer will be: 'a doctor someone selling jumpers in a shop selling shoes in a shoe shop papers in a paper shop someone who looked after trees & bushes at a garden centre' etc; 'the list of things it would have been possible for you to do is never fucking ending it goes on forever' Clare decides, because it is the openness of the future in general that is in the past (Smith, 2001, pp. 207–8). But if the 'future in the past' is a periphrasis for death[8] it is also a way of naming something basic about the tense conditions of stories, that what is to come is already in the past, and this makes it quite unlike the passage of time in lived experience. Clare repeatedly comes up against the link, or the difficulty of linking, life and stories, and in particular she returns to the analogy between death and a story that stops:

> [I]t is like reading a book yeah like say you were reading a book any book & you were halfway through it really into the story knowing all about the characters & all the stuff that's happening to them then you turn the next page over & halfway down the page it just goes blank it stops there just aren't any more words on it & you know for sure that when you picked this book up it was like a normal book & had an end a last chapter a last page all that but now you flick through it right to the end & it's all just blank. (Smith, 2001, p. 190)

This is what it would take to make a book properly representative of the unexpected death in life: the impossible disappearance of a future you could see was there. There is, in other words, no possible analogy between the visible materiality of what is to come in writing and its invisibility in life. The thought, however, is prompted by a memory of Thomas Hardy's novel *Tess of the D'Urbervilles* (1891), a novel, as Clare knows, preoccupied with fate, with the notion that the future is scripted. Her memory is of an episode in which Tess looks at herself in the mirror and 'suddenly she thinks that we all know our dates of birth but that every year there is another date that we pass over without knowing what it is but it is just as important it is the other date the death date' (Smith, 2001, p. 188). The 'death date' helps to bring into focus the temporal structure that is at stake in the tension of living and writing: it offers an impossible viewpoint, a perfective viewpoint that knows a sequence as a whole, and that cannot be known, from within an unfolding or incomplete sequence. This is the tension of completion and incompletion, of perfective and imperfective, or as Derrida would have it, of structure and event[9] that characterizes all thinking about time, and which finds expression in the simple unfolding of a story, any story, because writing is governed by a future anterior structure in which what happens has already taken place.

The Literality of Letters

The visible, graphic dimensions of words, and the blank spaces that surround them are important aspects of what is *meant* in these novels. *Hotel World* finishes with the letters of Sara Wilby's Woooooooo-hoooooooo falling into the void of blank pages that follow from the end.[10] The literal falling of words obviously means to reproduce for words what happens in the story world – the fall of Sara Wilby into the silence of the dumb waiter – but it also serves to remind us that Sara's only being is verbal. Like Anna's upside down letters in *There but for the* the fall of letters finds some very literal descriptions *Hotel World*, as Sara's fall is being literalized as letters that fall out of words. The key section for this interplay, between the becoming-form-of-content and the becoming-content-of-form, is Else's narrative in the novel's second section. Else, whose vowels have fallen out of her request for change (Spr sm chn?) is interested in shorthand, and with well-paid secretaries 'filleting the words, and their wastepaper baskets overflowing with the thrown-away i's and o's and u's and e's and a's' (Smith, 2001, p. 46). Like Anna's literalization of inversion, Else's literalization is a kind of graphic metaphor, a making visible in writing something that can only be heard, the dropping of vowels, or perhaps finding in shorthand the written equivalent of something spoken. She imagines filleted letters as bits of paper, as litter in fact: 'She imagines the pavement littered with the letters that fall out of the half-words she uses' (Smith, 2001, p. 47). As well as there being a literalization of the falling away of letters, there is here a kind of literalization of the meaning of the word litter, as letters, so that writing is both the tenor and the vehicle of the metaphor. Letters, she imagines saying to police concerned with the litter, are biodegradable: 'they rot like leaves do' (Smith, 2001, p. 48). Like the literalization of 'literal', the literalization of litter also seems to be one of Smith's recurrent concerns, linked, in this case, to the question of what is permanent and what passes – of what endures into the future as art and what is disposable. Literature, she says in *Artful*, is 'Litter-ature!'[11]

These constituents of the metaphorical universe, the falling out of words and letters and the analogy they form for the falling out of life into death, the blank space and the blank page, and the relationship between writing and silence, help us to understand the last things that Sara Wilby says before she descends into eternal silence, at the end of the opening section of the novel:

Here's the story.

Remember you must live.
Remember you most love.
Remainder you mist leaf.

(I will miss mist. I will miss leaf. I will miss the, the. What's the word? Lost, I've, the word. The word for. You know. I don't mean a house. I don't mean a room. I mean the way of the . Dead to the . Out of this . Word. (Smith, 2001, p. 30)

Here again is the question of the 'the' as the graphic trailer of a blank space to come, to be completed. She will miss the world, but she cannot find the word, or rather she can only find the word 'word'. In this cryptic summary of the story, the transposition of letters leads to a disintegration of sense, the breakdown of life and leaf. As Sara falls out of the world, the world falls out of her sentences, and the letter 'l' falls out of the word 'world', which fills the blank that follows the 'the'. A stuttering end. These graphic encodings of the philosophical problems of futurity, the graphic and grammatical forms of completion and incompletion, make the physical marks of writing into a philosophical enquiry. Its topic, stated in grammatical terms, is the tension at the heart of time between the perfective and the imperfective, or time seen from the outside and time lived from the inside, an enquiry that can only be conducted in a world in which time is made visible by the form of writing.

CHAPTER FIVE

Queer Metamorphoses: *Girl meets boy* and the Futures of Queer Fiction

KAYE MITCHELL

Chapter Summary: This chapter reads Ali Smith's *Girl meets boy* (2007) through its source text – the Iphis and Ianthe story in Ovid's *Metamorphoses* – and considers the uses of the notion of metamorphosis, with its emphasis on both continuity and change, for contemporary conceptions of queerness and for what might be called a post-identity politics. After examining the significance of the Iphis and Ianthe story within the history of representations of lesbianism, the chapter proceeds to an analysis of the metamorphic imagery of Smith's novel, focusing on the exuberant descriptions of desire as transformative, and the repeated use of watery motifs to indicate both fluidity and force. Finally, the chapter seeks to situate *Girl meets boy* as a *queer* fiction – albeit one indebted to a longer tradition of *lesbian* writing – and suggests that, in its affirmative, future-focused aspects, *Girl meets boy* poses a challenge to the negative preoccupations of much recent queer theory.

Keywords: gender, identity lesbian fiction, metamorphosis, Ovid, queer theory, sexuality

This chapter offers a reading of Ali Smith's 2007 novel *Girl meets boy*, attending in particular to the novel's treatment of metamorphosis and its exploration of gender and sexual fluidity. I consider how Smith uses Ovid's story of Iphis and Ianthe, from the eighth-century *Metamorphoses*, to elucidate and develop late twentieth- and early twenty-first-century conceptions of queerness – notably undefined and/or 'unintelligible' manifestations of gender (Butler, 1990, 1993, 2004; Mitchell, 2008), queer temporalities and spaces (Halberstam, 2005; Ahmed, 2006; Dinshaw, 2009; Freeman, 2010), non-normative sexualities, and post-identity politics. My central suggestion, here, is that the concept of metamorphosis – the history and resonances of which I will briefly trace – might prove a more productive, less fraught way of 'queering' identity than the erstwhile critically dominant concept of performativity. While performativity has too often (erroneously) been conflated with 'performance', thereby presuming the presence of a pre-existent (and more or less unified, agential) subject (see Butler's comments in Osborne and Segal, 1994), metamorphosis emphasizes transformation, fluidity, flexibility and the permeability of the boundaries between subjects, genders (and, indeed, between species) – while still expressing an investment in, even a longing for, some kind of continuity, sameness and belonging that we might call 'identity'.

In addition, I want to read *Girl meets boy* as a *queer fiction*, rather than a 'lesbian novel', and to suggest that the former constitutes a productive and welcome development beyond the latter. In choosing to rewrite a story from the *Metamorphoses*, a work obsessed with categorization (type, species, class, boundary) and with category-crossing or violation, Smith produces, in turn, a novel that asks us to reflect upon the pitfalls and potentialities of category and identity – whether that is the categorization of gender and sexuality, or the genre affiliations of the text itself. *Girl meets boy* also, I argue, stands as a creative contribution to the theorization of queerness in the twenty-first century – notably challenging queer theory's recent preoccupation with negative affect and backwardness and offering instead, in the reimagining of the notoriously 'playful', self-conscious, unserious Ovid (Hardie, 2002, p. 1), something much more joyous, affirmative, and forward looking.

Girl meets boy forms part of Canongate's 'Myths' series – other titles in the series include *Weight* (2005), Jeanette Winterson's version of the Atlas and Heracles story, and Margaret Atwood's *The Penelopiad* (2005), which gives a voice to Odysseus's apparently dutiful wife, Penelope (in Atwood's version her motives are provocatively muddied). 'Myth', as it is employed in *Girl meets boy*, is something both limiting and liberatory: giving rise to restrictive, normative gender roles and identities, yet also allowing for forms of fantasy, pleasure and (self)transformation. Myths are not merely employed here, they are also questioned, interrogated. As Anthea (protagonist, and quizzical, modern-day Ianthe) asks:

> Do myths spring fully formed from the imagination and the needs of a society, [. . .] as if they emerged from society's subconscious? Or are myths conscious creations by the various money-making forces? For instance, is advertising a new kind of myth-making? Do companies sell their water etc by telling us the right kind of persuasive myth? Is that why people who really don't need to buy something that's practically free still go out and buy bottles of it? Will they soon be thinking up a myth to sell us air? And do people, for instance, want to be thin because of a prevailing myth that thinness is more beautiful? (Smith, 2007, pp. 89–90)

'Myth', here, expands to encompass various kinds of cultural persuasion and manipulation; it intervenes between subject and world; it distorts self-perception; it services the economy. Read in conjunction with Angela Carter's damning of myths as 'consolatory nonsenses' in *The Sadeian Woman* (1979), this suggests how myths might both placate – producing a kind of false consciousness – and unsettle; yet myth may speak also *'from* the imagination' and *'to* the needs of a society' (something that Carter, too, recognizes, of course) (Carter, 1979, p. 3). More pertinently, myth is pervasive, unavoidable. Thus, when Anthea says, 'I'm lucky. I was born mythless. I grew up mythless', Robin (the Iphis of Smith's novel) replies: 'No you didn't. Nobody grows up mythless [. . .]. It's what we do with the myths we grow up with that matters' (Smith, 2007, p. 98). Myths cannot be dodged, but they can be reworked, reinterpreted. Agency is here reintroduced in the act of storytelling and this self-reflexive avowal – 'it's what we do with the myths we grow up with that matters' – might stand as a comment on Smith's own practice of reinvention in *Girl meets boy*.

Iphis and Ianthe

What kind of story is the Iphis and Ianthe story, and what kind of myths (about gender and sexuality in particular) does it partake in and give rise to? Coming in book nine of Ovid's vast treasury of tales of transformation – 'Of shapes transformde to bodies straunge' (Nims, 2000, p. 3)[1] – the Iphis and Ianthe story relates the history of a girl raised as a boy, who then falls in love with another girl. As her father cannot afford the greater cost of raising a girl, the baby's mother, urged on by the goddess Isis, declares the child a boy at birth, and the parents call her Iphis, a name that 'did serve alike to man and woman bothe' (Nims, 2000, p. 245). Iphis is conveniently ambiguous in her gender appearance – 'The garments of it were a boayes. The face of it was such / As eyther in a boay or gyrle of beawtie uttered much' (Nims, 2000, p. 245) – and all goes well until she is betrothed to be married to her childhood sweetheart, Ianthe, and realizes that she cannot be the 'husband' that Ianthe is expecting on her wedding night:

Iphys loves whereof shee thinkes shee may not bee
Partaker, and the selfesame thing augmenteth still her flame.
Herself a Mayden with a Mayd (ryght straunge) in love became.

Shee scarce could stay her teares. What end remaynes for mee (quoth shee)
How straunge a love? how uncoth? how prodigious reygnes in mee? (Nims, 2000, p. 246)

The various translations of the Iphis story all stress the strangeness, unnaturalness and impossibility of Iphis's love for Ianthe. Even in Fleur

Adcock's 1994 re-telling Iphis laments: 'What future is there for me – for a woman / in love with a woman, a freakish and unheard-of / passion?' (Hofmann and Lasdun, 1994, p. 220). In Golding's 1567 translation, quoted above, the use of the word 'prodigious' suggests something 'monstrous' (Traub, 2002, p. 284), and precedes a soliloquy in which Iphis compares her impossible love to love between animals: 'A Cow is never fond / Uppon a Cow, nor Mare on Mare. The Ram delyghts the Eawe', etc. (Nims, 2000, p. 246). Perhaps unsurprisingly, then, critical responses to Ovid's tale of Iphis and Ianthe have been, as David Robinson notes, 'widely divergent' (Robinson, 2006, p. 165), ranging from claims that 'Ovid's narrative displays immense sympathy with Iphis's plight' (Hallett, 1997, p. 263), to suggestions that this particular story stands as 'Ovid's most damning denunciation of homosexuality' (Makowski, 1996, p. 30). Smith's generous verdict, delivered via Robin's re-telling of the Iphis and Ianthe story to Anthea, is that 'Ovid's very fluid, as writers go, much more than most. He knows, more than most, that the imagination doesn't have a gender. He's really good. He honours all sorts of love. He honours all sorts of story' (Smith, 2007, p. 97).

In fact, this story, despite its brevity and its fantastical nature, is an influential – and fraught – one in the history of literary representations (and wider perceptions) of lesbianism. As Valerie Traub asserts:

> The trope of impossibility, signified by Ovid's story of Iphis and Ianthe, epitomizes the fate of female-female love up to the end of the eighteenth century. The *amor impossibilis* is not reducible to a discursive figure like the friend or the tribade, but rather functions as a thematic convention within a long literary heritage. Related to both the rhetoric of idealized love in the friendship tradition and the convention of sex transformation in the discourse of tribadism, the *amor impossibilis* is, like them, derived from classical models and, like them, undergoes substantial transformation during the renaissance of *lesbianism*. (Traub, 2002, p. 279)

In Ovid's text this is very clearly an issue of *sexual* impossibility (not the impossibility of *love* between Iphis and Ianthe – which already exists – or the impossibility of their marriage, which is arranged and about to take place). As Robinson emphasizes, Iphis's love is not impossible 'for the typical reasons': 'a watchful guardian, jealous husband, strict father, unloving beloved. No, Iphis and Ianthe are both unmarried, both in love, their fathers both approve, indeed are hastening the match' (Robinson, 2006, p. 171). It is not social or cultural obstacles that pose the problem, but rather the perceived unnaturalness of lesbianism – it is nature that stands in the way: 'lesbian sex is an oxymoron, it cannot happen, it is literally, physically impossible', glosses Robinson (2006, p. 171). Diane Pintabone ascribes this idea of lesbian sex as 'impossible' to a Roman understanding of sexual behaviour as either active (penetrative, masculine) or passive (receptive/penetrated, feminine) (Pintabone, 2002, p. 267) but, as Traub suggests, this is a 'thematic convention' with a 'long literary heritage', and it is picked up even in late twentieth-century accounts of what Judith Roof has termed 'the "inconceivability" of lesbian sexuality in a phallocentric system' (Roof, 1991, p. 245; see also Butler, 1990, pp. 156–7).

In Ovid's tale, the 'impossibility' of Iphis and Ianthe's relationship is resolved by the goddess Isis who, intervening at the last moment, turns Iphis into a boy, and the story ends with the joyful marriage of the newly male Iphis and his bride, Ianthe:

> Next morrow over all the world did shine with lightsome flame,
> When Juno, and Dame Venus, and Sir Hymen joyntly came
> To Iphys mariage, who as then transformed to a boay
> Did take Ianthee to his wyfe, and so her love enjoy. (Nims, 2000, p. 248)

In the twenty-first century *Girl meets boy*, lesbian sex is 'impossible' only in the view of the obviously sexist and ignorant friends of Anthea's sister, Imogen: 'See, that's what I don't get, Dominic says shaking his head, serious. Because, there's no way they could do it, I mean, without one. So it's like, pointless' (Smith, 2007, p. 69). And Imogen, still struggling to assimilate the new information about her sister's relationship with another woman, thinks: '(Oh my God my sister who is related to me is a greg [Greg Dyke], a lack, unfuckable, not properly developed, and not even worth making illegal) (There are so many words I don't know for what my little sister is)' (Smith, 2007, p. 70). This issue of naming connects to both identity and (im)possibility – language identifies, categorizes, makes possible – yet when Imogen demands of Robin, 'what's the correct word for it, I mean, for you?', Robin replies simply, 'The proper word for me, [. . .] is me', asserting her right to exist beyond such categories and denominations (Smith, 2007, pp. 76–7).

The 'impossibility' is, additionally, partly sidestepped by figuring sex in metamorphic and metaphorical terms that eschew the active/ passive, penetrator/penetratee model (of which, more later). In *Girl meets boy*, then, Smith takes this tradition of reading lesbianism as 'impossible' and turns it on its head, seeking both to re-naturalize nature (rescuing water, that paradigmatic natural 'product', from the grips of a grasping corporation in a subplot about a bottled water company) and to emphasize the *naturalness* of female same-sex desire. In *Girl meets boy* even homophobic abuse can metamorphose into something more benign, natural and beautiful – the arrow pointing to 'LEZ' on Robin's schoolbook becoming, thanks to her embellishment, the 'trunk of a tree', the letters themselves surrounded by 'hundreds of little flowerheads, [. . .] like the letters are the branches of the tree and they've all just come into bloom' (Smith, 2007, p. 73). For if Ovid's tale (in its various translations) insists on presenting female same-sex desire as impossible, it nevertheless holds out the conceptual and political possibilities of metamorphosis – and it is this inheritance that Smith most concertedly takes up.

Metamorphosis, Identity, Queerness

Writing in 2002, Marina Warner claimed that the idea of metamorphosis 'is thriving more than ever in literature and in art' (Warner, 2002, p. 2), a point we might see as borne out by Ovid's return to popularity in the late twentieth and early twenty-first century – as evidenced by the success of Ted Hughes's *Tales from Ovid* (1997), the Michael Hofmann and James Lasdun collection of poetic re-writings of Ovid, *After Ovid* (1994), the reissuing of the Golding translation by Penguin in 2002, the publication of the *Cambridge Companion to Ovid* (also in 2002), and the appearance of various new translations and critical works (see Hofmann and Lasdun, 1994, p. xi) – as well as by the scope and reception of Warner's own work. Philip Hardie also suggests that postmodernism allowed Ovid to come back into favour – that what previously had been criticized as 'superficial wit and an irredeemable lack of seriousness' in his work could be 'reassessed in the light of a postmodernist flight from realism and presence towards textuality and anti-foundationalism' (Hardie, 2002, p. 4). Significantly, the Ovidian conception of metamorphosis, according to Warner, 'runs counter to notions of unique, individual integrity of identity in the Judaeo-Christian tradition' and this might provide another reason for the popularity of Ovid in the contemporary period – a period in which the very concept of identity has become both a preoccupation and a problem (Warner, 2002, p. 2). Warner notes how 'contemporary writers' – she mentions Salman Rushdie, Toni Morrison, Marie Darieussecq – 'are increasingly plotting their fictions against the normative models of the unified self' and using conceptions of metamorphosis to help them do this (Warner, 2002, p. 203).

At first glance, metamorphosis proposes a process of flux and change ostensibly incompatible with 'identity', which implies sameness, continuity. If (shared) identities permit us membership of a group, then metamorphosis seems to place us beyond such facile belonging. As Caroline Walker Bynum asserts:

> The question of change is, of course, the other side of the question of identity. If change is the replacement of one entity by another or the growth of an entity out of another entity in which it is implicit, we must be able to say how we know we have an entity in the first place. What gives it its identity – that is, makes it one thing? (Walker Bynum, 2005, p. 19)

Yet her reasoning suggests, of course, that no conception of identity is possible without a conception of metamorphosis – the two are mutually reinforcing; and indeed, Walker Bynum proceeds to argue that, in order to get the more 'labile' sense of identity that she maintains we require:

> What we need to think with are not images of monsters and hybrids, creatures of two-ness or three-ness, stuck together from our own sense of the incompatibility of aspiration and situation, culture and genes, mind and body. What we need are metaphors and stories that will help us imagine a world in which we really change yet really remain the same thing. (Walker Bynum, 2005, p. 188)

According to the paradox being presented by Walker Bynum, it is change that facilitates continuity; we are transformed and yet elements of the pre-transformation self persist and develop; to be is simply to be changeable, transient. Ovid's *Metamorphoses* is comprised of such stories and, in taking up this conception of metamorphosis, Smith edges towards such a 'labile' sense of identity. Throughout *Girl meets boy*, there is an emphasis on the ability of all things to change, to mutate, and desire, above all things, is transformative (this is also frequently the case in Ovid's *Metamorphoses* where desire compels a change of body or species, or where the transformation is a punishment for illicit desires):

> Her hand opened me. Then her hand became a wing. Then everything about me became a wing, a single wing, and she was the other wing, we were a bird. We were a bird that could sing Mozart. It was a music I recognised, it was both deep and light. Then it changed into a music I'd never heard before, so new to me that it made me airborne, I was nothing but the notes she was playing, held in air.

> [. . .] I was sinew, I was a snake, I changed stone to snake in three simple moves, stoke stake snake, then I was a tree whose branches were all budded knots, and what were those felty buds, were they – antlers? were antlers really growing out of both of us? [. . .] I was a she was a he was a we were a girl and a girl and a boy and a boy, we were blades, were a knife that could cut through myth, were two knives thrown by a magician, were arrows fired by a god [. . .].

> We were all that, in the space of about ten minutes. Phew. A bird, a song, the insides of a mouth, a fox, an earth, all the elements, minerals, a water feature, a stone, a snake, a tree, some thistles, several flowers, arrows, both genders, a whole new gender, no gender at all and God knows how many other things including a couple of fighting stags. (Smith, 2007, pp. 101–4)

In the course of these passages detailing their love-making, agency shifts from one to the other ('her hand opened me [. . .] I changed stone to snake'); they are first joined ('everything about me became a wing [. . .] and she was the other wing') and then fused ('we were a bird'); the boundaries between them are blurred, becoming radically, exhilaratingly permeable; there are moments when the individual self is utterly transcended ('I was nothing but the notes she was playing'); and throughout the focus shifts from 'her' to 'me' to 'she' to 'he' to 'we' to 'I', and so on, in a metamorphic process of individuation and de-individuation, assertion of self and loss of self. Smith's giddy transformations echo Ovid's pace and ebullience and reference his use of nature imagery and the supernatural; as in Ovid, the human/animal boundary is violated ('were antlers really growing out of both of us?'). To this Smith adds a self-reflexive focus on the shifting metamorphoses of language ('stoke stake snake') that figures desire as both the apotheosis and the breakdown of linguistic description.[2] 'Phew', indeed.

Furthermore, while Ovid's take on gender is rather conventionally binaristic – when Iphis becomes a boy she develops a 'larger pace' (stride), 'Her strength encreased, and her looke more sharper was to syght. / Her heare grew shorter, and shee had a much more lively spryght, / Than when shee was a wench' (Nims, 2000, p. 248) – Smith presents gender as much more radically indeterminate: 'I was a she was a he was a we were a girl and a girl and a boy and a boy'. Robin and Anthea are 'both genders, a whole new gender, no gender at all' and the imagery here darts peripatetically between the conventionally masculine/phallic (arrows, snakes, blades) and the conventionally feminine (flowers, birds, earth, a song). In describing Robin, Anthea likewise inverts gendered characteristics:

> She had the swagger of a girl. She blushed like a boy. She had a girl's toughness. She had a boy's gentleness. She was as meaty as a girl. She was as graceful as a boy. She was as brave and handsome and rough as a girl. She was as pretty and delicate and dainty as a boy. She turned boys' heads like a girl. She turned girls' heads like a boy. She made love like a boy. She made love like a girl. She was so boyish it was girlish, so girlish it was boyish, she made me want to rove the world writing our names on every tree. (Smith, 2007, p. 84)

'Girl meets boy' here in the person of Robin, and a traditional, heterosexual romance story metamorphoses into a story of gender mixing and fluidity. 'Robin Goodman' is the girl with the gender ambiguous name (like 'Iphis'), the girl who is a *good man*, and whose name is also an intertextual reference to Puck (Robin Goodfellow) in William Shakespeare's *Midsummer Night's Dream* (1600) – a figure similarly associated with fantasy, transformation, and erotic trickery, and one arguably possessed of indeterminate gender.[3] Furthermore, while, in Ovid's story, Ianthe remains ignorant throughout of the true gender of her intended (and therefore unproblematically heterosexual in her desires), Smith focalizes her version through Anthea/Ianthe, making her aware from the outset of the 'deviance' of her desire for Robin/Iphis and happily complicit in the attempt to bring this desire to fruition.

Throughout *Girl meets boy*, the notion of metamorphosis is most strikingly signalled by the novel's central motif of water. Again, the metaphor of water/thirst for desire is present in the original. In Golding's translation, Iphis bewails the fact that, 'The day of Mariage is at hand. Ianthee shalbee myne, / And yit I shall not her enjoy. Amid the water wee / Shall thirst' (Nims, 2000, p. 247); Fleur Adcock renders this simply as 'I shall be thirsty amid water' (Hofmann and Lasdun, 1994, p. 221). Smith's version of this, as Robin tells the Iphis and Ianthe story to Anthea, is that, 'It'll be like standing right in the middle of a stream, dying of thirst, with my hand full of water, but I won't be able to drink it!' (Smith, 2007, p. 96) In fact water proves significant throughout Ovid's *Metamorphoses*, with lakes and pools playing key roles in certain stories (most notably, perhaps, that of 'Narcissus and Echo'), and the very 'fluidity' of water making it the perfect symbol of metamorphosis – changeable, reflective, elusive, evanescent and yet able to wear away rock.

Water and watery motifs are used throughout Smith's novel to emphasize both fluidity and the pervasiveness and inevitability of metamorphosis. Water is something that cannot be contained, despite the attempts by the bottled water company, Pure, for which Anthea and her sister work, to treat it as a commodity; it remains resolutely natural, incorruptible. In the 'creative' meeting, one of the company lackeys notes, 'How water is smart, how water is graceful, how water, since it can change shape and form, can make us versatile [. . .] and how we're all actually about seventy-five per cent water. We need to suggest that water IS us' (Smith, 2007, p. 38). Water, then, offers a model of identity – 'water IS us', we are water – that takes us back to nature and to the body, without producing essentialized, fixed identities, instead emphasizing both flux ('it can change shape and form') and force.

Water is also used throughout to describe desire. Thus, Anthea describes her first night spent with Robin as 'our first underwater night together deep in each other's arms' (Smith, 2007, pp. 81–2). Falling in love is like 'a storm at sea': 'the ship that I was opened wide inside me and in came the ocean' (Smith, 2007, pp. 44–5). Later, Anthea reflects that:

> I was like a species that hadn't even realised it lived in a near-desert till one day its taproot hit water. Now I had taken a whole new shape. No, I had taken the shape I was always supposed to, the shape that let me hold my head high. (Smith, 2007, p. 81)

There is both change and continuity here, a new identity and the persistence of the old one: the transformation allows Anthea to take 'the shape I was always supposed to', just as many of Ovid's transformations allow the transformed individual to assume the shape that best expresses what they already were (for instance, Lycaon, the wolf man, is already a beast, a cannibal, and his new form merely reflects that). Water can take any shape, which might make it appear the most passive

of elements, yet it can also actively shape things – run grooves in mountains, erode cliffs: 'Was I briny', asks Anthea, 'were my whole insides a
piece of sea, was I nothing but salty water with a mind of its own, was I
some kind of fountain, was I the force of water through stone?' (Smith,
2007, p. 102). Like the sexual descriptions that I cited earlier, this watery
language eschews the logic of penetrating/penetrated (and thus, by
extension, of masculine/feminine), so that erotic experience renders the
body liquid, malleable but forceful; finally, watery motifs here express
the saltiness of bodily fluids, a body dissolved in desire, the boundaries
between bodies likewise dissolving.

In addition to the high-flown metamorphic imagery of desire, love
and erotic encounter to be found throughout *Girl meets boy*, we find also
the notion of metamorphosis put in the more prosaic, pragmatic service
of feminist and anti-capitalist politics. The graffiti messages that Robin
and Anthea (signing themselves 'Iphis and Ianthe', 'the message girls' or
'the message boys') leave all over Inverness concern the inequalities that
women face all over the world and all repeat the slogan 'THIS MUST
CHANGE' (Smith, 2007, 133). So 'change' is here overtly politicized –
and people are urged to bring about change (to be agents of change), not
merely to allow change to happen to them – a key development from the
Ovid source text, where most of the transformations are done *to* mortals
by gods. Smith's use of metamorphosis in this novel might then be read
as bearing out Rosemary Jackson's description of 'the modern fantastic'
as 'a subversive literature' (Jackson, 1981, p. 7), or Brian McHale's claim
that 'the fantastic' (in literature) 'precipitates a confrontation between
real-world norms (the laws of nature) and other-worldly, supernatural
norms' (McHale, 1987, p. 75). In fact, I would suggest that Smith goes
further in challenging what might count as 'real-world norms' and in
using fantastic *descriptions* and *imagery* – rather than, strictly speaking,
fantastic *scenarios* – to reflect on real-world conditions; the novel combines fantastic imagery with a grounding in the 'real' world of work,
relationships, family tensions, mobile phones, weight anxieties, popular
television, casual bigotry and nasty corporations. The popular cultural
references, in particular, root the novel in the politics of the present,
despite its borrowing of transhistorical motifs of metamorphosis and
despite Canongate's claims, in the blurb accompanying the series,
regarding the 'timeless' and 'universal' nature of myth.[4]

Andrew Feldherr writes of Ovid that 'if metamorphosis generally
marks the limit of what is consistent with the moral seriousness of heroic
epic, this is the line on which [Ovid's] *Metamorphoses* dances' (Feldherr,
2002, p. 169). The fantastic, transcendent descriptions of love-making in
Girl meets boy are juxtaposed with starkly polemical passages about globalization, homophobia and feminism – *Girl meets boy*, too, 'dances' on
the line between playful invention and 'moral seriousness'. In particular,
Smith's debt to second-wave feminism is clear – notice, for example, her

empathetic handling of the body issues of Anthea's sister, Imogen – and her use of playful, experimental language and imagery in the service of feminist values implies a critique of an unmitigated 'play' that is *not* in the service of some politics or other, even while her exuberant embrace of gender fluidity shows a debt to feminism's third wave.[5] Thus, Smith associates the fantastic – here: fantastic transformations – with desire, in a bid to capture the 'other-worldly' experience of love, while resisting Ovid's more conservative romantic denouement of a marriage smiled upon by mortals and gods alike. In *Girl meets boy* this elaborate public celebration of the relationship between Robin and Anthea is merely fantasized – played out in detail, with grandparents returned from the dead on a fibreglass boat, and magical music that makes the cathedral 'leap and caper' (Smith, 2007, p. 158) – before Anthea confesses:

> Uh-huh. Okay. I know.
>
> In my dreams.
>
> What I mean is, we stood on the bank of the river under the trees, the pair of us, and we promised the nothing that was there, the nothing that made us, the nothing that was listening, that we truly desired to go beyond our selves.
>
> And that's the message. That's it. That's all. (Smith, 2007, p. 159)

The move, here, from the transcendent, the fantastic, to the simple, even the banal ('Uh-huh [. . .]. In my dreams'), is a touching deflation that, again, brings us back to the real, the here and now. This is a happy ending, then, that acknowledges the transience, the provisionality of all such 'endings', and that refuses public recognition or endorsement in favour of private, intimate avowal.

Conclusion: Queer (fictional) futures

Girl meets boy builds on crucial past developments within lesbian fiction: the shift from 'deviant' to 'defiant' portrayals of lesbianism (that is, portrayals of it as *natural*) that Gabriele Griffin situates in the 1970s (Griffin, 1993a, p. 62); the flowering of what has been called 'the lesbian postmodern' (exemplified by the work of Jeanette Winterson) in the 1980s and 1990s (Doan, 1994); the lesbian manipulations of genre and popular fiction discussed by Paulina Palmer and Sally Munt, among others (see Palmer, 1993, 1999; Munt, 1992, 1994; also Griffin, 1993b); and the more recent critical interest in lesbian historical fiction stimulated, to no small degree, by the success of Sarah Waters (see Doan and Waters, 2000). Yet Smith is rarely identified as a 'lesbian novelist' in the way that Waters is; certainly she is not seeking to write lesbians into history, here, in the way that Waters has done, but rather using a transhistorical story of same-sex love – with its persistent myths of 'impossible' lesbian desire – in the service of a very twenty-first-century understanding of identity, sexuality and relationships. And if the self-reflexivity and formal fragmentations of her work owe something to postmodernism – Richard Bradford, for example, names Smith as one of the 'New Postmodernists', alongside contemporaries such as David Mitchell and Toby Litt (Bradford, 2007, p. 48) – then this is writing less obviously in the 'fantastic' vein than, say, Winterson's or Carter's, although both are clearly important and influential writers as far as Smith is concerned. In her (feminist, anti-capitalist) politics, Smith manifestly rejects both what Wiegman has called 'a cultural visibility framed by the commodity aesthetic', the move towards 'cultural' rather than political 'forms of collective identity engagement' (Wiegman, 1994, pp. 3, 4), and the 'radicalism [. . .] attuned to the demands of the marketplace' that Bradford attributes to the 'New Postmodernists' (Bradford, 2007, p. 48). If postmodernism – new or old, lesbian or otherwise – provides a vital back-history to Smith's writing (and certainly informs her work stylistically), it cannot fully account for it in the present.

In addition, I would suggest that it is more productive to read Smith's oeuvre as 'queer', rather than as 'lesbian' (similar arguments might be made about the work of Patricia Duncker and A. M. Homes, for example). Such a designation signals a move beyond identity politics and a more general concern with non-normativity, allowing, therefore, for queer readings of texts which are not directly *about* homosexual relationships and characters; Smith's *The Accidental* (2005), for example, strikes me as an interestingly queer deconstruction of the post-9/11 family, particularly when read alongside Ian McEwan's notably heteronormative *Saturday* (2005). By using the term 'queer', here, I am deliberately invoking a 'category in the process of formation' – or perhaps more accurately, deformation – a (non) category necessarily possessed of a 'definitional indeterminacy' (Jagose, 1996, p. 1). 'Queer' demarcates 'not a positivity but a positionality *vis-a-vis* the normative' (Halperin, 1995, p. 62); queer is an 'open mesh of possibilities, gaps, overlaps, dissonances and resonances, lapses and excesses of meaning when the constituent elements of anyone's gender, of anyone's sexuality aren't made (or *can't* be made) to signify monolithically' (Sedgwick, 1994, p. 8). The exuberantly metamorphic love scenes of *Girl meets boy* seem to speak to Sedgwick's definition of queerness in particular. Above all, queer theory has concerned itself with the need for, in Butler's words, 'a radical critique of the categories of identity' (Butler, 1990, p. ix): this is the challenge that queer theory took up – but has frequently struggled to fulfil. Smith's response to that challenge is to reinvent a story that *predates* the conception of sexuality *as an identity* in the service of a *post-identity* politics – but a post-identity politics that harbours, still, a desire for identities and a strategic need for them; this is the desire for both continuity and change, belonging and transcendence, that metamorphosis facilitates.

Queer *fiction* becomes also, on this reading, an eschewing of originality, in favour of creative *re*writings, copies that disrupt the original (to use, again, Butlerian terminology – see Butler, 1991) and that draw attention to practices of rewriting, rereading, reimagining, reinvention. What messages there are in this novel concern the agency offered by *storytelling* as a process both metamorphic and redemptive. As Anthea avers, towards the close of *Girl meets boy*:

> [I]t was always the stories that needed the telling that gave us the rope we could cross any river with. They balanced us high above any crevasse. They made us be natural acrobats. They made us be brave. They met us well. They changed us. It was in their nature to. (Smith, 2007, p. 160)

Such storytelling encodes not only a kind of agency but also an optimism distinctly at odds with much recent queer theory, which has displayed a marked preoccupation with loss, trauma, melancholy and shame in its investigations of queerness and queer lives in the past and in the present (see, for example, Cvetkovich, 2003; Love, 2007; Munt, 2007; Halperin and Traub, 2009; Ahmed, 2010).

Such joyous storytelling as Smith's preserves also the open-endedness and boundary-crossing so vital to the early queer theory of Sedgwick and Butler. Ovid's poem ends on an 'assertion of inextinguishable vitality [. . .] – against ruin, against disappearance' (Warner, 2002, pp. 16–17). Smith's novel – which garnered effusive reviews describing it as 'glorious' (Gunn, 2007), 'blissful' (Davies, 2007), 'exuberant' (Fitzgerald, 2008) and 'effervescent' (Taylor, 2007) – likewise closes on a poetic paean to the principle of metamorphosis and the (queer) hope that it holds out, a paean to:

> The story of nature itself, ever inventive, making one thing out of another, and one thing into another, and nothing lasts, and nothing's lost, and nothing ever perishes, and things can always change, because things will always change, and things will always be different, because things can always be different. (Smith, 2007, p. 160)

The shifts in tense here – from 'can' to 'will' and 'will' to 'can' – signal the endless possibilities of metamorphosis and stress reinvention, recycling, reincarnation as processes both natural and artistic; 'change' is presented, here and throughout *Girl meets boy*, as both a vital, organic principle and a moral responsibility (the responsibility to *make* a difference). The novel makes of metamorphosis a queer process of proliferation and generation, making and unmaking, that gestures towards some better future. Yet Smith's queer utopianism, even as it anticipates José Muñoz's glossing of queerness as 'the warm illumination of a horizon imbued with potentiality', 'an ideality that can be distilled from the past and used to imagine a future [. . .], a longing that propels us onward' (Muñoz, 2009, p. 1), always feels the pull of the present, and always tempers its grandiosity with modesty: 'And that's the message. That's it. That's all' (Smith, 2007, p. 159).

Narrating Intrusion: Deceptive Storytelling and Frustrated Desires in *The Accidental* and *There but for the*

ULRIKE TANCKE

Chapter Summary: Ali Smith's most recent novels, *The Accidental* (2005) and *There but for the* (2011) boast remarkably similar scenarios: each centres on the intrusion of a stranger into a seemingly sheltered middle-class family's home. At first glance, these scenarios beg to be read in symbolic or metaphorical terms, that is, at a thematic level, turning the novels into allegories of contemporary mores, anxieties and concerns. This chapter, by contrast, centres on the narrative techniques by which these scenarios are rendered. Crucially, in each of the novels, the central enigma is not resolved; that is, the reader's presumable expectation of narrative resolution is thwarted. With this mechanism of 'narrative deception', the 'intruders' ultimately assume a revelatory function that exposes our penchant for straightforward narratives of progress and clearly identifiable developments, and our disinclination to acknowledge the uncomfortable realities of violence and desire that shape human actions. Ultimately, the novels can be understood as replacing the postmodernist fascination with the virtual with a disturbing 'reality principle'.

Key words: Hyperreality, post-9/11 fiction, postmodernism, traumatological fiction, violence

Ali Smith's most recent novels, *The Accidental* (2005) and *There but for the* (2011) boast remarkably similar scenarios: each centres on the intrusion of a stranger into a seemingly sheltered middle-class family's home. In the case of *The Accidental*, the Smart family's holiday in Norfolk is disrupted by the appearance of the mysterious Amber; in *There but for the*, the Lees' Greenwich dinner party takes an unexpected turn when one of their guests, a young man called Miles, locks himself into their spare room, refuses to leave and subsequently develops into a public and media attraction.

At first glance, these scenarios – sudden upheavals disturbing privileged middle-class existence – beg to be read in symbolic or metaphorical terms, that is, at a thematic level. Critics have frequently noted the references to the Iraq war and the global War on Terror that abound in *The Accidental* and have therefore read it as an allegory of the Western sense of self in the wake of the 9/11 terrorist attacks (see Tew, 2007, p. 211). In a similar vein, reviewers of *There but for the* have typically pointed out the ways in which the novel's erratic punning, philosophical commentary and contemporary allusions make it a literary reflection on 'the way we are now' (Churchwell, 2011). Moreover, with their recurrent use of wordplay, numerous intertextual references and broad range of cultural allusions, both novels seem to exemplify postmodern playfulness and self-referentiality. At the same time, however, the novels' thematic distinctness is offset by their narrative set-up, which, in each case, hinges on the event of the intrusion and is structured along the alternating points of views of the various characters affected by it.

The plot device of cataclysmic intrusion appears to create a natural parallel to the contemporary upheavals which both novels intermittently hint at, most notably the events of 9/11, the resulting War on Terror, and the interconnected upheavals of a globalized world. Philip Tew cites *The Accidental* as one example of 'traumatological' fiction (see Tew, 2007, p. 211), and both novels can indeed be read as expressive of a particular, discernible postmillennial climate. Yet, while at first glance both *The Accidental* and *There but for the* employ references to contemporary events, rather than commenting on a particular zeitgeist or sociocultural condition, they explore the way in which such reference points – and the way in which we respond to them – function as indicators of our own perceptions, prejudices and preformed judgements. Moreover, the novels combine identifiable thematic reference points with a seemingly easily decodable narrative structure revolving around the mysterious intrusion; a structure that responds to the reader's desire for clear-cut cause-and-effect scenarios, thus misleading us in a double sense. Hence the novels' contemporary resonance and thematic set-up is designed as a complex narrative red herring that we easily latch on to and that thereby exposes our penchant for immediate associations and simple categorization.

The first level at which this narrative deception takes place is that of form. *The Accidental* initially appears to chart a conventional developmental trajectory, in which Amber figures as a catalyst for change in relation to the four characters whose perspectives the narrative alternately engages with. This idea is suggested by the headings 'beginning', 'middle' and 'end' given to the novel's three main parts. Each of these is further subdivided into four separate chapters in which the family members take turns to tell a part of the story from their respective points of view. In addition to this tripartite structure, however, the narrative also boasts experimental elements which disrupt the seemingly straightforward plot line. For instance, Amber's profound impact on each of the characters and the degree to which she unsettles their existing beliefs and senses of self is also communicated by the fragmentary nature of much of the novel's language, which boasts chapters beginning in mid-sentence (Smith, 2005, pp. 7, 109), passages written in verse (Smith, 2005, pp. 173–7) and stream-of-consciousness (Smith, 2005, pp. 37–8, 259). The novel's three sections, alternately focalized through Astrid, Magnus, Michael and Eve, are framed by Amber's first-person account in the short prefatory and intermittent chapters following each of the three parts, in which she reflects on her mysterious origins, their interweaving with contemporary socio-political events and – in an indirect manner – comments on her role vis-à-vis the characters. However, the structure of the novel's main plot as a whole – its neat chronological trajectory from beginning to middle to end – suggests a straightforwardly teleological narrative development. This tension indicates the complexity of the novel's structure and its implications: *The Accidental* seems to simultaneously offer both teleology and non-linearity; the reader is tricked by the suggestion of linear chronology and teleology into believing that we are dealing with a clear-cut narrative set-up of cause and effect.

In a similar vein, *There but for the* misleads the reader as to its narrative set-up. With its four sections revolving around the incident at the Lees' dinner party and its aftermath, the reader expects Miles's unlikely behaviour to be eventually explained and resolved. Yet what we are given instead are individual narratives, each connected with Miles the character – those of a woman, Anna, whom he met on an organized trip as a teenager; Mark, the gay picture researcher who took him along to the party in the first place; the grandmother of his first sort-of-girlfriend who died at 16; and Brooke, the 10-year-old daughter of a black couple who were also guests at the dinner party. These individual narratives, however, merely play with these connections rather than integrating them in a believable cause-and-effect manner. At first glance, this implicit commentary on '[t]he way things connect' (Smith, 2005, p. 196) is all the reader is left with at the end of the novel, as the scenario remains largely unresolved. The novel's enigmatic – and, importantly, elliptic – title underlines this ambiguity, suggesting ostensive presence ('there') but at the same time undermining it with its incomplete concession ('but for the').

The narrative structure of Smith's novels thus urges us not to take the apparently pivotal event signalled by Amber's and Miles's appearances at face value, but rather identifies the underlying agenda it is designed to serve. It crystallizes the narrative deception at work in the novels: their intrusion urges a reading along the lines of a turning point or life-changing event for the people concerned (see Germanà, 2010,

p. 88). At a closer look, however, it can more fruitfully be conceptual-
ized as a narrative means designed to lend credence to the characters'
developments and decisions and as a technique that draws attention
to the overarching emphasis of the texts on violence and desire. In that
sense, Amber and Miles, respectively, function as a narrative device in
a double sense, that is, the deception works at two levels: in the case
of *The Accidental*, Amber seems to aid our understanding of the text as
a narrative of turning points, and she allows the characters to be presented as experiencing a pivotal encounter. Similarly, in *There but for the*
Miles's intrusion into the Lees' home works as a narrative device that
binds together the stories of a disconnected set of characters who have
in some way been in contact with him, but that ultimately leaves us with
an aporia at its centre. In each case, the reader is implicitly asked to look
elsewhere for the novel's genuine concerns, while the disruptive event
at its core merely signals that we are invited to look further than the
superficial level of plot.

To start with *The Accidental*, the most readily accessible plot level of
Amber's appearance is offset by the novel's distinctly contemporary fla-
vour. There are occasional hints at current political and cultural affairs
and intermittent references to recent events and developments, most
notably the Iraq war in the aftermath of the 9/11 terrorist attacks and the
war crimes committed by US soldiers at the Abu Ghraib prison, which
came to media attention in 2004. These contextual reference points
neatly appear to situate *The Accidental* in the category of 'post-9/11' fiction. One possibility to make sense of this characteristic is to read the
plot device of Amber's intrusion and its cataclysmic nature as a natural
parallel to the events of 9/11, demonstrating, in Tew's words, '[a] traumatological emphasis . . . foregrounding conflict and intimacy in the
apparently narrow bounds of domesticity' (Tew, 2007, p. 211). However,
I will argue that this apparent parallel is doubly misleading. The novel's contemporary reference points function as narrative red herrings
that are designed to trick the reader into falling prey to – and hopefully
acknowledging – their desire for clear-cut categories and messages.
The scenario is clearly more complex than merely signifying a simple
mimetic reflection of global geopolitical and sociocultural upheaval in
the family unit.

Significantly, the way in which allusions to contemporary events are
rendered in the novel highlights the fact that the characters are only
affected by these events in a vicarious fashion. Their exclusively medi-
atized access problematizes the ethical relevance of suffering which
ultimately remains remote. For instance, in one of the 'Eve' sections
of the novel, the narrative explicitly invokes the Abu Ghraib incidents.
Eve's mental memory of the photographs of abused Iraqi prisoners and
American military personnel ostensibly enjoying sadistic torture games
exemplifies the ethical implications of globally transmitted images of
atrocities. Pondering the degree to which she has been desensitized

to the emotional impact of pictures of that kind, the narrative voice observes that

> The more pictures she saw, the less they meant something that had happened to real people and the more it became possible to pile real people up like that anywhere you wanted and have your picture taken standing smiling behind them.

> She could still clearly see it, the photograph of the dead man in the bodybag and the grinning girl soldier, . . . She didn't know what to do about the looking, whether to keep on looking or to stop looking . . . She was living in a time when historically it was permissible to smile like that above the face of someone who had died a violent death. (Smith, 2005, pp. 285–6)

Eve's response to the images – her vacillation between fascination and abjection, examining and looking away – reflects the complex and ambiguous significance the Abu Ghraib pictures have assumed in the public perception of the War on Terror – an oft-met argument is that the spectator's gaze itself involves a degree of complicity in the deeds (see Hesford, 2006, p. 30).

The idea of complicity is also hinted at in the above passage, when the narrative voice registers Eve's uncertainty about 'looking' (Smith, 2005, p. 286). Importantly, this complicity is a function of the narrative strategy: complicity is mediated through Eve's free indirect discourse. Her unease about the voyeurism entailed by the pictures is immediately followed by a narrative gesture of distancing, as Eve's voice contextualizes her reaction as part of a large-scale cultural climate of willing acceptance of atrocities. This is clearly a move to shift responsibility onto the anonymous plane of a particular historical moment which 'permits' the kinds of images Eve contemplates. Of course, this is not to say that Eve bears any concrete responsibility for the events she visually remembers; rather, her stance appears problematic in view of her earlier admission that she feels 'a bit guilty, albeit in a measured way' (Smith, 2005, p. 91) about the Iraq war. Her professed guilt occurs in a situation where it is clearly an inappropriate designation of her response and only serves the self-image she purports to create. Paradoxically, asserting her alleged culpability here appears as a self-congratulatory move of seemingly accepting blame in order to present herself as exceptionally self-aware and morally sensitive.

In making this point, *The Accidental* does not propose moral relativism; to acknowledge the trivial nature of violence and atrocities is not to say that we should not try to empathize with suffering remote from our own lives, or that we should ignore the structural inequalities and political power struggles that cause suffering worldwide. However, what the novel does suggest is that individuals' implication in violence and cruelty starts much closer to home and that professed moral outrage at things far beyond our personal sphere of influence may all too easily make us overlook our own capacity for inflicting violence and suffering. It is this uncomfortable recognition that is triggered by Amber's appearance, for characters and readers alike.

The novel's final sentence – Amber's unsettling self-presentation: 'I'm everything you ever dreamed' (Smith, 2005, p. 306) – can be read as an analeptic explanatory device that generates a complex and unsettling reading of the novel that brings my last point to the fore. As the nod towards the Freudian unconscious implicit in this comment suggests, Amber externalizes urges and desires that are lying dormant in the characters and exposes unacknowledged facets of their personalities. Externalizing their submerged impulses, she acts as a catalyst forcing the characters to acknowledge those aspects of their personalities that point not only to individual flaws, but to disturbing constants of the human condition: our inclination to self-delusion and our innate capacity for violence.

Amber's role can be traced in an exemplary fashion with regard to Magnus. Initially, his strategy to cope with his feelings of guilt in contributing to his classmate, Catherine Masson's suicide is to replace, in his imagination, the 'real Magnus' with the idea of 'hologram boy', that is, an artificially recorded, three-dimensional image and thus, effectively, a disembodied version of himself. The self-image as 'hologram boy' is a reassuring fantasy, whereas his real, embodied equivalent is inescapably implied in the girl's death:

> He himself is a hologram. He has been created by laser, lenses, optical holders, a special vibration-isolated optical table. He is the creation of coherent light . . . The real Magnus is this, now, massive, unavoidable. The real Magnus is too much. He is all bulk, big as a beached whale, big as a floundering clumsy giant . . . Magnus himself is all bad. He was bad all along though he didn't know it. He believed in his own coherent light. He was wrong. He was bad. He was bad all through . . . The end. It is because of him. He showed them what to do. They did it. They put her head on another body. They sent it round the email list. She killed herself. Magnus is shocked every time he thinks it. What really shocks him is that nothing happens. Nothing happens every time he thinks it. Didn't it matter? Doesn't it? They took her head. They put it on the other body. Even though it was a lie it became true. It became more her than her. (Smith, 2005, pp. 37–9)

The 'real' Magnus's sense of guilt crystallizes in his corporeal presence. This material immediacy reflects a similar mechanism with regard to the manipulation of the girl's photo, where a seemingly harmless and disembodied computer application (cutting and pasting the photo) is rendered in terms of an inherently violent act. Crucially, Magnus does not succeed in keeping up his self-image as 'hologram boy'; rather, his complicity in the girl's death manifests itself in *his own* body. This becomes obvious as the above-quoted passage continues:

> He thinks of it now. He gets stiff. Up he comes, up he goes. Every time he thinks of himself standing looking at the picture they made, on his own, in his room. He was in on the whole thing. Every time, up he comes again. Ah. He is so fucking monstrous. He can't stop. He has tried. Try harder, ha ha. It was hilarious. The way her head was on the neck. The way the breasts were angled . . . Now he is laughing again, stiff as hell. (Smith, 2005, pp. 39–40)

Magnus's body betrays his complicity in the girl's abuse: his uncontrollable laughter and his erection contradict what he knows to be morally appropriate, but his physical responses are too powerful to be reined in. Magnus's experience of his body revolves around its abject materiality (Weiss, 1999, p. 42); it culminates in his disturbing erection, which enacts an unsettling merger between sexual desire and death, whose nexus is the corporeal immediacy of both phenomena.

At first glance, Amber's appearance in Magnus's life reads like a way out of his self-loathing and guilt-ridden sexual anxiety. From their first encounter, Amber makes drastically upfront advances on Magnus and eventually seduces him several times. In so doing, of course, she latches on to the root of his abjection – his sexual response to the girl's death. At the surface level, the text appears to suggest that Amber has a healing effect on Magnus, replacing his association of sexuality and guilt with an affirmative version of sexual encounter, reconciling him with his adolescent sexuality and eventually even enabling him to '[tell] it all [the story of the girl's suicide] to Astrid . . ., or as much of it as he knows and as much of it as he can, beginning at the beginning' (Smith, 2005, p. 258). However, this seemingly conciliatory tale of redemption through therapeutic sharing of experience sits uneasily with the dark undertones that permeate Magnus's sexual encounters with Amber.

Again, the narrative operates with a dual hermeneutics that makes it difficult for the reader to pinpoint its overall drift. At one level, Amber does seem to have thoroughly transformative effects on Magnus, rescuing him from the brink of suicide and subsequently introducing him to the pleasures of meaningful sexuality, thereby apparently breaking the connection between his sexual urges and his involvement in Catherine Masson's death that previously burdened him. Yet the textual rendition of this evaluation also reveals the cracks that undermine this exclusively positive vision. For one thing, Magnus's fond appreciation of Amber's role in his life is couched in fictional terms, suggesting that the idealized account the reader is presented with is an embellished version of the reality:

> Amber = everything he didn't even know he imagined possible for himself.

He will be able to remember this all his life, this losing his virginity to, learning all about it from, an older woman; the kind of thing that would happen to a boy in a classic novel or something but is really happening to him, the kind of thing that he will be able to tell someone over a beer in a quiet pub, leaning on the counter, speaking low, moved by his own memory of it when he is much older, a man, in his late twenties maybe or his thirties. (Smith, 2005, p. 153)

However, the text leaves it open whether their sexual encounters are genuinely entirely positive in nature. While Magnus's perspective presents them as miraculous and life changing (Smith, 2005, pp. 141–2), the narrative is also suffused with undercurrents of vulgarity and violence, such as when it quotes Amber's frequent public innuendos ('A hard time! Give it to me!' [Smith, 2005, p. 136]) and her crudely explicit remarks ('We'll be away about an hour, long enough for me to ravish him sexually then bring him back safely, is that okay?' [Smith, 2005, p. 143]). Readers are made to share the reaction of the other characters, 'laughing like they think it's a hilarious joke' (Smith, 2005, p. 143), at the same time as they are inevitably complicit in Amber's brash honesty, knowing full well that her comments are no mere bravado. The self-deception that Magnus falls prey to, exclusively focusing as he does on Amber's positive impact, is thus both replicated and undermined from the point of view of the reader.

Moreover, their relationship ultimately continues the sex-death nexus that has been established with Magnus's unwitting sexual response to his memory of the pornographic version of Catherine Masson's photo. Magnus and Amber's first meeting takes place as Magnus is about to commit suicide by hanging himself with a shirt on a beam on the bathroom ceiling. The scene creates a multilayered set of associative connections between Catherine Masson's tampered photograph, online pornography and Magnus's death wish: the 'full-looking, soft-looking knot' (Smith, 2005, p. 54) on Catherine's school tie parallels the slipknot Magnus creates with the shirt to hang himself; the 'dark hair' (Smith, 2005, p. 54) of the internet porn model whose body Magnus copied and pasted onto Catherine's photo is taken up by the description of Catherine's 'brown hair' (Smith, 2005, p. 54) and, in turn, Amber's 'yellow angelic hair' (Smith, 2005, p. 55). The description of Amber as an 'angel' (Smith, 2005, pp. 55, 56) is undermined when the chain of associations comes full circle as Amber is depicted as 'very beautiful, a little rough-looking, like a beautiful used girl off an internet site' (Smith, 2005, p. 55).

As this narrative set-up suggests, with its random set of associations and crude physicality, Amber and Magnus's sexual relationship also hints at the violent potential inherent in sexuality and desire and thus, obviously, links in with Magnus's earlier experience of his sexual urges as brutal, monstrous and destructive. In other words, Amber's appearance signifies that the body, far from being an elusive entity that can be imaginatively transcended, is a capacity to be reckoned with. This individual experience of inflicting harm on other's bodies stands in contrast to the novel's interspersed references to the Abu Ghraib incidents, that is, globalized images of violated bodies: even if both engage virtual media, the former cannot remain virtualized and boast a tangible material presence.

Amber's ambiguous effect on Magnus – triggering a degree of self-reflection, but at the same time unearthing the disturbing dimensions of his desires and behaviours – is paralleled in her encounters with the other family members. In Astrid's case, Amber appears initially to have an even more straightforwardly salutary effect, as she triggers a cascade of revelations, about being bullied at school and about her desire to reconnect with her biological father. Yet again, Amber's role in Astrid's development cannot be taken at face value, that is, as a psychological healing process. In fact, Astrid's budding self-confidence with regard to the group of girls who have bullied her at school gains a sinister dimension when she fantasizes about Amber taking revenge on her behalf. Semi-conscious just before going to sleep, Astrid imagines Amber turning up at each of the girls' houses in turn and violently attacking them in retribution ('Amber slaps [Zelda Howe] hard across the face' (Smith, 2005, p. 133), she 'swings [Lorna Rose's] legs so she falls over' (Smith, 2005, p. 133) and she 'pushes [the swing chair] hard backwards so that Rebecca falls out of it on to the lawn' (Smith, 2005, p. 133)). Amber's brutal attack foreshadows her concluding self-designation – 'I'm everything you ever dreamed' (Smith, 2005, p. 306) – when she precedes her violence with the ominous remark: 'believe me I am your worst nightmare welcome to hell' (Smith, 2005, p. 133). The fact that this is all happening in Astrid's unconscious suggests that Amber functions here as an externalization of the former's unacknowledged impulses and desires, which follow the primitive logic of 'an eye for an eye'. This is highlighted by the fact that the narrative initially marks out the scene as a product of Astrid's imagination ('She sees *in her head* . . .' [Smith, 2005, p. 132], 'Then *maybe* Amber goes . . .' [Smith, 2005, p. 133; emphasis added]), only to gradually withdraw any such perspective-allocating expressions, so that the reader is tempted to read the scene as an account of facts rather than a pleasurable fantasy of revenge.

These ambiguities culminate in Amber's encounter with Eve, which externalizes submerged facets of Eve's personality. In one sense, Amber appears to be a catalyst for Eve's suppressed desires for non-conformity and escape, undermining her average existence as a middle-class, working mother in an almost farcically clichéd manner when she kisses her (see Smith, 2005, p. 202). Yet Eve's subsequent behaviour is anything but a liberating or self-affirmative move, but exposes a hidden layer of violence and destructiveness in her character. Immediately after their kiss, Eve throws Amber out of the house (pp. 202–3), without giving a reason, and much to her family's dismay. More importantly, the end of the novel sees Eve abandoning her family to go on a round-the-world trip and eventually travel to the United States to visit her dead father's house. The sense of destructiveness is heightened as her trip progresses: while in the United States, she randomly intrudes into an American family's home, a seemingly pointless move which reflects and repeats Amber's equally unmotivated and sudden presence in the Smarts' holiday home. The scene is deliberately set up in such a way as to create parallels between Amber's intrusion and Eve's imitation of it, such as when Eve explains her sudden presence with the fact that her 'car broke down' (Smith, 2005, p. 297; cf. 64), is mistaken for different people as fits the family members' expectations of their day, or when she replicates Amber's sociopathic disregard for politeness by frankly voicing her opinion of the mother in front of the daughter ('Your mother is an absolute nightmare bitch from hell, Eve said' [Smith, 2005, p. 298]) and stuffing her pockets with food that is being prepared for the family's dinner party that evening.

As the narrative trajectory culminates in the metaphorical collapse of Eve and Amber into one, it exposes a disturbing set of human universals – the capacity for violence, the ruthless pursuit of self-interest and the unavoidable propensity to inflict hurt on others. In this sense, Tew is right to state that the novel 'positions the traumatological within the realm of one's underlying fears and desires' (Tew, 2007, p. 213). Eve's narrative underscores this in an indirect fashion, as it exemplifies the human inclination not to acknowledge the tangibly material dimensions of 'fears and desires'. This becomes particularly pertinent in view of Eve's escape and its inflections with her professional identity as a writer of so-called autobiotruefictinterviews (Smith, 2005, p. 81), in which she imaginatively recounts the lives of war victims if they had in fact lived. In a subtly ironic manner, her narrative dubs her decision to abandon her life in the United Kingdom as 'tak[ing] a gap year from her own history' (Smith, 2005, p. 286). In addition to the allusion to fashionable parlance ('take a year out' [Smith, 2005,p. 287]), the phrase also situates Eve's behaviour in a broader discourse of history and historiography in the context of her work as a writer. She decides to take her 'gap year' when she is 'on her way to a press conference about the Families Against the Thievery of Relatives' Authenticity group', which opposes the format of her 'autobiotruefictinterviews'. The response that Eve has prepared reads like a manifesto for postmodern historiography: '*Who is to say what authenticity is? Who is to say who owns imagination? Who is to say that my versions, my stories of these individuals' afterlives, are less true than anyone else's?*' (Smith, 2005, p. 286). However, the novel contrasts this notion of history as storytelling with Amber's scathing indictment of Eve's pursuit: 'all these endless fucking endless selfish fucking histories . . . I ought to punch you in the effing ucking stomach . . . That'd give you a real fucking story to tell' (Smith, 2005, p. 196). Amber's drastic derogation points out the category difference between history as a linguistic construct and real events with tangible, physical impact (even though these can, of course, never be accessed in unmediated form). Eve's 'history', by contrast, overlooks the violence inherent in historical events – although it is exceptionally pertinent in the case of the subjects of her work; after all, the real-life figures she uses as her fictional characters are all dead, that is, they paradigmatically exemplify the violence of history – and thus merely delivers a pretence at reality. Amber's vocal opposition to Eve's reductive understanding of history thus crystallizes the novel's meta-critical impetus: Amber signifies the urgent philosophical necessity to assert the primacy of reality over its linguistic representation. To perceive reality as 'a function of language' (Pols, 1992, p. 6) is an ultimately reductive move that renders the subject matter of any narrative insubstantial and irrelevant. The novel thus stages a critique of the postmodernist anxiety about the impossibility of knowing the real. Paradoxically, it does so by drawing attention to our increasing engagement with the hyperreal in which its juvenile characters – Magnus with his online activities and Astrid with her determination to approach her surroundings through the lens of her digital camera – are entrenched. To the extent that Amber functions as an externalization of the characters' submerged desires, she also highlights that the virtual is dangerous in that it deceives us about the fact that violence, guilt and the body cannot be escaped from.

There but for the similarly questions the postmodern conviction of linguistic constructedness by juxtaposing reality – exemplified by Miles's physical presence in the Lees' home – with various layers of discursive formations. The scenario is complicated in *There but for the* because of the fact that there is no interaction between Miles and the other characters after he has locked himself away in the Lees' spare room (apart from some trivial encounters revolving around food provision and the like). As a result, he does not function as a catalyst figure in the sense that Amber does but, while physically present throughout and variously connected to each of the characters through whose perspective each section of the narrative is filtered, Miles operates as a lens that sheds light on the other characters and legitimizes them being in the spotlight. What this narrative set-up suggests, ultimately, is that the unlikely plot twist of his intrusion is just that – an improbably twist that is not to be taken at face value, let alone be accorded any deep significance of its own. Instead, the novel's genuinely disturbing message lies elsewhere: like *The Accidental*, it pinpoints the dark sides of the human psyche and of human desires.

Most obviously, *There but for the* offers scathing social satire, with the Lees' Greenwich home (complete with 'authenticated c17th door[s]' [Smith, 2011, p. 107] and a spare room 'which we were about to turn into a badly needed study for our daughter who has important exams this coming year' [Smith, 2011, p. 105]) and their dinner party symbolizing the problematic implications of urban gentrification. As Genevieve Lee's letter in a Sunday paper's 'Real Life' section suggests, Miles's intrusion into their bourgeois sanctuary has resonances of the Freudian uncanny, turning the familiar into something strange:

> It is strange having a stranger in the house with you all the time. It makes you strangely self-aware, strange to yourself . . . Perhaps in some way metaphorically we are all like this man 'Milo' – all of us locked in a room in a house belonging to strangers . . . [W]e do not know when our home will feel like home again. (Smith, 2011, pp. 106–7)

These reflections may read like glib yet seemingly profound philosophizing in view of her overall self-congratulatory tone; however, in the context of the novel as a whole, her 'strange self-awareness' can be read as a gesture that the reader is asked to share, that is, it epitomizes the stance that the narrative provokes.

What the various narrative strands of the novel expose, after all, is a set of uncomfortable observations on our contemporary reality and on the human condition at large that the reader is both complicit in and invited to reflect upon. One thematic level at which these observations occur is established by the references to global migration and refugees which are developed across different narrative strands. The first person whose perspective is recounted at the start of the novel, Miles's teenage travel companion Anna, used to work for immigration authorities recording asylum seekers' claims and their justifications. Anna's account of the poignant stories she was commonly told – 'thirteen Afghanis and . . . two Iranians hidden in [a] lorryload of lightbulbs' (Smith, 2011, p. 59) – highlight the inability of traumatic experience to be rendered via language (see Whitehead, 2004, p. 4):

> A lot of the people Anna had seen had trouble speaking, either because of translation problems, or because a rain of blows had made them distrust words. Or both. Translation was sometimes itself a little rain of blows. How could what had happened to them be possible in one language, never mind be able to be retold in another? (Smith, 2011, p. 59)

As Anna recounts that the refugees' gruesome stories were typically 'judged not credible' (Smith, 2011, pp. 59, 60), the narrative draws on trauma to exemplify the instability of representation and the manipulative uses to which it can be put. More importantly, however, the thematic level established in her narrative is also used to express universally valid facts about the human condition when she observes that: 'In any language, it was almost always about what home was' (Smith, 2011, p. 59).

The refugee topic is taken up in the following part of the novel, which recounts the events preceding Miles's disappearance to the spare room, largely from Mark's point of view. The shallow dinner party conversation initially reiterates liberal platitudes about the benefits of a globalized world ('a more or less borderless world. And that's as it should be' [Smith, 2011, p. 146]), only to then – at Brooke's deadpan intermission – express the need for borders and divisions as a fundamentally human desire: 'everywhere needs some defence against people just coming in and overrunning the place with their terrorisms or their deficiencies . . . Humankind has needed fortifications since the start of humankind started' (Smith, 2011, p. 146). While this standpoint is ostensibly ridiculed through its awkward and redundant verbiage, the reader is thereby asked to admit his or her own investment in similar scenarios of division. In so doing, the narrative expresses a hard-to-admit constant of human living-together, namely that a borderless world is a utopian vision. The later admission of the same dinner guest that '[m]oney and power' are 'the real magic words' (Smith, 2011, p. 151) may similarly jar with common liberal credentials, yet at the same time pinpoint a fundamental truth about the human condition. Ironically, the complacent voice of petty bourgeois capitalism that utters this statement is not merely ridiculed, thus focusing the novel's social critique in an indirect fashion.

Thus contrasting conflicting human desires – the need to belong and the necessity to differentiate oneself from others and to exert power over others – the novel suggests that there is no redemptive solution to these oppositional drives. This is where the significance – or rather, the non-significance – of the Miles figure becomes apparent: we may expect his intrusion to function as a trigger for far-reaching social critique, yet his merely vicarious appearance in the narrative means that he is not a social revolutionary of nonconformist activist, but an ultimately enigmatic figure who remains an unresolved mystery at the novel's centre. While we might expect him to crystallize the novel's social critique, the narrative works in a more complex and indirect fashion, thus suggesting that there is no solution to 'the pressing human dilemma: how to walk a clean path between obscenities' (Smith, 2011, p. 159). We inevitably confront a 'reality principle' (Tew, 2007, p. 212) in which 'obscenities' have to be reckoned with.

This constitutive 'reality principle' is also the point where the key concern of *There but for the* dovetails with that of *The Accidental*. While they draw on the essentially 'traumatological' nature of the contemporary cultural moment, the novels expose fundamental constants of the human condition – in other words, historical continuities. Instead of clearly identifiable turning points or 'transfiguring events' (Siegel, 2005), be it in individual lives or in the culture at large, they display a continuity of violence and desire that the narrative consistently draws attention to, and to which there is no available solution. This is not to say that the novels are defeatist in their ethical position; rather, they demand an unflinching acknowledgement of – and, by implication, an ethical response on the part of the reader to – the fact that violence, destructive desires and the like are 'part of our species-typical psychology rather than a psychological aberration' (Müller-Wood and Wood, 2010, n.p.). The deceptive nature of the novels' set-up lies in the fact that, structurally and through the narrative perspective, they trick us into believing that their concern is with fantasies when it is really about material reality, and that they revolve around key cultural concerns when they really focus on individual, and hence localized, desires. The novels' significance as commentary on post-global British culture lies in their characteristic oscillation between stylistic and structural sophistication and their deceptively indirect promotion of a more 'realistic' alternative to the postmodern hyperreal. The figures of Amber and Miles invite us to become 'strangely self-aware' and to honestly acknowledge the destructive impulses inherent in human nature. In so doing, they emphasize, as John Gray puts it, that 'the human animal will stay the same: a highly inventive species that is also one of the most predatory and destructive' (Gray, 2002, p. 4).

'The Space That Wrecks Our Abode': The Stranger in Ali Smith's *Hotel World* and *The Accidental*

PATRICK O'DONNELL

Chapter Summary: In this chapter, I consider Ali Smith's *Hotel World* (2001) and *The Accidental* (2005) as novels that contest the singularity and homogeneity of identity and the homologous entities of family, nation and world. Using Julia Kristeva's philosophical reflection on the figure of 'the stranger' as the other within and without who contests notions of identity as singular, I discuss Smith's two novels as portrayals of persons and events upon which an uncanny contingency intrudes, thus initiating a series of consequences in which identities are destroyed and remade. What occurs within the confined spaces of a hotel or a vacation home in these novels extends outwards to a cosmopolitan world inhabited by strangers, contextualized by a history in which the past is always present. Smith's novels thus point toward alternative futures in lives that include alterity and proceed otherwise.

Keywords: domesticity, history, identity, temporality, the stranger

Strangely, the foreigner lives within us: he is the hidden face of our identity, the space that wrecks our abode, a time in which understanding and affinity founder. By recognizing him within ourselves, we are spared detesting him in himself. A symptom that precisely turns 'we' into a problem, perhaps makes it impossible. The foreigner comes in when the consciousness of my difference arises, and he disappears when we all acknowledge ourselves as foreigners, amenable to bonds and communities.

(Kristeva, 1994, p. 1)

Julia Kristeva's familiar, yet subtly inverted description of the foreigner reckons that the stranger who lives within 'ourselves' (the pluralization

of identity is not accidental), once recognized, spares us from 'detesting him in himself'. In the double move that Kristeva generates, the
stranger releases us from hating 'his' singularity, or the radical particu-
larity of an intransigent otherness that would otherwise be located as
the enemy within. She thus formulates a movement between a series
of differentiated entities that exist only in relation to an opposite-to-
be-undifferentiated: self/other; guest/host; stranger/familiar; foreign/
domestic; singular/plural. In Kristeva's thought, it is not so much that
these (old) binaries can be simply collapsed into each other on the road
to utopian community, as it is that one only exists by virtue of the continued existence and mutual incorporation of the other: they are *bound*
to each other, and it is only in the recognition of that bond or debt that
their continued coexistence remains possible. There will always be foreigners, strangers, guests, just as there will always be citizens, hosts and
kin: 'we' are temporarily both and all at one point in time or another.
These are positions occupied in an array of mutable circumstances
threaded with contingency, and for Kristeva only a pluralization of
identity makes possible the eccentric, disturbing presence of the one
whose difference makes possible the collectivity of the many.

We might consider Ali Smith's novels as a fictionalization of this
philosophical sketch, or more accurately, as its projection in time
and space, its dialecticisation through character, act and language.
The two novels by Smith under consideration here, *The Accidental*
and *Hotel World*, are equally concerned with the spatial economies of
estrangement in two realms that share the status of being temporary
housing – that of a holiday cottage in Norfolk inhabited by the Smart
family, and a hotel in an unnamed city where the accidental death of a
young chambermaid has occurred. The transitional spaces of the two
novels are not entirely domestic, although domestics (in the double
sense of hired help and the members of a family) pass through them;
nor are they entirely foreign, though their temporariness as sites of
visitation necessarily means that strangers who have crossed county
or city borders or workers who maintain their simulated domesticity are their primary navigators. Smith clearly intends for the tightly
parochial and deadly confines of the 'Global Hotel' of *Hotel World* to
be viewed ironically within the context of cosmopolitan worldliness
and the company of migratory strangers who inhabit the planet, and
the rustic but treacherous dwelling of *The Accidental* to be seen as a
site where the dysfunction of the family and the familiar takes place
within a simulation of a domesticated natural order. When the superficial complacency of these social orders is destroyed by unforeseen
events (a sudden death; the arrival of a stranger), the consequence are
catastrophic in a root sense – a *sudden* overturning that signals a disruption of temporality and, as we shall see, an opening onto a recognition of others as members of a community founded on contingency.
Like the novels themselves, in which generic boundaries are crossed at

random and linguistic play abounds, the venues of hotel and home in Smith's fiction are hybrid spaces that contain, or fail to contain, collisions and collusions between self and other, families and strangers, the foreign and the domestic. Only occupied for a time and in time, they are conflated regions where past, present and future are conjoined (the titling of the chapters of *Hotel World* as verb tenses providing the clue), and where the insights to be afforded by viewing room, house, family, nation, world as homologous entities are explored in Smith's symptomatic, affect-laden characterizations.

Within these hybridized, restricted areas, event and occurrence are minimal. What is said and what happens (a fall in a dumb waiter; dinner with a stranger; sexual intercourse; throwing a camera off a bridge; the offer of hospitality) exist as the visible, symptomatic manifestations of sporadic encounters with otherness. These occurrences – coming about variously as the consequence of random acts of hospitality, or accident, or alienated outburst – suggest the degree to which, in Smith's fiction, life is contingent and essentially out of control, the thin veneers of 'housing,' domesticity, family and self shown up for their fragility when temporal and experiential continuums are ruptured by an instantaneous event.

The entirety of *Hotel World* is premised upon such an event. A young chambermaid, curious about an anachronistic appurtenance in a contemporary hotel, crawls into a dumb waiter in a moment of play, and falls to her death. Speaking from beyond the circumstances of her demise and conducting a vexed dialogue while she can with her own corpse, her memory and capacity to speak fading fast, she describes her own mortality as a falling out of language: 'I climbed inside the, the . . . I forget the word, it has its own name' (Smith, 2001, p. 6), she reflects. Likewise, she expresses a thirst for detail, as if in dying she had lost the 'realism' of the quotidian and its pertaining dialect:

> Because now that my breath, you might say, has been taken I miss such itching detail all the time . . . A mouthful of dust would be something. You could gather it any time, couldn't you, anytime you like, from the corners of rooms, the underneaths of beds, the tops of doors. The rolled up hairs and dried stuff and specks of what-once-was-skin, all the glamorous leavings of breathing creatures ground down to essence and glued together with the used-up leftover webs and flakes of a moth, the see-through flakes of a blue bottle's dismantled wing. You could easily (for you can do such a thing whenever you choose, if you want) smear your hand with dust, roll dust's precious little between a finger and a thumb and watch it stencil into your fingerprint, yours, unique, nobody else's. And then you could lick it off; I could lick it off with my tongue, if I had a tongue again, if my tongue was wet, and I could taste it for what it is. Beautiful dirt, grey and vintage, the grime left by life, sticking to the bony roof of a mouth and tasting of next to nothing, which is always better than nothing. (Smith, 2001, pp. 4–5)

Sara Wilby (her last name ironically indicative of the identity she once was and will never be again) mourns her passing in this linguistically rich grasping at lost language and self-definition. She longs for the 'leavings' of mortal life, the dust in which she could commemorate her corporeality even as she marks the temporariness of language and corporeal existence – the 'what-was-once-skin', the elided or forgotten word 'ball' between 'dust's precious little' and 'between a finger and a thumb'. While alive, Sara has silently fallen in love with a woman who repairs her watch, its hands 'stuck at ten to two' (Smith, 2001, p. 17), and who is 'surrounded by watches in cabinets, watches in cases, watches all up and down the walls . . . all of them stopped, with their hands pointing to different, possible, times of day' (Smith, 2001, p. 18). Noting that 'the only working watch in the shop that morning was on her arm, ticking into the warm underside of her wrist' (Smith, 2001, p. 18), Sara thus connects affect and affection with the spectacle of present time passing away into the instantaneousness of contingency, as compared to the 'dead time' of the stopped watches and the dead battery of her own timepiece bearing the name of 'Sekonda' (Smith, 2001, p. 18). Giorgio Agamben's commentary on the 'dead time of modernity' illuminates the implicit comparison that Sara is making here between the living, present instant of falling in love, as well as falling in death, and the dead, past time of stopped watches and lost detail. Agamben writes that 'dead time' is 'homogenous, rectilinear and empty'; for him, it is time 'sanctioned by modern mechanics, which establishes the primacy of uniform rectilinear motion over circular motion', a form of temporality 'abstracted from experience' (Agamben, 1993, p. 16). Many of Smith's characters encounter forms of otherness and heterogeneity that rupture the mechanistic or 'dead' temporal continuum of contemporaneity. One of the epigraphs that Smith chooses for *Hotel World*, taken from Christopher Jencks's *The Architecture of the Jumping Universe* (title unattributed in the novel) underscores the ways in which death or accident in Smith's fiction ironically disrupts the continuities of 'dead time': 'Traditional religions emphasize constancy, the Modernists with their mechanistic models emphasize predictability, but the cosmos is much more dynamic than either a pre-designed world or a dead machine . . . each jump is a great mystery' (Jencks, 1997, pp. 7–8).

Through Sara's double-voiced discourse (in a chapter entitled 'Past,' she is her living self passing into death speaking to her dead self eager to be done with life), Smith compounds the conundrum of identity in relation to the temporality that haunts her fiction. Identity is only known by virtue of the dust of its mortal remains that indicate a breach of time's continuity. The self is composed of an other who is the embodiment of self-estrangement in the confrontation with mortality where the body decays and language falls away. And, the experience of living and its recollection only occurs in relation to time's winding down, the 'ends' of time, voice and language within the short view.[1] In effect, Sara speaks from the 'time' in between life and death which provides her with a perspective on identity as doubled, always its own other, though unnoticed in the continuous 'dead time' of everyday life that is sundered by a catastrophic instant.

In *Hotel World*, the story of Sara's unfortunate fall catalyses the remaining four narratives, each echoing her plummeting out of language and existence. In 'Present Historic', Else (Elspeth Freeman), a homeless woman possibly suffering from tuberculosis, observes the street scene as she panhandles outside the Global Hotel and 'imagines the pavement littered with the letters that fall out of the half-words she uses (she doesn't need the whole words)' (Smith, 2001, p. 47). 'Future Conditional' is told from the perspective of Lise, formerly the hotel receptionist, who is at home in bed suffering from an undiagnosed illness several months after Sara's death and who feverishly recalls an extension of hospitality on the street to Else by inviting her to stay for free at the hotel one night. In 'Perfect', Penny, a reporter who is staying at the Global Hotel in order to write a review of its services, meditates at length on the universality of death while alone in her room ('She hated her imagination, it was full of snakes, dead animals, and unexpectedly beautiful smashed-up pianos' [Smith, 2001, p. 151]). Her encounter with Else, who is confusedly departing from the hotel in the middle of the night, leads to a series of revelations about estrangement and indebtedness as the two women take a meandering walk through the novel's unnamed town. Clare, Sara's sister who has come to the Global Hotel in order to discover how it was that her sister died months earlier, is portrayed in 'Future in the Past' as attempting to discern the 'logic' behind the chaotic indeterminacy of a freak accident in recalling her sister's past and its imagined relation to a future she is never to have. In 'Present', which serves as the novel's epilogue, a camera-eye narrator roams among the inhabitants of the city near the vicinity of the Global Hotel, pausing for a moment to focus upon the young woman in the watch repair shop who pockets Sara's unredeemed watch as a memento of the young woman she has silently observed watching her outside the shop. Thinking about Sara, 'she can feel small wings moving against the inside of her chest, or something in there anyway, turning, tightened, working' (Smith, 2001, p. 235), a past memory of a then-present moment in which '[s]he wasn't ready. The timing was wrong' (Smith, 2001, p. 235).

The narratives of *Hotel World* are thus premised upon a series of accidents, missed encounters, bad timings, temporary alliances and unintended consequences, such as that which occurs when Else leaves the bath water running in her hotel room as she departs in the middle of the night, leading to the flooding of the room and the subsequent firing of an innocent chambermaid who is unfairly penalized for Lise's random act of kindness. Underlying the events and eventualities of the novel is the evanescence of time passing and the indeterminacy of the future, which speak to Smith's interest in drawing the connection between temporality and the encounter with alterity that, to invoke Kristeva once more, is at once a form of self-estrangement. In effect, the rupturing or missing of time, the collusive temporalities of the accident or the spontaneous encounter, the overlapping of future onto past and present onto future – these 'times out of joint' open outward onto occasions where 'affinity founder[s]' and radical difference emerges. The linkages between Sara's fall, Lise's illness and her encounter with the homeless Else, Penny's 'nighttown' adventures with the same, Clare's traumatic return to the scene of her sister's death, and the recollections of the unnamed 'girl who works in the watch shop' (Smith, 2001, p. 233) are primarily not those of cause and effect or Dickensian circumstance. Instead, the principles of the novel are bound to each other by virtue of another temporal logic where the collision of the familiar with the uncanny and a convergence with forms of otherness – ranging from that of the nomadic stranger to one's own mortality – underlies the detail of the quotidian.

Together, the narrators of *Hotel World* form a 'community of strangers' brought together by chance – an accidental, ad hoc community, to be sure, and one that only comes into being through incidental contact – but one that evinces signs of the global cosmopolitanism the novel's title implies. As Anthony Appiah has written, contemporary cosmopolitanism rests upon two interlinked concepts:

> One is the idea that we have obligations to others, obligations that stretch beyond those to whom we are related by the ties of kith and kind, or even the more formal ties of shared citizenship. The other is that we take seriously the value not just of human life but of particular human lives, which means taking an interest in the practices and beliefs that lend them significance. People are different, the cosmopolitan knows, and there is much to learn from our differences . . . As we shall see, there will be times when these two ideals – universal concern and respect for legitimate difference – clash. (Appiah, 2006, p. xv)

The temporary connections that several women in the novel forge in the wake Sara's demise can be viewed as 'bonds of obligation' falling well outside those of 'kith and kind' or 'shared citizenship': a professional journalist takes responsibility for seeing a confused homeless woman through a night of wandering; a hotel receptionist offers hospitality to a beggar; a woman suffering from a mysterious illness considers her own mortality in light of that another woman whom she barely knows; a shopkeeper imagines a future with a dead woman with whom she has had a momentary encounter, as a customer, while she was alive.

This is a community radically different from that of the social order in any normative sense, and it is one that, as Smith makes clear in the novel, is contingent, even risky – involving as Appiah suggests, the distinct possibility of 'clash' or conflict, registered in *Hotel World* through the class, linguistic and perceptual differences that collide with each other when the women come into contact. Penny, for example, is both 'repelled and energized' by her contact with the corporeal detritus of unknown and unseen strangers she encounters while wandering through the night with Else (Smith, 2001, p. 163). Sitting on a concrete bench with the exhausted homeless woman, she regards a hair that has blown into 'her open mouth': 'It wasn't her own hair, or the woman in the coat's. It was long. It was someone else's entirely. Penny picked it out, disgusted. Then she held it up in front of her' (Smith, 2001, p. 162). The scrutiny of a strand of hair – one of those 'leavings' of bodily exist-ence that Sarah commemorates – leads her to the recognition of the 'foul . . . queasily exciting . . . humdrum . . . exotica of others' lives' and 'the knowledge that she could be brought together with someone else . . . by a literal thread, by something with the thinness, the genetic randomness, the intimacy of a single hair from a single other thread' (Smith, 2001, p. 163). Penny's reflection reveals the deep contradictions of the cosmopolitan community of strangers in *Hotel World* manifested on the level of bodies and bodily remains coming into contact: both inti-mate and disgusting; a product of both avoidance and embrace, leading to a form of knowledge borne as much of voyeurism as genuine interest and investment in the life of the other; and above all, always contingent, always temporary.

The texture and complexity of this cosmopolitan time-space is most fully rendered in the remarkable final chapter of *Hotel World* told from the perspective of a telescopic camera eye that zooms out to reveal the matrix of the novel's world and zooms in to focus on specific inhabitants of the town, awakening to a new day. These include the girl in the watch shop 'just out of the shower', 'a man whose son drove off yesterday, leav-ing him waving on the pavement' (Smith, 2001, p. 232), a 'builder . . . sitting on a plank sticking out of a loft extension three storeys up in the air. He is about to wake any people still asleep with his drill' (Smith, 2001, p. 233), or a 'woman who was struggling along the road yesterday' opening 'one of the awkward things she was carrying then. It is a plastic container of orange juice as big as her upper body' (Smith, 2001, p. 233). These focalizations of the everyday local are foregrounded through an envisioning of receding global, national and urban landscapes haunted by the ghosts of the deceased:

> High in the north on a street in a town in the misty, cold-bound Highlands, the ghost of Mrs M. Reid is back in front of what used to be her shop, where she sold sugar-sticks and humbugs, gums and liquorices, peppermints, loz-enges, chocolates moulded into new shapes . . . Down the country and over the border, speeding away from the massed northern ranks of the ghosts of centuries' worth of anger-wakened warriors baring their wounds and waving their warty shields, the ghost of Diana, Princess of Wales, historic and royal ghost, . . . ghost again today on the pages of this morning's *Daily Mail* . . . is

smiling shy and sweet as a girl, in a tiara . . . Low in the south in the hazy city the faded shade of Solomon Peavy . . . resentfully woken and set loose again every time someone reads the poem written to his memory by Ben Jonson . . . is loitering in the reconstructed Globe Theatre . . . Anywhere up and down the country, any town (for neatness' sake let's say the town where the heft and scant of this book have been so tenuously anchored) the ghost of Dusty Springfield, popular singer of the nineteen sixties, soars, sure and broken, definite and tentative, through the open window of a terraced house on the corner of Short Street. (Smith, 2001, pp. 226–9)

The narrative of the specific ghost who haunts the novel, Sara Wilby, is contextualized within a larger haunted history and a landscape populated by a random, miscellaneous assortment of fellow-travellers united in paradox. Both opaque and defined, both soaring and anchored, these phantoms embody the self-contradictory universality of their mortality and utter difference from each other implicit in the specificity of their life-details that delimit their ontological status as those-dead-previously living, and their timely linkages to those-living-who-will-be-dead. This is the cosmopolitan habitus of *Hotel World*, which concludes with a striking 'hauntology' of a world in which multiple temporalities are conflated in the instant (the *Daily News* resurrecting Diana's ghost at every moment), and spatial domains (house, hotel, city, nation, region, planet) are homologized.[2] The world of the Global Hotel is saturated with the reminder, made evident through various ghostly encounters, that living is, in its details, a continuous succession of fortuitous and disastrous encounters with alterity, border-crossings, sudden falls and uncanny moments that reveal the stranger within. To which, the novel suggests in its closing words, one can only respond with an identity-pun, an outburst of affect that grasps at the paradox: 'Woooooooo-hooooooooo' (Smith, 2001, pp. 3 and 238).

The stranger who occupies the 'space that wrecks our abode' comes home to roost with a vengeance in Smith's *The Accidental*. Divided not according to verb tenses but to story-arcs ('The Beginning', 'The Middle', 'The End') interspersed with the brief monologues of a floating narrative presence named 'Alhambra', the novel relates the intrusive presence of a seemingly innocent stranger, Amber, who comes to stay for a time at the holiday cottage of the Smart family, and who sets about transforming (or destroying, depending upon one's perspectives) each of their lives. Amber can be viewed as the uncanny other who each family member either desires or abjects, but the question of her agency in the novel is an open one: the dysfunctional Smart family is already on the road to ruin before the events of the novel begin, and Amber may be either the active instrument of wreckage or a neutral catalyst whose mere presence magnetizes inherent destructive forces. Eve, the mother, is unhappy in a marriage to a husband (her second) whose philandering is becoming increasingly flagrant; a bestselling author, she is engaged in the work of prosopopoeia (giving voice to the dead or inanimate) in books that 'take the ordinary life of a living person who died before his or her time in World War II – but a voice that tells his or her story as if he or she had lived on' (Smith, 2005, p. 81). Ironically, however, her own voice (or her ability to ventriloquise those of others) has been stilled by writer's block.[3] Her life and identity, like her writing, is effectually not her own. Michael, her husband, is a walking parody of the middle-aged, amorous literature professor whose behaviour leads to his firing. Magnus, Eve's oldest child from her marriage to Adam Berenski, is a guilt-ridden teenager who has been involved in a schoolroom prank that leads to the suicide of a classmate. Her daughter, Astrid, poised on the edge of adolescence, obsessively 'tapes' her life through the lens of a digital camera, as if recording it makes it more real.

Intimate relationships develop between Amber and each member of the family during her short stay, each leading to multivalent changes: she becomes a life-mentor and friend to Astrid, a seductress to Michael as well as to the previously uninitiated Magnus, a daughter to be saved from a troubled past by Eve. Out for a walk one day, Amber takes Astrid's precious camera and throws it over a bridge: is the destruction of this prosthesis a matter of spontaneous sadistic play, or does it compel Astrid to free herself from a mechanical device for self-expression? Michael is terminated from his position because of a complaint from a student with whom he has had relations, but for Eve, the last straw is Michael's visible consorting with Amber: does this portend the destruction of a marriage, or a new life (and new authorial energies) for the stalled writer? Magnus, who serves as the family's conscience and who is well aware that 'Everybody' in the family 'is in broken pieces which won't go together, pieces which are nothing to do with each other, like they all come from different jigsaws' (Smith, 2005, p. 138), might be seen as the victim of a sexual predator in his relationship with Amber. However is their affair the first step on Magnus' road to adulthood and his willingness to take responsibility for his role in the suicide of a young girl? And Michael, in the end, is bereft of family and employment, but nevertheless experiences a sense of release: has he been saved from the parody of bourgeois existence that he has embodied up to this point in time?

All of these questions revolve around the identity of Amber, the stranger, who has arrived at the site of domesticity in the form of a contingency, the real or contrived 'accident' of a broken-down automobile. Amber's name indicative of the colour of a warning signal, and contrarily suggests in other meanings a preservative or self-defensive function (trees exude the resin called 'amber' to protect themselves from insects). Thus, nominally, Amber is she who comes from the outside to the inner domain of the family, 'wrecked' by novel's end as various parties scatter into the alternative futures that the annihilation of the family unit entails. As 'the accidental', she is the embodiment of contingency – the untimely and unforeseen, the small event that has fatal consequences, the sudden arrival of the catastrophic. In certain moments, she appears to be wholly self-invented, arising as if from nowhere out of an erased past, telling Eve that 'when she was in her twenties', driving a Porsche '[o]ne sleeting winter night, the week before Christmas', she has accidentally run over and killed 'a girl of seven wearing a little winter coat' who has suddenly run onto the road (Smith, 2005, pp. 100–1).[4] Amber implies that she has been escaping this event and the 'self' associated with it ever since, as she roams without direction from place to place, a nomadic entity born of accident, her life a skein of contingent relations with strangers.

Yet, as much as she is a stranger and an outsider to those with whom she comes into contact, for each member of the Smart family, she is also the multifarious embodiment of 'knowledges' – sexual, historical, biological, public, identificatory.[5] To Magnus, for example, she adds to the sexual knowledge she confers upon him a multidisciplinary wealth of information ranging from quantum physics to etymology:

> He and Amber have had discussions about how light is part particle, part-wave structure, how time is bending . . . Amber knows about Egyptian, Etruscan, Aztec everything. She knows about car electronics, solar radiation, the carbon dioxide cycle, things in philosophy. She is an expert on those wasps which inject other insects with paralysis so that their own grubs can feed off something still alive. She knows about art, books, foreign films. She spoke for ages one afternoon in the attic about an Irish playwright who listened at the cracks in the floor of the room he was renting, to hear the people in the kitchen of the house he was staying in, so he could put the kind of speech that people actually used into his plays. (Smith, 2005, p. 150)

The playwright referred to is John Millington Synge, but what is notable in this passage is the range of Amber's miscellaneous knowledge, as well as how her recounting of a literary anecdote portraying an author who converts living human speech into writing in an eerie reversal of Eve's invention of voices for those dead before their time. As 'the accidental', Amber's nomadic knowledge has been randomly acquired and is spontaneously imparted, yet apt to each individual in the Smart family she encounters, as if the externality of information or the simulation of an invented past could serve as a mirroring counterpart to the identities of Astrid, Magnus, Michael and Eve.

To Eve, Amber brings knowledge of an event in which a child dies by accident before its time, giving rise to a recognition of the mother she has never been to children who are entirely other than imagined by the fantasy of happy domesticity. Her sudden manifestation brings to Michael a recognition of his native parochialism (an English professor, he notes that '[t]here wasn't much call for accidence in English, which had lost its inflexion tendencies in the Middle English period' [Smith, 2005, p. 71]), and what he has been missing both in his marriage and his affairs with young women. To Magnus, she brings a recognition of the elemental and paradoxes of time and space that both acculturates and particularizes his sense of reality, enabling a movement beyond the bondage to guilt toward a sense of connection and worldly futurity. Under Amber's influence, observing a 'nondescript tree', he can 'note to himself now' that its leaves 'are connected to its branches are connected to its bigger branches are connected to its trunk' (Smith, 2005, p. 156); such connectedness, he reflects, extends to

> all living things by virtue of being things which respond to photosynthe-sis = all food, fossil, fuel in both the past and the present: and if there's a past and a present then there's probably (and definitely possibly) a future, and the notion of a future and Magnus and all. (Smith, 2005, pp. 156–7)

And to Astrid, especially in the seemingly senseless act of destroying her camera, Amber is the force propelling her toward a form of expe-riential agency that is both apocalyptic and hopeful in her capacity to confront various 'ends'. Toward the conclusion of the novel in the sec-tion entitled 'The End', Astrid reflects on the demise of a planet 'actu-ally getting darker' (Smith, 2005, p. 233), on the end of her family life as she has known it (literally signified in the vandalizing of the family residence, perhaps by Amber, that occurs while they are on holiday), and on the end of her childhood as she contemplates her nominal trajec-tory into the future: 'Astrid is two vowels short of an asteroid. Asterid the asteroid' (Smith, 2005, p. 215). Yet all of these ends are at the same time not ends, but 'the beginning of everything, the beginning of the century, and it is definitely Astrid's century, the twenty-first century, and here she is, here she comes, hurtling through the air into it with the responsibility to heatseek all the disgustingness and insanity' (Smith, 2005, p. 234).

Amber is the stranger without and within who brings both knowl-edge of self and a knowledge of alterity that opens out spatially onto a planetary reality and temporally onto a future that seems both certain in its existence and radically indeterminate in its direction. In effect, Amber's presence, like Sara's accident, leads to the spontaneous crea-tion of a community of strangers both gathered around and scattered by the person or event that has generated a confrontation with the alterity within and without. From *Hotel World* to *The Accidental*, we can observe a development in Smith's discourse of contingency that manifests an increasing dependency on 'the accidental' to rupture the homogeneous narratives of self, family, nation and world such that a future beyond these, different from these, might come to pass. At the same time, like *Hotel World*, *The Accidental* suggests that futurity depends equally upon a recognition of the continuous presence of the past in the figure of Alhambra, who may be Amber's off-double (as one name nearly, but not quite, phonically and anagrammatically incorporates the other), and who records her conception in 1968 in the movie theatre for which she is named. As Alhambra's narrative proceeds in the interstices of the narratives of the Smart family and their encounters with Amber, it increasingly enlarges its context from the locality where the narrator is born, to that of British cinematic and national history in the 1960s and 1970s, to the history of film as a reflection of world history in the twentieth century, and finally to a vision of The Alhambra, the tenth-century palace built in Granada, destroyed and rebuilt over the centuries by many cultures such that, as the abode of a continuous succession of 'strangers', it stands as a symbol of a transient cultural temporality:

> It was Moorish. It was Arab. It was Berber. It was Muslim. It got ruined. They restored it. It was very briefly Jewish. It was very briefly Gypsy. The Christians threw the Muslims out. The Catholics kept the palace but put a church on top of the mosque. Poets loved it. Writers loved it. Painters loved it. Nineteenth-century tourists loved it . . . The writer John Ruskin said it was too Christian to be art. The designer and architect Owen Jones studied it, then built the Crystal Palace. The circus promoter P. T. Barnum built himself a mansion based on it. The mansion didn't last. It burned down in the end. The people who built cinemas gave some cinemas its name. Like the one I was conceived in. Now we're back at the beginning. (Smith, 2005, pp. 305–6)

Serving as the voice of history (but a particular kind of history involving cinematic renderings of diverse cultural moments and the paradisiacal fantasy of empire that the 'Heaven on earth' [Smith, 2005, p. 306] of The Alhambra symbolizes in this passage), Alhambra contextualizes the contemporary domestic drama experienced by the Smart family when the stranger invades. Smith is careful to place the destruction and reanimation of familial identities that the novel charts, concluding with the narrative of Eve becoming another Amber to a young woman she meets on her own nomadic travels, within the framework of a larger global history marked by change, cultural hybridity, violence and repurposing. While one aspect of this history registers a desire for forms of domain, homogeneity and permanence that signify (for some) 'heaven on earth', an entirely different version of history resides in the cycles of cultural demolition and construction, the 'hauntology' of the ever-present past, and the work of an uncanny contingency in historical process which informs, at bottom, the making of identity in the future. For Smith, the stranger – the allegorical embodiment of cultural and historical contingency – is the visible reminder that 'we', in time, are always composed otherwise.

CHAPTER EIGHT

Idiosyncrasy and Currency: Ali Smith and the Contemporary Canon

DOMINIC HEAD

Chapter Summary: This chapter places Ali Smith centrally in the debate about literary value and the construction of the contemporary canon. It is argued that the risk of complicity in academic work about contemporary writing – of reinforcing the judgements of the publishing industry, and the vested interests that produce those judgements – is ameliorated in a form of criticism that concerns itself simultaneously with the *construction* of the contemporary as well as the process of academic evaluation and the tentative business of canon formation. A parallel set of concerns is found in Smith's major novels, *Hotel World, The Accidental* and *There but for the,* in which her aesthetic, presented as an oblique form of satire, facilitates a critique of vested interest. This critique implies a self-consciousness about how the problem might define/confine her expression, and this tacitly identifies the dichotomy about value at the heart of the critique of the contemporary as, in some senses, Smith's central topic. The chapter concludes by implying that the co-presence of the creative writer and the academic critic in university English departments might bring into focus a shared dilemma about valuing contemporary literature.

Keywords: canon, contemporary, creative writing, university English, value

The study and analysis of contemporary fiction is, in some crucial respects, quite different to other fields of English literary study and criticism. The central problem here concerns literary value, but this is more complex than is sometimes thought. A typical approach to the problem might be to acknowledge that the study of the contemporary is vulnerable to hindsight, but the problem is more complex than this, because the study of the contemporary is also, simultaneously, the study of the *construction* of the contemporary. Indeed, the critic is helpless to get beyond or behind this prior construction. It may sometimes be possible to identify and celebrate the work of a neglected contemporary novelist, but this is a random happy circumstance, and a rare event, given the sheer volume of material that is produced each year: no critic can have an all-encompassing knowledge of the terrain, and a genuine command of the field. More usually, critics of the contemporary are responding to the canon that emerges from the predilections of agents, publishers and reviewers, all of whom are pre-empting the current emphases of literary prize culture. Thus, the field of analysis of the contemporary is inextricably linked with commerce and the control of cultural capital.

There are two broad responses to this problem. The first option is to mount a critique of the way literary critics contribute, perhaps inadvertently, to the establishment and preservation of cultural capital. The second option is to try and embrace the formal and aesthetic qualities of the contemporary, while retaining a consciousness of it as a constructed phenomenon. To write a form of criticism, that is, in which two (potentially competing) notions of value are simultaneously in play. This adds another dimension to that sense of provisionality in the criticism of the contemporary: it is not just that we are speculating, offering hunches in valuing particular writers; beyond that, conscious of the artificiality of the thing that we deem still to be worth valuing (aesthetically), we ponder the ways in which it is constructed and how the construction requires that we attend to the overshadowing question of financial value, vested interests, and our role in forging that link between aesthetics and commerce.

This chapter seeks to illustrate this problematic area of defining the contemporary by using Ali Smith as a case study. The deliberation contributes to the debate about the general problem concerning the way in which contemporary writers are hailed during their lifetimes, and are identified as canonical in some preliminary way, something that has already happened for Smith: *Hotel World* won the 2002 Encore award, and *The Accidental* was awarded the Whitbread Novel of the Year in 2005. Both novels were shortlisted for the Booker Prize and the Orange Prize. Historically, it has sometimes been the case that novelists disappear from view in subsequent generations, despite having been celebrated by contemporaneous critics and reviewers because of their currency. Being 'of' the moment – that is being steeped in context and therefore seemingly highly relevant in their day – does not guarantee a lasting reputation for novelists.

The key point here is to show how Smith's form of satirical writing – which in the novels considered in this chapter involves the invention of outsiders capable of puncturing the bubble of selfish privilege – gives her an original purchase on her context: it is an aesthetic (a literary value) which facilitates a critique of vested interest (that other kind of value). I'm conscious that this might seem to sidestep the problematic area I have identified above, where there is a potential conflict – or, at least, a rich area of contradiction – between the value we identify in a writer's craft, and the value assigned to them in the marketplace. Yet Smith's own critique of vested interest implies a self-consciousness about how the problem might define/confine her expression, and this tacitly identifies the dichotomy about value at the heart of the critique of the contemporary as, in some senses, Smith's central topic, and therefore *itself* a fundamental feature of her aesthetic.

The full implications of this, involving an assessment of the balance of style and context in Smith's novels, are treated towards the end of this chapter. This analysis begins with a reading of *There but for the* (2011), and then traces similar concerns in both *The Accidental* (2005) and *Hotel World* (2001), working backwards through the most substantial fiction in order to demonstrate how Smith's idiosyncratic style and quirky perspective facilitates her (often satirical) commentary on contemporary life. Central to this analysis is the attempt to contextualize that central aspect of Smith's work – the critique of privilege – and to trace its development. In this discussion I draw on some of the more perceptive reviews of these novels, with an eye to how Smith's reputation has been built up outside academe.

On the face of it, Smith's originality is hard to pin down. By the time of *There but for the*, reviewers were apt to play the game of identifying her literary antecedents. Concerning Smith's central conceit, the guest who outstays his welcome, Sarah Churchwell (in *The Observer*) found echoes of Molière's *Tartuffe* (1664), as well as of a 1939 Broadway hit by George S. Kaufman and Moss Hart, *The Man Who Came to Dinner* (Churchwell, 2011). Perhaps the reviewers' other most remarked-upon feature is the overly clever 9-year-old, Brooke Bayoude, lover of puns and language play, whose precocity makes her, according to Charles McGrath, 'a sort of cross between Lewis Carroll's Alice and one of Salinger's child savants' (McGrath, 2011). Yet the most obvious aspect of the literary recycling is the self-borrowing: the dinner guest who doesn't leave is anticipated, as a device, by the interloper on a family holiday in *The Accidental*; and the precocious child by Astrid, in the same novel. For a writer often hailed as inventive and original in her earlier work, this sense of revisiting tried-and-tested conceits and devices, in *There but for the*, might seem surprising.

Behind the conceits and devices, however, there is a beguiling account of the anomie at the heart of contemporary society in this novel (perhaps Smith's major theme). What is interesting about the treatment of this theme in the three novels considered here is that the satire, and the portrayal of two-dimensional characters, is enriched by the intervention of her more humanized characters (such as Mark Palmer in *There but for the*, or Amber in *The Accidental*). Further than this, the plight of these characters is interwoven with the context that is the focus of Smith's satire – competitive centre-right democracy – which thus emerges as an inevitable delimitation for her frustrated, unfulfilled figures who cannot transcend the baseness of the context that imprisons them. There is also a sense that Smith's implied stance is delimited by the same context. For example, as is shown below, she has been criticized for her predictable liberal sympathies. Yet it is not always easy to see what other alternatives are available to her, without jettisoning realism altogether. Moreover, the novels sometimes betray an acute understanding of their own limits; and, insofar as that becomes a self-conscious aspect of the novels, it is one way of accounting for her apparent literary recycling.

This kind of contextual/stylistic delimitation does not explain away some of her weaknesses, however. Theo Tait's sharply critical review of *There but for the*, in the more considered and retrospective manner of reviews in the *London Review of Books*, poured cold water on some of the more enthusiastic earlier reviews. In doing so, Tait questioned some of the book's stylistic and satirical credentials, calling it 'whimsical, tepidly experimental and desperately predictable in its sympathies' (Tait, 2012, p. 32). In particular, he criticized the set-piece dinner party, which had been 'repeatedly praised by reviewers for puncturing middle-class philistinism and smugness'. He considers this 'nonsense', because 'her characters are so stupidly tactless and frequently evil that their values come entirely pre-punctured'. Although Tait qualifies this estimation of the writing by uncovering some of its qualities, he does not dilute the essential judgment of the book's satirical thrust, which serves 'simply to rain down simple-minded pieties on the unfortunate reader' (Tait, 2012, p. 33).

It is possibly the most sympathetic character in *There but for the* who facilitates a more interesting deliberation in the dinner-party scene, a deliberation which I take to be the novel's central idea. Mark Palmer, who has brought Miles Garth to the Lees' dinner party, is an artfully created 'damaged' character, whose homosexuality has marginalized him as much as has his hypersensitivity. Whereas Miles, the guest who doesn't leave, becomes the means through which the broader social anomie is revealed – his gesture appropriated by different people and groups, hungry for meaning (witness the various banners carried by those keeping vigil, 'Milo For Palestine', 'Milo for Peace', 'Milo For Troops Out Of Afghanistan', and so on [Smith, 2011, p. 315]) – Mark Palmer is more fully cultivated as a figure of suffering and lost opportunity. He is haunted by memories of his dead lover, but most especially by his mother, who committed suicide when he was at school (Smith, 2011, p. 163). The other dinner-party guests discuss him when he leaves the room, and realize that his mother was a famous painter, Faye Palmer. Brooke Bayoude's parents give an account of her most famous work, 'History Sequence 1 to 9', which

> begins with the faraway woman in the chair and, as you come closer, progress from canvas to canvas, you see that the woman is tied at the wrists and ankles to the chair, and then that she looks like she is crying, and then

that what she is crying is blood, and as you come closer still you see that her eyes are a bloody mask. (Smith, 2011, pp. 164–5)

As the sequence progresses, in Bernice Bayoude's account, the close-up of the face, 'when you see that the eyelids have been sewn shut, with foul little bloody little black stitches', is followed by a close-up of just the stitches, and then, in the final canvas, the artist 'goes beyond the mask, right into the eye, and there's no eye in there, the socket is empty, there's a foul-looking insect and it's eating the lining of the socket' (Smith, 2011, p. 165). Terence Bayoude explains that Faye Palmer had taken the idea from an actual account of a tortured war prisoner, and had reflected on 'what it means to have to bear the knowledge of inhumanity, having to bear it communally' (Smith, 2011, p. 165). The clear allusion to Francis Bacon in Faye Palmer's work is made explicit a couple of pages later (Smith, 2011, p. 167). Her paintings are described by Bernice as 'shocking to the core', but also 'shockingly beautiful' (Smith, 2011, p. 166). And this idea of an overpowering painting sequence comes soon after Mark's reported reflections on feeling degraded by internet images, which in their banality produce 'a new level of Dante's inferno, a zombie-filled cemetery of spurious clues, beauty, pathos, pain, the faces of puppies, women and men from all over the world tied up and wanked over in site after site, a great sea of hidden shallows' (Smith, 2011, p. 159). It is this random, affectless plenitude which generates 'the pressing human dilemma: how to walk a clean path between the obscenities' (Smith, 2011, p. 159). This, perhaps rather obvious contrast between different kinds of image, signals what I take to be Smith's main concern in this novel: forms of representation, and the responsibility of art to try and detach itself from the mire of commerce and exploitation. Or rather, the concern is manifested as an anxiety about the capacity of art to detach itself in this way, and this speaks to the larger question of the literary marketplace, and the construction of the contemporary canon: in this moment Smith implicitly registers her own anxiety as a prize-winning novelist about finding fresh modes of intervention.

More particularly, in relation to this episode, Smith is patently concerned with what form of artistic representation might be said to incorporate the kind of reflection on artistic responsibility that is assigned to Faye Palmer's sequence of paintings, the reflection on 'what it means to have to bear the knowledge of inhumanity, having to bear it communally' (Smith, 2011, p. 165). There is an invitation, here, to think about the novel in this connection, and particularly about *this* novel. The possible formal analogy with the painting sequence, with its progressively more detailed point of focus, is relevant in a basic way, but does not give much purchase on Smith's mode of writing, since all novels work progressively to enrich understanding of the identity and circumstances of the depicted characters. Neither is the contrast between the painting sequence and the internet's 'great sea of hidden shallows', immediately helpful (Smith, 2011, p. 159): that contrast seems to promote the idea of a new visceral form of artistic shock, in which the power of the image works with artistic form to provoke a reaction. Such an effect might stand in opposition to the desensitizing effect of the internet image, where the sheer proliferation of obscenity – or of that which was once deemed to be obscene – renders it banal. But Smith does not employ shock in this way.

And yet, in a less visceral sense, that combination of form and message to provoke a reaction in the face of desensitization *is* actually Smith's method. Her novels employ periphrastic narrative methods, and offbeat circumstances, in order to probe the truth of social inequality. In *There but for the*, the artistic method is itself productive of suffering for those who are closest to it – the artist who commits suicide, and Mark, the son, whose life is blighted by the loss of his mother. And the gesture of Miles Garth, locking himself in the spare bedroom at the Lees' dinner party, might also be taken as emblematic of the artist's role, putting himself through something in order to produce debate. His withdrawal from the bigoted and hypocritical evening's conversation seems like a local gesture of protest; but it is appropriated and infused with wider signs of protest by the followers of Miles, as he achieves celebrity status. It is the enigma, the obliquity of his action that signals the need for some kind of social *reaction*, which is amplified in the responses of his followers. Of course, he provokes a multitude of responses – for example, there are banners appropriating his protest, in addition to the 'causes' cited above (Smith, 2011, p. 315). The huge response his unexplained protest/gesture calls forth implies a hunger for meaning, and an urgent need to find a rallying point for what is a muddle of unfocused protest. This points to a widespread social absence, another aspect of Smith's analysis of the internet age where again 'the pressing human dilemma' is 'how to walk a clean path between the obscenities' without any recognizable moral anchor (Smith, 2011, p. 159).

One way of explaining the fabulistic aspect of Miles' gesture is by analogy with the role of the artist/writer, and the same function can be assigned to Amber/Alhambra in *The Accidental*. This 'barefoot delinquent angel' (in the words of one reviewer) produces redemption for the Smart family, the members of which (with the possible exception of 12-year-old Astrid) do not seem obviously deserving cases for angelic intervention and redemption (Hughes-Hallett, 2005, p. 53). The stereotypical presentation of lecherous stepfather Michael, the lecturer in English literature, makes him the least interesting character in this connection, although his falling in love with Amber does produce an important lesson in emotional literacy.

Emotional literacy indeed is what Amber teaches. This is most obvious in the case of Magnus, on the verge of suicide when Amber arrives, because of the guilt and horror he feels at his involvement in the suicide of a classmate. His role in the ghastly cyber-bullying of this girl, teaching some other boys how to superimpose the picture of her face on a pornographic image, is perhaps the most prominent instance of desensitized obscenity in Smith's oeuvre. Amber's cure is to seduce him, a lesson in the difference between vital consensual sex, and the dehumanized image viewed without consciousness of its possible emotional connotations. In this sense, Amber performs the novelist's role, encouraging psychological growth in the character that is not expressly demonstrated in the narrative.

This same process applies to the mother Eve, whose writing career is quintessentially unethical. Her series of popular fictionalized biographies, based on the premise of imagining the afterlives of victims of World War II as if they had not died, has produced inevitable tensions with, and distress for, the families of her subjects. That she is suffering from writer's block at the outset of Smith's novel implies a subconscious guilt that parallels that of her son and her husband. At the end of the novel, still blocked, and prolonging the period of not working, Eve travels to America and seems set, as Eleanor Birne has astutely observed, to take on Amber's role, 'intruding in a middle-class family house' (Birne, 2005, p. 31).

The cathartic function that Amber performs for Astrid has to do, again, with the image, and with perception and engagement. The clinching moment is when Amber throws Astrid's video camera off a footbridge. On the face of it, the lesson seems fairly straightforward: Astrid is obsessed with filming the world rather than living in it. In a more general sense, the life lessons for the characters have to do with avoiding forms of mediation that obstruct engagement. When the Smarts return from holiday to find their home completely emptied by burglars this is particularly clear. For Astrid, the loss of the letters from her father to her mother, which she had hidden under her bed, is the most poignant hardship. But she finds she is relieved to be without them, and free of the anxiety of trying to interpret her parents' backstory through them (Smith, 2005, p. 232).

Yet there is something more self-conscious about the topic of mediation, and this is where *The Accidental* becomes most interesting, formally. In her *Times Literary Supplement* review, Sophie Ratcliffe identifies this aspect of the novel very clearly. When Eve Smart seems to be emulating Amber at the novel's conclusion, Ratcliffe suggests that 'the recurrence of the trope of the mysterious stranger has an almost stifling effect. The novel's coda, returning to the flickering cinematic Alhambra, suggests that the Smarts may have been a projection of her never-ending film-spool' (Ratcliffe, 2005, p. 20). The frame structure certainly has this effect of recontaining the novel within the cinema scene, while also returning us to the moment of Amber/Alhambra's conception. To the extent that Amber's agency enacts the author's own morality, this is a frame tale which reminds us of the authorial function, but which agonizes about that too: there is something distinctly disturbing about the

reminder that the novel, in its repetitive tropes, some of which interrogate critically the social function of film and image, resembles a 'never-ending film-spool'.

The double bind that is located here is succinctly accounted for in
Ratcliffe's comparison between Smith and Iris Murdoch:

> [W]hile, for Murdoch, the novel offered a suitable alternative to systema-
> tised ethical theory, Smith's parodic, patterned deliberacy reveals her suspi-
> cion of the ways in which the novel, it its attempt to comprehend or express
> the problem of particularity, might, accidentally, swamp the instances it is
> trying to preserve. (Ratcliffe, 2005, p. 19)

This is an accurate way of accounting for the differences between the
two writers, which also signals why the comparison is worthwhile:
Smith's concern about the ethical function of the novel, less sanguine
than Murdoch's, helps pinpoint her deliberation about the contemporary, a point to which I shall return. But first I wish to pursue some more
specific examples of Smith's concern about how the novel might 'swamp
the instances it is trying to preserve'.

A clear thematic indication of this concern, and an instance that
underscores the distinction between Smith and Murdoch, occurs in
Hotel World (2001) when the homeless Else reflects on the novel form.
She likes reading poetry in the local town library, but not novels:

> She can't be bothered with novels any more. She has read enough novels to
> last a lifetime. They take too long. They say too much. Not that much needs
> to be said. They trail stories after them, like if you tied old tin cans to your
> ankles and then tried to walk about. (Smith, 2001, p. 51)

The tendency of novels to 'trail stories after them' might be another
way of articulating the Murdochian cultivation of contingency, and that
celebration of the combination of order and chaos built into the very
form of the novel in Murdoch's conception of its moral purport. It is that
'uncontainability' of the contingent stuff of life that provokes further
thought. Smith finds her own way of provoking thought beyond the
frames of her novels, but not with the amplitude of plot and character
that is characteristic of Murdoch.

The apparent anti-novel argument in *Hotel World* is developed in the
penultimate section, 'future in the past', narrated by Clare Wilby, sister
of Sara Wilby, the chambermaid who falls to her death in the dumb
waiter, and whose ghost narrates 'past', the opening section. In her
stream of consciousness, recollections about Clare's reading of Hardy's
Tess provoke uncomfortable thoughts about her sister's death, even
though her ultimate judgement of the novel is damning: 'an old long
book with all those boring bits about fate I can't remember anything
else out of it except the horse getting killed & the baby & the man with

the moustache' (Smith, 2001, pp. 188–9). It is not the complexity of the emplotment, nor the substance of the philosophical argument that lives on from the novel, as far as Clare is concerned – those, perhaps, are the kind of features that might constitute tin cans tied around the ankles. Instead, the elements that live on for her are the powerful vignettes, and the arresting extractable ideas, such as the reflection about the death date, the 'date that we pass over without knowing what it is' (Smith, 2001, p. 188). These embody the significant afterlife of the novel; and this is comparable to Smith's own method, where the significant, suggestive moment, in the manner of a good short-story writer, is made to carry her larger ideas.

It is perhaps easier with hindsight, after the publication of *The Accidental* and *There but for the*, to identify the self-consciousness evident in *Hotel World*, and the claim Smith is making for her own method. By making her marginalized characters celebrate the poetic, the vignette, the moment, and by making them identify with these literary features as more directly relevant to their own circumstances, she is making a large claim for her own method against the usual conventions of the social-conscience novel. Clare Wilby's comments on *Tess* in *Hotel World* quoted above embody the best example of this. Yet they are paralleled by Astrid's process of relinquishment in *The Accidental* – learning to give up her desire to order the world through film, or to horde her father's letters to her mother as a key to explaining their lives. These anti-narrative impulses also have something in common with Brooke Bayoude's fascination for facts that do not need to link up in *There but for the*; and also, more obviously, with her delight in puns. And what is true of these characters is also true of the way they are treated by Smith: she is more interested in the moment than in conventional character development.

This puts a fresh complexion on Giles Foden's review of *Hotel World*, which detects a formal enactment of 'postmodern aspects' that dismantle the conventional portrayal of character: 'I have never seen the tenets of recent literary theory (the impossibility of the coherent subject, or substantive character, for instance) so cleverly insinuated into a novel' (Foden, 2001). If we accept what I take to be Smith's rationalization of her method – that she circumvents an in-depth treatment of character in order to focus on the essence of a situation – then this may not betray a conviction about the instability of identity or the impossibility of the coherent subject. Rather, in a nice (but important) distinction, it might identify contexts in which the luxury of bourgeois identity formation cannot occur.

This, perhaps, is where the contrast with Iris Murdoch becomes most telling. In her best known statement about the moral credentials of the novel, 'Against Dryness', Murdoch saw the Welfare State as embodying 'a set of thoroughly desirable but limited ends', which had also induced 'a lassitude about fundamentals'. Because the Welfare State had seemed to bring 'a certain struggle to an end', the 'manifold virtues of man and society', Murdoch felt, were no longer in view (Murdoch, 1961, p. 18). For the novelist, this made the truly contingent nature of social life hard to capture, with the consequence that the novel had been reduced to two inadequate alternatives in the twentieth century. This is Murdoch's famous dichotomy between 'crystalline' and 'journalistic' forms (Murdoch, 1961, p. 20).

With hindsight, this might seem a luxurious moment, when the problems with the social novel could be identified, and the prescription for a remedy could be offered within the pages of a short essay. If the social connections remained, upon which Murdoch's formula for a reinvigorated novel of society would seem to depend, is it the case that the 'post-consensus' era, with the collapse of those assumed social connections, makes things that much more complicated? It is interesting to speculate that the best known novels about the new era of individualism, such as *Money* (1984) by Martin Amis, or Jonathan Coe's *What a Carve Up!* (1994), depend upon a much more elaborate manner of formal invention than that which was proposed by Murdoch. Of course, the line in the sand dividing 'consensus' from 'post-consensus' fiction is much hazier than this implies. Yet, within a gradual trend in British fiction since 1950, Smith stands at the end of a scale in which social atomization has become increasingly more prevalent in the novel of society.

This places Smith in an interesting, and intermediate position in a consideration of character and the ethics of the novel, since the complex narrative unfolding usually associated with ethical fiction is not a prominent feature of her work. In fact, there may be a degree of scepticism, in Smith's treatment of character, about the extent to which a character in a novel can be the vehicle of moral debate. However, this should not necessarily be taken to indicate a point of contact with the hostility of some post-structuralist criticism towards the very ideal that a moral dilemma can be encoded in the situation confronting a fictional character. Smith's position, or rather the position that seems to emerge from her novels, is not so much that language and ideology determine character, or that the individual is constructed through discourse, or that the idea of the coherent self is a myth to be exploded. Neither is she suspicious of the tendency of the novel to cultivate empathy for the putative coherent self. What she does, instead, is imagine situations in which the self is impoverished or foreshortened by circumstance, so that the reader's empathy is fuelled by the recognition that this or that identity, as imagined and depicted, has been unfortunately curtailed. This is true of all of Smith's sympathetic characters. It is especially so, for example, of those marginalized figures in *Hotel World*, Else, Lise and Clare: their (limited) situation defines them. It is the ghost of Sara Wilby – the experiential world having been denied her – who epitomizes this aspect of Smith's work.

This explains why there is a relative lack of the moral dilemma in Smith's fiction, as a focus of narrative interest, as one would find in Murdoch; or before Murdoch in Conrad; or after her in McEwan, where a settled life – that of Henry Perowne in *Saturday* (McEwan, 2005); or Joe Rose in *Enduring Love* (McEwan, 1997) – is threatened by contingency, but ultimately reclaimed through galvanized action. By contrast, the characters I have discussed in this chapter are too marginalized to experience the luxury of a neatly defined moral dilemma, and are usually disempowered, so that a resolution through overt human agency is not always possible. And this is one explanation for the fabulistic elements of *There but for the* and *The Accidental*, where, in the absence of more circumscribed moral concerns as points of focus, much larger ethical questions, hazily defined, are suggested by the actions of Smith's catalyst characters, Miles Garth and Amber/Alhambra. Amber, for example, functions to reveal, gradually, that which is concealed beneath the surface relations and activities of Astrid's family: there is no moral crisis.

Smith's method does sometimes provoke criticism, because the absence of detail in the treatment of character and circumstance can leave her implied political sympathies overexposed. As one reviewer summarized the characters in *Hotel World*: '[T]hey lead their lives in such a vacuum (Smith offers only cursory background on any of them) that they seem mere mouthpieces for the author's vague, simplistic, leftist rage' (Upchurch, 2002). However, in the account I am giving of her particular method, where the conventional moral dilemma is unavailable, and where the larger ethical framework *necessarily* seems overblown or hazy by comparison, this kind of exposure of the author's politics may be an inevitable consequence.

Beyond this, there may also be something more subtle about the author's stance than is implied in 'leftist rage'; and this brings me back to the area of discussion with which I started this chapter, concerning literature, value and the contemporary. To frame this element of the discussion, I want to return to Ratcliffe's suggestion, in the review cited above, that there is a crucial difference between Murdoch and Smith in their views about the ethical capacity of the novel: where Murdoch is determined to embrace and explore the novel's ethical potential at a formal level, Smith is apt to ironize the novel's ethical credentials while simultaneously drawing upon them. This distinction, which implies a greater hesitancy and ambivalence on the part of Smith vis-à-vis the novel's social power or relevance, identifies that aspect of the contemporary to which she most clearly responds: the doubt about agency and the fear of complicity in the knowledge class.

The key instance of this hesitancy considered above is the parallel between Amber's catalyst role in *The Accidental*, and the author's own morality, highlighted in the frame that emphasizes the authorial function – with the novel coming to resemble a 'never-ending film-spool' – but which simultaneously makes us uneasy about that potentially manipulative function. The fabulistic element of both *The Accidental* and *There but for the* distracts slightly from this anxiety, but it remains an element that is implicit in the design of these novels, by virtue of the implied authorial position in each case. I read this self-consciousness – which I am presenting, chiefly, as a formal attribute – as an implicit aspect of the novelist's anxiety in the era of literary prize culture: that he or she may be a beneficiary, or even product of the entrepreneurial post-consensus society that is responsible for that cultural moment where the literary prize achieves a new form of pre-eminence, and becomes a dominant factor in the literary marketplace. For novelists, like Smith, who are also sharply critical of the social effects of the broader social moment, and the new forms of inequality that have emerged in the post-consensus years, the fear of complicity – and to an extent the fact of complicity – has to be reckoned with.

This dilemma is similarly acute for the academic critic of contemporary literature. As I said at the beginning of this chapter, the unique critical problem, here, is that the study of the contemporary is also, simultaneously, the study of the *construction* of the contemporary. Accommodating themselves to the impossibility of disengagement from the commercial nexus, critics of the contemporary require a particular kind of self-consciousness, unless they are engaged, merely, in a critique of the way literary critics contribute to the establishment and preservation of cultural capital. The more productive response, I have suggested, requires a dual performance, attentive to the aesthetic qualities of contemporary production, while fully cognizant of its constructed (and therefore potentially complicitous) nature. We therefore need to consider the extent to which academic critics, whether consciously or unconsciously, have recognized in Smith's themes and formal techniques a set of concerns about the contemporary context and the knowledge class which closely mirrors their own concerns. The parallel could reveal self-preoccupation, and a failure of critical insight which might call Smith's emergent standing in the contemporary into question. Approached in a more positive spirit, the parallel might suggest the kind of productive cross-fertilization between the creative and the critical that justifies the response of both spheres to the intellectual dilemma of the contemporary, and which suggests the consolidation of an increasingly consonant knowledge class. (Here I am referring to the developing critical enthusiasm for Smith's work within academia, not the [sometimes hostile] critical responses of broadsheet reviewers.)

There is, however, another context which is relevant to the corresponding concerns of critical and creative writing: that of the new role assumed by many prominent British writers, as teachers within the university system. At the end of an earlier period of austerity for the Humanities, Bernard Bergonzi reflected on the future for English, in the light of the theory wars of the 1980s, the false political hopes raised by the theoretical revolution in the academy, and the ways in which liberal approaches to English had been exposed as somehow lacking the requisite professional credentials. Interestingly, from the perspective of the late 1980s, before the sudden and ubiquitous emergence of creative writing programmes in British universities, Bergonzi could reflect that 'teaching and writing seem to me to go badly together and I would advise young aspiring writers to seek some quite other mode of employment' (Bergonzi, 1990, p. 9). Bergonzi's analysis of the problems facing English as a discipline in 1987–8 (when the final version of the book was written) is anticipated in his perception of the road not taken:

> Looking at more persistent and committed writers who have taught in English departments, one observes that sooner or later most of them do what [John] Wain and [Kingsley] Amis did and get out. I am thinking now of those British writers who attempt to combine literary production with the academic teaching of mainstream literature. The American system of employing poets and novelists to teach 'creative writing' offers the writer a different relationship with the academy; on the face of it a more direct and sustaining one, even a form of patronage, though with its own attendant dangers. (Bergonzi, 1990, p. 9)

The question to ask is whether or not aspects of Bergonzi's utopia of an 'ideal unity' have indeed been delivered in the era of taught creative writing (Bergonzi, 1990, p. 9). Smith's comments on university teaching are pertinent, here. She disliked working as a lecturer in English at Strathclyde University intensely, a job which made her ill with chronic fatigue syndrome: 'I hated my job so much, when I came out of it and decided to leave, a lot of things got off my back' (Gapper, 2003). However, her accounts of teaching creative writing, as opposed to English literature, while far from unequivocally enthusiastic, are more ambivalent. All teaching seems to make her ill: for example, the anticipation of teaching a creative writing workshop gives her irritable bowel syndrome (Smith, 2001, p. 24). Yet her explanation for this reaction involves a reflective self-critique:

> I can't make up my mind whether this is a commonsensical and protective physical urge from the notion that writing is always best done in a room with a pencil and nobody watching, or a perverse and antisocial response, the response of the lazy and the vanity-ridden person. (Smith, 2001, p. 24)

Smith tempers her visceral antipathy for teaching with the suggestion that this might be a personal, and antisocial reaction, which means that the creative writing workshop might comprise a platform for a more social investigation of the writing process. This need not have any bearing on the tone or mood of the writing, or, indeed, any implications for its social or communal purport. But it does demonstrate Smith's anxiety about her role in the community of writers, an anxiety underscored by the era of taught creative writing in British universities. The fact that the quotation above comes from a creative writing coursebook demonstrates a partial commitment, at least, to the institutionalization of creative writers.

Earlier in this chapter, I presented the institutionalization of writers, and the consequent emergence of ethical dilemmas shared by creative practitioners and academic critics, as either an insular mirroring process, or the means by which responsibility might be more adequately articulated. At the very least, the self-consciousness inspired in critics of contemporary literature by virtue of their proximity to practice (and practitioners) seems to create the potential for the kind of relevance and engagement that Bergonzi, quite understandably, could not envisage in 1988. For the critic, the dilemma concerns how value is constructed, and the (perhaps unwitting) role the critic plays in canon formation; for the practising writer, the dilemma centres on how one *is valued*, and the degree to which the canons constructed within academia co-opt the writer (perhaps unwittingly) into a protected circle of professionalism, distancing him or her from their personal engagement with social reality, the stuff of fiction. Smith's ambivalence about the creative writing workshop articulates the dilemma from the creative rather the critical end of the spectrum.

These reflections on the critic's function are inspired by my reading of Ali Smith's analysis of the novelist's function within her novels, and the shared contextual pressures that writers face within the confines of contemporary regulation. Outside academe, this might seem a parallel that is flimsy, or self-regarding. However, in the new era of critical practice in the study of the contemporary, where British writers (including Ali Smith) now rub shoulders with their would-be critics, the parallel seems compelling to me. Nevertheless, given the rapidity with which creative writing has been embraced, these shared concerns and anxieties remain to be fully examined. But we can recognize some of the problems that ensue; and that, of course, is the precondition for their solution.

CHAPTER NINE

'The Uncanny Can Happen': Desire and Belief in *The Seer*

MONICA GERMANÀ

Chapter Summary: Ali Smith's play *The Seer* (2006), explores the vacuity of modern life whilst making specific references to the question of contemporary Scottish identity. Belief and desire are the central themes around which the plot of Smith's playful drama unfolds. A frequent motif in her writing, throughout Smith's work desire embodies a subversive drive, which catalyses a process of epiphanic awakening, a revelation which exposes the ethical and aesthetic purposes of the pleasure of language. In *The Seer* language is exposed in its ambiguity: a tool for deceit, language can manipulate people and their beliefs. But language, too, in its poetic function serves the purpose of filling the social vacuum left open by the postmodern condition, reasserting the importance of community and communication. Catalysed by the encounter with the other, the *jouissance* of language is central to Smith's work, and, in particular, as this chapter elucidates, *The Seer*, a play about the regained ability to see, hear, feel for, and ultimately, speak to each other.

Keywords: desire, *jouissance*, poetic language, Scottish theatre, *The Seer*, the uncanny

Consider sunbeams. When the sun's rays let in
Pass through the darkness of a shuttered room,
You will see a multitude of ways
Inside the sunbeam, moving in the void,
Seeming to be engaged in endless strife,
Battle, and warfare, troop attacking troop,
And never a respite, harried constantly,
With meetings and with partings everywhere.

(Lucretius 2. 114–20)

My epigraph from Lucretius's poetic description of what would be later defined as 'Brownian motion' may appear strangely placed at the threshold of an essay that promises to discuss the relationship between desire and belief in Ali Smith's play *The Seer* (2006). Yet, as this chapter will elucidate, in *The Seer* Smith investigates the potential of a new ontology of emotions, evoking the possibility of departing from the simulacral vacuum mourned by some postmodernist writers through the emotional awakening that lies at the heart of the play. The mechanics of desire, the drive that, in various ways becomes the key to the self-renewal that thematically underpins *The Seer*, are akin to the erratic – and yet, unstoppable – motion of the particles of light described by Lucretius: in a similar fashion, I would argue, the invisible particles of desire destabilize accepted norms, shaking up the emotional apathy that threatens to annihilate the self, while building intangible links with the other.

The 'metaphysics of desire' (Belsey, 1994, p. 8) repeatedly return to haunt Smith's writing, in fiction as in the other genres she has worked with. Take, for instance, these stanzas from the song 'Half an Apple', which Smith wrote for *Ballads of the Book*, a collaborative project reinterpreting the traditional form of the Scottish ballad:

First I take an apple
I cut it down the middle
I eat my half of apple
And I leave the other half for you
It's just one thing that I can do.

Or I can set the table
Like in an ancient fable
Where somebody is summoned
By a knife and fork and spoon and thin air
I mean someone who isn't there.

(Various Artists, 2007)

In many ways the lyrics from this piece of music offer an appropriate, if retrospective, introduction to the themes explored by Smith in *The Seer*. Music, and particularly traditional Scottish music, is both theme and dramatic technique in *The Seer*. The lyrics of the song establish an intertextual reference to 'Thomas the Rhymer': the allusion to the apple, the ominous fruit Thomas receives from the Queen of Elfland, is not accidental. Just like the traditional ballad of 'Thomas the Rhymer', the song 'Half an Apple' is about absence, and, in particular, the paradoxically present absence conjured up by the object of one's desire. Absence and distance, literal or metaphorical, are important conditions of desire in its purest form; as noted by Catherine Belsey in relation to Jacques Derrida's treatment of desire in *The Post Card* (1980), 'The existence of this correspondence assumes an absence, the separation of the lovers'

(Belsey, 1994, p. 69). Smith's deployment of the spectral motif to convey the notion of absence in the song, as well as her metaleptic use of the pronoun 'you', may remind us of similar strategies and shared preoccupations with the spectrality of desire in her novel *Hotel World* (2001). The lyrics hint to desire's ambiguous relationship with belief, pointing to the impalpable bonds that exist between emotion and reason and to the ontological complications that desire introduces in our set of beliefs; underlying 'Half an Apple', then, is a question about the 'real' and the dubious authenticity of desire: is what we want real? Is what we believe in real? Can we believe in what we want? This chapter will not attempt to provide answers to these questions, so much as to unveil the complex ways in which *The Seer* articulates the conflict between authentic and simulated desire.

Throughout the two acts, the play self-consciously interrogates easy assumptions about the boundaries of self and of one's world(s). *The Seer* starts off with Iona and Neil, presented as the quintessential modern middle-class Scottish couple: unmarried young professionals sharing the mortgage for a trendily furnished flat. Enclosed in the solipsistic superficiality of their hollow world of online shopping, gastro-pretentiousness and futile gadgetry, their relationship has reached an emotional plateau. What is shaping to be an ordinary night at home after a day at work is shaken up by a set of intrusions on the stage. This is also, of course, the starting point of *The Accidental* (2005), where the arrival of Amber at the Smart's holiday home sets in motion the characters' individual crises, and likewise, it returns in the plot of Smith's latest novel, *There but for the* (2011), which uses the unwillingness of a guest to leave a dinner party as the inciting incident for the parallel narratives that form the novel. In *The Seer* the first intruder is Janie MacDougall, a con-artist who ends up impersonating Iona's sister, Kirsty, by simply turning up on the couple's doorstep and weaving her way into their life. Since the real Kirsty never appears on the stage, Janie is referred to as Kirsty throughout the play (and this chapter). Just before the end of the first act, the second intruder, Sabrina, apparently a member of the audience, comes on stage, prompted by one of Kirsty's pseudo-spiritualist tricks: Neil and Iona believe she is a ghost. In the second act, while Kirsty is offstage, the third intruder, Janice, another member of the audience, joins the actors on the stage, though Neil and Iona understand her to be their neighbour, Mrs Henderson. When she comes back on stage, Kirsty falls instantaneously in love with Janice. After yet another interruption from the couple's neighbour, Mrs Henderson, with everybody else back to their respective lives and worlds, Neil and Iona are left alone, as they were at the beginning of the first act, but they are not unchanged.

Devised to erode the boundaries between the world of the play and the 'real' world, *The Seer*'s metatheatrical/metaleptic strategies interrogate the authenticity of Neil and Iona's world and its relationship to whatever other worlds may exist outside it. Simultaneously, such ontological interrogation points to the significant role played by desire, the absence of which is implicitly lamented in the consumerist world of twenty-first-century Scotland, and the significance of authentic desire in the construction of the real. As Leo Bersani rightly observed in his influential study of desire, '[w]e probably first experience desire in our lives as a naïve confusion of the self with the world' (Bersani, 1984, p. 5); that is, the insurgence of desire troubles the equilibrium previously established by the desiring subject and their world. Indeed, if we turn to Jacques Lacan's psychoanalytical analysis of the 'structures' of desire, we are reminded of the dramatic process produced by the self's desire for the other, which, in Lacan's work, plays a crucial role in the rise of the symbolic order: 'man's desire is the desire of the Other' (Lacan, 1977, p. 264). Yet what Lacan's theory of desire also emphasizes, is the paradoxical quality of desire, which, in essence, can never be fulfilled. The satisfaction of desire would, logically, lead to the end of the self's vital drive. Instead, Lacan explains, desire operates in a way that it only consumes itself, perpetuating a deferral of its own fulfilment, and thus ensuring that the self may always experience that sense of 'lack' that produces desire:

> Desire is that which is manifested in the interval that demand hollows within itself, in as much as the subject, in articulating the signifying chain, brings to light the want-to-be, together with the appeal to receive the complement from the Other, if the Other, the locus of speech, is also the locus of this want, or lack. (Lacan, 1977, p. 263)

Desire thus reiterates itself endlessly, constantly drawing attention to the missing object of one's desire. Ehsan Azari explains this process further:

> When the object is within reach, we do not desire it. In other words, we don't wish to have something that is already in our possession. This makes desire slip from one object to another, and the object we are about to possess, has to be rejected. Such refusal allows fixation to move onto another object. (Azari, 2008, p. 12)

One could argue that the capitalist/consumerist economic system is designed to exploit the human desire's capability for constant renewal and therefore stimulate the perpetuation of longing for new objects of desire. Indeed, as Bersani had already suggested at the end of the twentieth century:

> [E]ven in a society which realizes our brightest, most exaltingly generous dreams of the human community, we may find ourselves haunted by the impulses of a self which we had too easily dismissed as an outmoded superstructure of a rejected form of social organization. (Bersani, 1984, p. 8)

In other words, the condition for desire does not necessarily, according to Bersani, depend on the relative or absolute potential fulfilment of an individual's wants. In fact, even in a hypothetical utopian scenario, desire may trigger an almost nostalgic longing for what we do not have any more, channelling our desire into (conservative) nostalgia or the longing for what no longer exists. Yet, more recently, critics have drawn attention to the threats posed to the self's *authentic* desire by the relentless modes of production and consumption of late capitalism. By manufacturing simulated desire – that is, desire designed to temporarily open a gap to be filled by a new product on the market – consumerism manipulates the subject's ability to feel desire, and consequently pleasure, with the quick fix offered by short-lived fads: rather than increasing the subject's fulfil-ment of the long-term goals of authentic desire, consumerism dilutes the intensity of desire and diverts the subject's consciousness away from that which leads to more meaningful achievements. As Goodheart argued in *Desire and Its Discontents* (1991), '[i]llimitable desire in its aggressive and perennially discontented consumption of objects becomes – in effect – nihilism. Objects cannot be discriminated and lose all their value. The totalized conception of desire in which objects are irrelevant makes of desire itself a vacuity' (Goodheart, 1991, p. 21). The saturation of desire may thus produce the opposite effect of the meaningful function of authentic desire and lead to the death of desire, or, if we prefer, boredom, 'the condition in which there are many things you can do; it's just that you don't want to do any of them. You are bored: desire is dead within you' (Irvine, 2006, p. 22). This is exactly the starting point in *The Seer*.

Presenting us with a couple whose apathy epitomizes the absence of desire in contemporary culture, the audience would easily identify the play's protagonists as an average couple of young professionals living anywhere in Western Europe. Through an insight into Neil and Iona's sexless, eventless, but in other ways flawless life – a life replete with the privileges that consumerism affords – the play focuses on the crisis of desire within the culture of globalized postmodernity. The dialogue between Neil and Iona is purposefully devoid of meaning and yet it is the vacuity of their relationship, their jobs, their so-called home that becomes the play's focal point. When Neil asks Iona, 'Is it focaccia or ciabatta?' (Smith, 2006, p. 8), the mundane question is made more ironic because of the dramatic emphasis Neil places on the bread dilemma, though the importance of the issue is simultaneously diffused by Iona's apparent ignorance of the difference between the two kinds of bread: instead of offering a definitive answer, she asks back, 'Which is the one you like again?' (Smith, 2006, p. 8). The scene exposes the lack of real tension and drama, as it plays out Neil's food allergies as whimsical manifestations of a character whose identity seems to be rooted in bogus medical conditions. The truth is, as Iona admits, that 'there's no horrible drama in our lives, like the couples you see on programmes on TV or in the papers' (Smith, 2006, p. 18). But this is exactly Neil's and Iona's 'horrible drama': although admittedly in good jobs, they can't afford to go travelling because of the mortgage (Smith, 2006, p. 26), they have no sense of community and don't even know their neighbours (Smith, 2006, p. 31). Their nondescript daily routines are only spiced up by the 'unexpected' arrivals of gifts they buy themselves online. As Iona explains:

> Easier than going to the shops. It's exciting. You pay for it on your credit card. So it doesn't seem like you're spending money at all. Then the next day or a few days later the thing you've bought comes through the door, like a present. (Smith, 2006, p. 27)

The reference to virtual shopping is significant here. Like most of the apparently pointless items that fill Iona and Neil's lives, it is their insignificant hollowness that questions the authenticity of desire in the play. In this context, online shopping is the metonym of a larger set of postmodern vacuums that *The Seer* unveils. The power of the internet and the control it exercises on the fabrication of simulated desires is a direct extension of the influence of advertising on the construction of the kind of transient desires that consumerism relies on. As John Berger observed in *Ways of Seeing* (1972):

> Publicity exerts an enormous influence and is a political phenomenon of great importance. But its offer is as narrow as its references are wide. It recognizes nothing except the power to acquire. All other human faculties or needs are made subsidiary to this power. All hopes are gathered together, made homogeneous, simplified, so that they become the intense yet vague, magical yet repeatable promise offered in every purchase. (Berger, 1972, p. 147)

The Seer, whose title can also be read as a self-conscious reference to the ability to see, or, as the case may be, to the blindness that affects our inability to recognize authentic desire, offers a similar reading of virtual shopping. The function of the internet in the play is precisely this: to highlight the postmodern subject's inability to identify or prioritize their desires. In a post-capitalist system when everything becomes available before demand, it is the mechanisms of production that determine our desires, and not the other way around.

While exposing the dangers inherent in a culture which, more and more, relies on the immediate satisfaction of computer-generated desire, Smith draws a link between the crisis of desire and community loss: the former's lack of authenticity leads to the ontological impossibility of the latter. A social group that relies largely on the internet to fulfil desire will make the existence of a local trade – and the community around it – redundant. Consequently, the play's locale becomes vague and bears no relevance to the significance of the story. Contemporary urban Scotland is evocative, in this sense, of Marc Augé's non-place, the quintessential spatial embodiment of the hyperreal, the place of transient experiences, epitomized, for instance, by 'the complex skein of cable and wireless networks that mobilize extraterrestrial space for the purposes of communication so peculiar that it often puts the individual in contact only with another image of himself' (Augé, 1992, p. 79). The problems with the crisis of desire therefore is linked to wider questions of authenticity, particularly in relation to the eradication of a local community that Augé's theory of 'non-places' may infer. Smith is particularly concerned with the anonymity and dislocatedness that affect contemporary society. Set against one of Augé's exemplary non-places, the corporate 'Global Hotel', her second novel, *Hotel World*, produces, besides other critical reflections, a commentary on the invisible communities stemming from the hyperreal cultures of twenty-first-century globalization. At the time of Augé's writing, the internet had only just begun to change people's lives. It had not yet changed the ways in which we decide what to eat for dinner or where we go for a drink. Nevertheless, his emphasis on the solipsistic alienation brought in by the 'complex skein of cable and wireless networks that mobilize extraterrestrial space for the purposes of communication' is particularly relevant to twenty-first-century virtual living. With no real acquaintance in their local community, it is significant that Iona compares her life with Neil with the lives of TV characters: in the hyperreal context of their experience, these fictional people are more real than their actual neighbours. It is no coincidence that, when Neil discusses his case studies, he overemphasizes their importance: 'my case-studies are to do with the new Scotland. They're vital' (Smith, 2006, p. 12). We do not in fact, get to know more about the crucial details that Neil's case studies are going to disclose about the 'new Scotland'. When Kirsty asks to hear more about such case studies, Iona can only say they are 'studies [of] [. . .] cases' (Smith, 2006, p. 34). The reference to 'new Scotland', however, suggests that this is in fact one of the larger issues affecting the characters in *The Seer*, as later reinforced by Neil's dialogue with Janice, when he justifies his reluctance to reveal details about his job: '[W]hat you do clearly isn't confidential or vital for the formation of contemporary national identity' (Smith, 2006, p. 82).

The Scottish question is further conveyed through the play's allusions to Scottish tradition. The very beginning of the play introduces these issues through the deployment of traditional Scottish music, which, apparently, only Iona is able to hear. The source of the tune is a mystery as the sound comes from the apartment below, which Iona believes to be temporarily empty, while the Hendersons, their neighbours, are on holiday. The play's title refers to popular superstition and, in particular, the bogus myth of 'Finn MacFinn the great MacFinn', who, according to Kirsty, was born on the grounds of the couple's block of flats. One of Finn's prophesies claims (in Kirsty's words) that:

> In the days, the terrible days, when a country made anew cannot honour its differences, cannot hear the many, many different voices all singing together

to make its own unique voice; in the days, the terrible days, when strangers will no longer be welcomed at the hearth of a Scottish home; the days, the terrible days, when sister will turn against sister and throw her out of her flat when she only wants somewhere to stay for a little while; ah, blessed I am not to see those days, for nothing shall follow them but calamity, calamity and selfishness all. (Smith, 2006, p. 31)

Kirsty's brief monologue draws attention to the question of belief and make-belief. To the impostor, who has craftily manufactured the superstition to convince Iona to let her stay, the 'seer' may be her passport to free accommodation. To Iona, the bogus prophesy brings home the 'truth' she has been looking for. In a piece of dramatic writing that self-consciously plays with language to undermine its reliability, the invisible seer allows Iona to believe in the inexplicable voices she has been hearing and collude with Kirsty's cunning plan.

The playful interrogation of superstition also establishes links with Smith's fictional work; the reference to the Brahan Seer appears, for instance, in her first novel, *Like* (1997):

When the Brahan Seer, ancient highland magician of the greatest powers, once foretold that if there were too many bridges over the River Ness, or if there were too many women in power in the nation, then terrible dire chaos would follow. I read in a book once that they halted work on the fifth bridge when word came that Hitler had invaded Poland. The Second World War, all because some people in the North of Scotland started putting together that one-too-many bridge. (Smith, 1997, p. 158)

Thus Ash, the unreliable narrator of the second part of the novel, exposes the manipulative power of superstition, pointing to its ambiguous hold on individuals' beliefs. In this sense, too, the play's impostor/enchantress, Kirsty, evokes her previous incarnation as Amber, the subversive *femme fatale* of *The Accidental* (2005) and a contemporary embodiment of the dangerous woman of many traditional Scottish tales and ballads. These thematic links perform an ambiguous function: though seemingly reminiscent – with a hint of nostalgia – of Scotland's folkloric past, they also deconstruct the solid foundations of a postmodern Scottish experience, exposing the simulacral qualities of Scottish culture against the backdrop of twenty-first-century globalization. Contemporary Scotland is in fact depicted as simultaneously devoid of beliefs and, most crucially, the *desire* to believe. The question of belief becomes particularly pressing when Kirsty intrudes into Neil and Iona's comfort zone, hoping to be able to impersonate a person familiar to Neil and Iona. The only truth about Kirsty seems to be that she is in fact a liar and, as Neil reads from a newspaper article, a con-artist, 'known under various aliases including Mirabella of the Marvels, Fortuna the Fabulous High-Wire-Walker and Sybilla-I-See-Everything', and wanted by the police for fraudulent activities (Smith, 2006, pp. 40–1). What is most disquieting about the affair is not so much that a con may try her luck pursuing her gain through deceit, but the fact that Iona does not recognize her own sister or, more plausibly, she is willing to identify the stranger as her sister. In this context, Kirsty subverts another strand of superstition, that of the changeling, which, in this instance, may fulfil desire, rather than cause havoc. Like Amber in *The Accidental*, whose elusive self comes to represent, in different ways, the object of desire of each member of the Smart family, Kirsty embodies the inciting incident, the catalyst for change that Iona has been longing for. Like Amber, Kirsty also resists identification, as suggested by her multiple names and forged identities mentioned in the newspaper article, and as she revealingly admits: 'I've got a very fluid sense of self' (Smith, 2006, p. 41).

Smith's experimentalism has frequently been discussed in relation to her self-reflective use of wordplay, puns, and the deliberate disruption of textual and narrative conventions that have informed her major works of fiction including the most recent *There but for the*. The absurdist sub-text and theatricality of *The Seer* is also underpinned by Smith's playfulness both with regard to the script and theatrical form. Towards the end of the first act, this becomes particularly evident with the so-called fall of the fourth wall, the imaginary barrier that separates the world of the play from the world of the audience, which collapses when Kirsty is able to see the audience who have come to see the play. To Neil and Iona, who cannot see the audience, but can only 'see' their wallpaper – which the audience, of course, cannot see – this is either another of Kirsty's tricks (Neil) or a hallucination (Iona) (Smith, 2006, p. 45). To Kirsty, however, that other world, the world beyond the invisible wall, becomes the only 'real' world, juxtaposed to the imaginary world of the play. Her personal address to the audience has a debunking effect on the ontological foundations of the play. Echoing Plato's allegory of the cave, Kirsty questions whether the Hendersons, Iona and Neil's neighbours, actually exist:

> Are the Hendersons a figment of your collective imagination? Basic philosophy, lesson number one – ready? If the Hendersons are sitting by themselves in a dark room, with nobody thinking about them, are they still the Hendersons? And – the big question – if you've never seen the Henderson's, have the Hendersons never seen you? (Smith, 2006, p. 49)

Smith's metatheatrical strategies, which occupy most of the second act of the play, have a dual effect. On one hand, in playing with the real/imaginary ontological hierarchies of the play's worlds, they interrogate the solidity of belief. Just like their case studies, their futile conversations over the merits of organic food and online shopping, Neil and Iona's only bond to their community may just be a simulacrum, a reference without substance. Simultaneously, in exposing the invisible barrier separating the two worlds, the continuous disruption of the suspension of disbelief undermines the very notion of boundaries. In this respect, too, Smith's play can be read along with other important examples from recent Scottish theatre, such as David Greig's *Europe* (1994) and Stephen Greenhorn's *Passing Places* (1997). Both plays, as Nadine Holdsworth has argued insightfully, deal with the question of national boundaries, and their significance in the context of late twentieth-century globalized geography:

> An increasingly globalised culture, new technologies, the dominance of multinationals persistently circumventing the boundaries of national econ-omies, the proliferation of transnational corporations such as the European Union and a growing global diaspora, all contribute to a climate which forces a spotlight on what the nation means to individuals. (Holdsworth, 2003, p. 26)

This can lead, according to Holdsworth, to either innovative ways of reimagining identity or a re-entrenchment of ethnocentric and nation-alist reactionary positions. In forcing the audience to consider the fine line that separates our world from the 'other' world, *The Seer*, argua-bly, involves readers and spectators to rethink the significance of fixed boundaries and our sense of belonging.

The play's engagement with problematic boundaries is conveyed through the multiple intrusions into the private world of Neil and Iona's home, pointing to the threat, frequently haunting Smith's narratives, that the 'other', the 'incomer', the uninvited guest, may pose to the stability of our world. The play complicates the ontological structure of its world further as Kirsty, herself an embodiment of the other, discovers the new world of the theatre's spectators. Kirsty's most pressing concern is with her new audience, a community that apparently refuses to acknowledge her existence. To counteract their apathy, Kirsty's dubious magic talk borrows the language of telepathic spiritualism:

> I, Maestra the Magnificent, am here among you tonight to prove once and for all that the uncanny can happen. And to reveal to you the mysterious marvellous multifariousness of the totally unseen invisible veiled connec-tions that run between all of us all the time. For as you sit there before me, though you don't know it, secret messages are transmitting themselves from you to me. Yes they are. I can prove it. (Smith, 2006, p. 51)

The ontological questioning put forth by Kirsty's discovery of the 'other world' destabilizes the foundations of all ontological certainties pertain-ing to the world of the play. Her call for a specific member of the audience sitting next to an empty seat invites Sabrina to join the stage just before the end of the first act. The disruption brought in by the apparent merg-ing of the two worlds prompts Sabrina to explain that '[t]here's room in the universe for all the different planes of existence' (Smith, 2006, p.

66), a gesture towards postmodernist aesthetics that seemingly comes from an audience responsive to such strategies. The metatheatrical wit that punctuates the interaction between the audience characters and the play characters on stage echoes the metafictional playfulness found in Smith's novels; Sabrina's statement that 'you've all been badly written' (Smith, 2006, p. 65) is later echoed by Janice, Sabrina's friend, who complains about the ways in which the characters appear to be manipulating a paying audience: 'What kind of play is this? You can't order an audience around like that! I'm going to write to the people who gave you your grant and ask them to revoke it. This play'll never tour!' (Smith, 2006, p. 89). But the fall of the fourth wall has also drastic consequences on the characters' identities. While Sabrina – who is a self-named 'awful English incomer' (Smith, 2006, p. 67) – claims to be 'the only one here on the stage who is really real', Neil's self-doubting grows into a radical ontological breakdown: 'I don't know any more. Am I a man? Am I a woman? Do the Hendersons exist?' (Smith, 2006, p. 67).

Against Neil's identity crisis, Kirsty's response to the other world is representative of a different kind of approach to the unexpected intrusion of the other. Upon seeing Janice for the first time, her awakened desire becomes a gateway for self-renewal: 'I feel like I could be anyone. I've never felt like this before. I feel all pure. I feel all new' (Smith, 2006, p. 85). The insurgence of authentic desire as a result of being in love clashes with the other ephemeral kinds of desire that the play previously manifested, particularly in relation to internet shopping. Belsey rightly observes that 'desire is [. . .] the location of resistances to the norms, proprieties and taxonomies of the cultural order' (Belsey, 1994, p. 6). Desire, therefore, is simultaneously what structures and unsettles the self and its relationship with the other. *Jouissance*, the ultimate goal of authentic desire, stems from the subversive drive that ultimately leads to happiness by way of a radical change. As Julia Kristeva explains:

> Happiness exists only at the price of a revolt. None of us has pleasure without confronting an obstacle, prohibition, authority, or law that allows us to realize ourselves as autonomous and free. The revolt revealed to accompany the private experience of happiness is an integral part of the pleasure principle. (Kristeva, 2000, p. 7)

Crucially, *jouissance* is rooted in manifestations of language that deviate from the norm: it is the intrusion of the semiotic – the irrational, less controlled, erratic order of language – that disrupts the structure of the symbolic, forcing the self to reach outward, towards the other. The random encounter with Janice produces this kind of 'revolt' in Kirsty's world. No longer confident in her self-fabricated world of lies, Kirsty's hesitant lines dismantle her linguistic confidence – 'Are you real? Do you exist? Am I making you up?' (Smith, 2006, p. 84) – and expose the fragile foundations of the symbolic, and the ontology of beliefs that the symbolic represents. Simultaneously, it is the *jouissance* produced by the encounter with the other that releases the subject from the constrains of the symbolic, renewing the self, instead, through the (temporary) breakdown of the barriers that separate the subject from the other:

Kirsty   Such beauty, such perfection, can't be real.

Janice   There's thousands of pounds here. I'm sure it's real.

Kirsty   And here you are, the real thing!

(Smith, 2006, p. 85)

While Janice's greed exposes the fallacy of the short-sightedness of the kind of greed produced by consumerism, Kirsty's desire, triggered by her falling in love with Janice, is what causes her system of beliefs to collapse, and, at the same time, renew itself. The scene displays the desiring subject's inability to see things – Kirsty does not see that Janice is only interested in her money – yet it also points out the fresh perspective offered by *jouissance* – 'I feel all . . . possible again' (Smith, 2006, p. 85) – and the destabilized ontology produced by the language of emotions.

The subversive marriage of language and desire has haunted Smith's writing since her debut collection of short stories, *Free Love And Other Stories* (1995). Here, the disruptive workings of desire run like a red thread through all the stories in the collection, but the distinct symbiosis between desire and language emerges strongly in 'The World with Love', the last story in the collection, where the narrator indulges in the excitement produced by the French words she has learnt to use to express her growing desire for a school friend. Significantly, it is only through the foreign sounds of another language that desire can be uttered and therefore acknowledged: 'You scared yourself with how much you were thinking about her. You thought of her with words that gave you an unnameable feeling at the bottom of your spine and deep in your gut' (Smith, 1995, p. 146). The unutterable truth about desire exceeds the boundaries of the familiar, bleeding into the unfamiliar territory of foreign words. In its indissoluble bond with language, love, as the authentic embodiment of desire for the other, becomes the antithesis of capitalism's manufactured kinds of commercial desire: compared to such market-engineered desires, which ultimately entrap the subject in the vicious circle of meaningless consumption, authentic desire, even when doomed to fail, never leaves the subject unchanged. Placing emphasis on the consumption of desire in contemporary popular culture, Belsey has commented on the commercial value of desire, particularly in relation to the enduring appeal of romantic love:

To the degree that the postmodern condition implies an unbridled consumerism, the cultural logic of late capitalism, pleasure for cash and a product to gratify every possible impulse – if not, indeed, to construct the impulse in the first place – love is a value that remains beyond the market. While sex is a commodity, love becomes the condition of a happiness that cannot be bought, the one remaining object of desire that cannot be sure of purchasing fulfilment. Love thus becomes more precious than before because it is beyond price, and in consequence its metaphysical character is intensified. (Belsey, 1994, p. 72)

In *The Seer* the discovery of the other world – or the world of the other – has triggered a different set of emotions, which, as Kirsty suggests, are both 'purer' and 'newer'. The old world – the world of the play – is revealed in its meaninglessness; what matters now is the new world: 'Who cares about the other world when this world is transformed, so different, so full of life, and love and Janice Henderson?' (Smith, 2006, p. 93) The uncanny has happened: it is the encounter with the unfamiliar that has subverted the rules of the familiar world. Read against the hyperreal context of the play, Kirsty's emotional awakening preludes to the rekindling of Neil and Iona's relationship at the end of the play.

As the encounter between two individuals from two worlds, which should have never logically intersected with each other, is made possible by the play's disruption of its own conventions, *The Seer* highlights the uncanny mechanics of desire. Though desire may derive from a lack within us, it is through the encounter with the other, the stranger, that we become aware of our longing for the object of our love. Troubling the inside/outside, self/other categorical oppositions, then, the discourse of desire shares the ambiguities of the Freudian uncanny. As Elizabeth Wright suggests:

> The emergence of the uncanny may be the moment which disturbs our narcissistic gaze, the moment which allows us to see that the old repression is futile, a waste of energy – 'uneconomic' in both its Freudian and its material sense, that a redirection of desire is called for. (Wright, 1999, p. 25)

As it approaches the end, a new kind of ontology, a set of 'real' emotions replaces the simulacra that haunted the world of the play since the beginning. In this respect, the play manifestly juxtaposes the pleasure produced by the tangible purchases from online shopping and compares it with a different kind of less palpable pleasure, the kind of happiness produced by the unexpected connection with the other. In turn, such newly awakened desire produces a different set of beliefs, proposing a view that the 'real', far from being a stable, monolithic category, may in fact be manipulated by our desires. The key issue is articulated by Iona when she blames Neil for denying her freedom to believe: 'You never let me believe what I want to believe! [. . .] You never let me believe what I need to believe!' (Smith, 2006, p. 91). In the end, however, *The Seer* reaffirms the notion that the 'real' is constructed by belief, which, in turn, emerges as a malleable framework subject to the desire for the other.

This becomes particularly evident when, at the end of the play, the traditional Scottish tunes that have haunted the couple's apartment from the beginning, become instrumental in re-establishing the broken communication with the other. Significantly, it is a karaoke machine that catalyses the positive resolution of the play's conflict:

Neil

     I will build my love a bower
     By a cool crystal fountain
     And round it I will pile
     All the wild flowers of the mountain.

Iona   *(moved)* Oh! Oh, Neil. I don't think I've ever heard you sing before.
Neil   That's because I can't, not really. I wish I could. I wish could sing better for you.
Iona   You can! That's so beautiful!
Neil   I'd sing you such beautiful songs if I could.
Iona   You sang perfectly. That was the loveliest song I've ever had sung to me.

(Smith, 2006, p. 96)

Thanks to this musical device, Iona realizes that Neil can sing, and Neil, in turn, remembers falling in love with Iona. Mediated through a reproductive device – itself a product of late twentieth-century technology and a symbol of globalized entertainment – the lines from the traditional ballad 'The Braes o' Balquhidder' are layered with significance: simultaneously looking back to the past tradition they belong to and forward to the future awaiting for Neil and Iona (and contemporary Scotland), the intertextual reference to the ballad self-reflectively draws attention to the function of poetic language in contemporary culture. When Iona claims that '[t]he old songs are the best' (Smith, 2006, p. 97), Kirsty corrects her: '[d]epending on their adaptability to new ways of singing them' (Smith, 2006, p. 97): a return to tradition would be too simplistic a way of recuperating a lost sense of national identity. The emphasis is on the use of contemporary strategies to adapt the old tunes to accommodate change; as Iona puts it in her toast at the end of the play: 'This is a world made new, by different eyes' (Smith, 2006, p. 101). The play asks us to reconsider the ways in which we may be failing to form solid bonds with the others, the neighbours we never see, the shops we never visit, the strangers we do not engage with. As Sara Ahmed reminds us, the etymology of 'emotion' reveals the dynamic drive of human sentiment, one which is suggestive of our need to belong in a place, but also connect to the others who may share that space:

What moves us, what makes us feel, is also that which holds us in place, or gives us a dwelling place. Hence movement does not cut the body off from the 'where' of its inhabitance, but connects bodies to other bodies: attachment takes place through movement, through being moved by the proximity of others. (Ahmed, 2004, p. 11)

In pointing to the importance of emotional awakening as a strategic way out of the postmodern impasse, *The Seer* departs from the play's initial emphasis on the loss of the real, as it draws attention to the individual's ethical responsibility towards the other. Explaining Baudrillard's critique of postmodern culture, Graham Matthews suggests that '[c]ommunication has become a circular process of endless replication and simulation in which meaning and value are eroded beneath the influx of images disconnected from their reality' (Matthews, 2012, p. 9). Moving in the opposite direction, the happiness generated by the rise of authentic desire in *The Seer* leads instead to the regained ability to see and speak to the other. The disruptive power of *jouissance*, first experienced by Kirsty as she falls in love with the absent Janice, has a knock-on effect for the remaining characters, but also, in line with the porousness of theatrical boundaries exposed earlier, on the world beyond the stage. In a circular fashion, just as it had started, the play ends with one of the traditional Scottish songs played by the karaoke machine. Neil and Iona do not sing, but simply wait, as the audience is invited to improvise a choir to the tune of a famous Scottish song.

'Sidekick Doubling the Tune': Writing Ali Smith in Norwegian

MERETE ALFSEN

It was the song of the flow of things, the song of the undammed river, and there with the fiddler was his sidekick, who doubled the tune and who, when he played alongside his partner, found in everything he laid hands on (whistle, squeezebox, harp, guitar, old empty oilcan and a stick or stone to bang it with) . . . the kind of music that. . . .

(Smith, 2007, p. 157)

This image of the fiddler and his sidekick from the wedding scene towards the end of *Girl meets boy* (2007) strikes me as a fitting metaphor for what goes on in the act of literary translation. The song of the flow of things is of course the source text. The translator, the sidekick playing alongside the master fiddler, doubles the tune using what she can find in her own language, the target language.

I have been a literary translator since 1986, at first translating mostly American writers including Alice Hoffman and Amy Tan. In 1992 my career made a leap when I was asked to translate Virginia Woolf's *Orlando* (1928). That book was awarded a prize for outstanding transla-tion, and was the start of my long-lasting literary relationship with Mrs Woolf. Soon I was also spending my days in the delightful company of Jane Austen, and have had the pleasure of writing five of her novels in Norwegian. Other British authors of 'mine' include Jeanette Winterson and A. S. Byatt, and of course, Ali Smith, starting with *Hotel World* (2001), which was published in Norwegian in 2004.

What I mean to do here is to try to show a few of the things I have laid hands on in order to play Smith's literary music in Norwegian. Translating Smith is a mind-bending undertaking. In fact, it is often not a question of translating in the traditional sense. The puns and the poetry and the playfulness have to be recreated, and it all has to be strictly idiomatic, not forced and too-clever language-bending, no 'translationese'.

One of the things I admire about Smith's writing is the way she lis-tens to what people really say. To the ways in which language is actually being used by the people to whom it belongs. And this is obviously the way her books should read in translated versions as well. That is what I mean by 'writing Ali Smith in Norwegian'. Then, of course, she takes the familiar words and phrases apart to see what is inside.

Here we go.

In *Hotel World* we meet Sara Wilby, a young girl recently dead. She has not yet left this world, she is still here, stuck in-between worlds. A ghost. The world is leaving her. The words are leaving her. Take this word 'ghost', a key word in *Hotel World*. It is commonly thought that Shakespeare's English is a very rich language, rich in words, while Ibsen's Norwegian, on the other hand, is poor, poor in words (which, in turn, would make a Norwegian translation from English second rate). In practice, however, the translator's problem is often the opposite. True to form, and like a true poet, Smith makes good literary use of a number of the many meanings carried by the word 'ghost' in English. It echoes in the text, accumulating meaning. Imagine, one and the same word for the Holy Ghost and the ghost of Dusty Springfield! That option does not exist in Norwegian. I had to choose different words in each context in order to give the immediate meaning. The cumulative and poetic effect of repetition is lost.

Another key word is 'change', also with multiple meanings. At the end of the first chapter in *Hotel World* is a section where three of the main characters are observed by the fourth, the ghost of Sarah.

> Here's a woman being swallowed by the doors. She is well-dressed. On her back she carries nothing. Her life could be about to change. Here's another one inside, wearing the uniform of the hotel and working behind its desk. She is ill and she doesn't know it yet. Life, about change. Here's a girl, next to me, dressed in blankets, sitting along from the hotel doors right here, on the pavement. Her life, change. (Smith, 2001, p. 30)

> Her er en kvinne som blir slukt av døra. Hun er velkledd. På ryggen bærer hun ingen ting. Kanskje skjer det snart en *omveksling i livet hennes*. Her er en annen kvinne, på innsiden, iført hotellets uniform og på jobb bak resepsjonsskranken. Hun er syk, men hun vet det ikke ennå. *Om veksling, livet*. Her er en jente, ved siden av meg, kledd i ulltepper, som sitter litt bortenfor hotellinngangen, her på fortauet. *Vekslepenger, livet hennes*. (Smith/Alfsen, 2004, pp. 34–5)

Close reading will reveal a slight shift in meaning here and there in the translation, as in the last sentence: 'Her life, change.' 'Vekslepenger, livet hennes.' The Norwegian phrase looks fine, but would translate back more like 'Small change, her life'. Not quite the same, admittedly. A bit smaller. There you go.

However, there is compensation to be had, too. Indeed, it comes from where Else sits, outside the hotel, begging for money. Else has learned to do without. Vowels, for instance, can be dispensed with: 'Spr sm chn?'

(Smith, 2001, p. 35). But Els(e), the frugal remnants of the name Elspeth happens to be the first three letters in the Norwegian verb 'elske' meaning 'to love'. A gift from the Norwegian language, freely given to Smith's text, where it truly belongs. She had to be Els, not Else, since Else is a common Norwegian name not lacking in anything.

Well. Next challenge, the word 'well'. A deep place to draw water from, but also the opposite of 'unwell'. Again, the English text plays on the different meanings – and there is no equivalent Norwegian option. 'Well' versus 'not well' in Norwegian has to be 'frisk' versus 'syk'. Honestly, as I told the author, I had no idea how to solve this. The only thing that came to mind was a Norwegian idiom, 'frisk som en fisk', literally 'well as a fish'. At least a fish is something in the depths, like a well . . . It worked! And have you got a fish that rhymes with 'syk'? –Well, we have a fish named 'sik' . . . And so, with just the tiniest bit of rewriting, I managed, in a way, to save the dichotomy of depth and a level place in the original.

One last example from *Hotel World* of what I like to call idiomatic revelations, or free gifts. It is from the last chapter, 'Present':

> The driving instructor is drinking Horlicks for breakfast; caffeine makes her jumpy. She is thinking of the feel of the learner driver up inside her. Her husband is having trouble with his tie. She is smiling and answering the questions he asks her, thinking of the feel of the push of the boy up amongst her clothes in her car.

> The learner driver is awake in bed going over the lessons he's had so far. Is she a good teacher? his mother asked him last night (his mother is paying for the lessons). Yes, he said. He blushed. She is a really good teacher, he said, she says I soon won't need dual controls and that with the right number of lessons I will easily pass. He has ten more lessons lined up. He is wondering what else he will learn. (Smith, 2001, pp. 231–2)

The idiom for 'easily pass' in Norwegian is 'stå med glans'. 'Stå' is the verb 'stand', but it is also used as a colloquial noun meaning 'hard-on'. And 'glans' means 'lustre', or in this context 'flying colours'. But then, you see, it is also 'glans' in the anatomical sense of 'glands'. Really, what more can you ask? Instead of the wholly innocent 'I will easily pass' you have 'stå med glans', which is perfectly idiomatic and correct, but at the same time draws in the reader's mind the unmistakable likeness of a penis, erect and eager. At this point the Norwegian text is funnier than the English one, but in a way that I would say is more than faithful to the original. Something is unavoidably lost in translation from time to time, but something is found, too. Here is another example; at the end of *Hotel World* is a poem, transcribed below, in English and in Norwegian. 'Rusk' means 'specks of dust'. 'Aske' means 'ashes'. Is this translation 'faithful to the original', or not?

remember	husk
you	du
must	må
live	leve
remember	husk
you	du
most	mest
love	elske
remainder	rusk
you	du
mist	rest
leaf	aske

Smith's sifting of language for human meaning often includes an exploration of grammatical structures. In *Hotel World*, grammatical tense defines the various chapters. In *The First Person and Other Stories* (2008) the grammatical person performs the same function in three of the collection's stories, but there is also a story called 'Present'. That title presents (sic!) the translator with a few problems. In this case, the Norwegian solution is not exactly brilliant, but the dilemma is rather classical, and I should like to include a discussion of it as an example of something the translator is very often up against. It also indicates how the translator's interpretation, her reading of the source text, determines the result.

In my reading, then, this story is essentially a sort of chamber play for three characters set in a country pub somewhere in England. A barmaid, a male guest who is interested in the barmaid, and the narrator, also a guest, observing what goes on between them. The time is November, pre-Christmas. The pub is already decorated for the holiday season. The title plays on three meanings of the word 'present' in English: 'gift', 'being present', and 'present' as in the grammatical tense. The story is about giving oneself as a gift to others, giving one's presence in the present, here and now. The English title incorporates all of these meanings quite effortlessly. The word 'present' is loaded to the hilt with meaning. This can't be done in Norwegian. Not as effortlessly, not idiomatically, only by a very forced and unpleasant bending and stretching of words. 'Gift' can be 'presang'; 'present' is a word in Norwegian and it does mean being present, but is not a colloquial term. And the grammatical tense is called 'presens'. The pregnancy of the English title cannot be matched. However, the pondering over it has at least made the reader/translator acutely aware of the many nuances of meaning that must be there in the story itself, also in the translated version. The Norwegian title became 'Gode gaver', literally 'Good gifts', or perhaps 'Blessings' (2009a).

So, unfortunately, no idiomatic revelation to save the day in this instance. And the translator must resist the temptation to mend it by choosing some unidiomatic, arty solution. Unless, of course, the source text allows for just that. Translating Smith is a *tour de force*, and once in a while one is required to go off-piste. Take, for instance, the breakdown of Professor Michael Smart in *The Accidental* (2005). A character in a novel who has a breakdown over almost twenty pages – in sonnets! I thought it might well be impossible, and that the book would never come out in Norway at all. To my astonishment, however, when I got down to it, the lines and rhymes just poured out of me. The poems were done in no time, and I think it unlikely that I'll ever have the opportunity to make such naughty rhymes ever again.

Speaking of naughty, I'll reveal to you what I think of as a hidden gem, albeit a very small one, in *Jente møter gutt* (2009b) (*Girl meets boy*). In the middle of the wonderful, racy lovemaking sequence (Smith, 2007, p. 102) is the well-placed expression 'down we went', meaning this and that. Strangely enough, there is no colloquial expression in Norwegian for 'going down on' in sexual terms, which is certainly part of the load of meaning here. What to do? But then – into the lap of the open-minded translator falls a true idiom, a phrase often used in folktales and tradi-tional literature, as Norwegian as the mountains and the fjords: 'Det bar til skogs.' It means approximately: 'Off into the woods'. It has all the speed and urgency of the original expression. And the best thing is, no one would have thought to read anything sexual into it outside of this context. Not every reader will catch the glint of this subtle little gem *in* the context either, but it is there!

When I first read at *There but for the* (2011), I thought: she's finally done it. She's finally gone and written an untranslatable book. It looked to me like something that ought not to be attempted. As a translator, one has to make up one's mind as to what is the sine qua non of a particular book, what simply has to be there in the new version for the translation to be worth undertaking. And I thought this time the wordplay and puns were just too much, and too fundamental to the whole structure of the book. From the start, the title presented itself as an insurmountable obstacle. There is no equivalent in Norwegian to the phrase 'There but for the grace of God go I'. And the four words, as we know, do not only make up an enigmatic and ingenious title, they also, typically of Smith, give the four main parts of the book their headings and their mean-ing. What turned me around was an inspiring discussion with Smith's Norwegian editor, Birgit Bjerck. We delved into the mystery of the book together, talking through it, and I came out convinced that it simply had to be done, and that *mystery* was a key word in the understanding and the rendering of it.

The title could not be translated. It had to be changed. The pleasing and meaningful connection between title and sections was lost. The sections must still have the first word of the first sentence as a heading, and that word must give the essence of the section, as in the original. That could be done. The four words no longer make up a phrase, so something both elegant and meaningful is definitely lost in translation – but the idea of the first word giving direction and meaning to the chapter survives, and idiomatically so. The Norwegian title is in keeping with Smith's text, inasmuch as it is a really juicy pun. The Norwegian equivalent of the military command 'at ease' is 'på stedet hvil'. Word for word it means 'in place rest'. The title of the book is a pun on this, På *stedet mil*, or 'in place miles'. It plays on the name of the unbidden guest, Miles, and also on the fact that he covers miles on the exercise bike in the guest room – 'in place', as it were. Also, and this is definitely the translator's reading, it connotes the biblical phrase of going the extra mile, which is what I think Miles is doing.

Then we are into the text itself, and the puns come at you hard and fast. Section 'There': 'Batter. Beat. Pound. Rain blows. Strange phrase, to rain blows. Somewhere over the rainblow' (Smith, 2011, p. 4). The reference cannot be kept, it doesn't work in Norwegian. However, out of my store of Norwegian phrases and usage, comes a substitute which works in exactly the same way, it startles the reader by combining something light, positive and optimistic with something nasty. 'Strange phrase, to rain blows' has a very straightforward translation into idiomatic Norwegian: 'Pussig uttrykk, å la slagene hagle' (Smith/Alfsen, 2012, p. 19). Then comes the line from the song, which I can't use. Instead, I make use of the second meaning of the word 'slag', 'blow', which can also mean 'kind, type'. We have a tradition of making 'seven kinds' of cookies for Christmas, 'sju slag'. This is the mark of a proper housewife and connotes domesticity, peace and good will, festive lights in the winter darkness. The Norwegian text goes like this: 'Pussig uttrykk, å la *slag*ene hagle. Sju *slag* til jul' ('Strange phrase, to rain blows [kinds]. Seven kinds for Christmas'). Note the extra bonus of the alliteration in the Norwegian text. Not always to be freely added, of course, but in a playful text like Smith's, definitely not amiss.

I remember thinking, while I was still questioning whether the book could be done at all, that if I could find a plausible solution to the Brooke/broke misunderstanding, there was a chance of success. Little Brooke is sitting on the front steps of the Lees' house in Greenwich when Anna approaches her.

> Hello, Anna said.
> I'm broke, the child said.
> Me too, Anna said.

(Smith, 2011, p. 13)

But what the child really said was 'I'm Brooke'. Oh, the sleepless hours I spent toying with what the child could possibly say in Norwegian. It had to be idiomatic *and* phonetically plausible. At long last, as so often happens, the solution was the simplest and most obvious one; idiomatic, yes, and plausible enough, although not phonetically perfect. I simply used the obvious word for 'broke', which is 'blakk'. It does in fact work, and is an example of how *idiomatic* is paramount.

The fourth and final main section of the book, where the 'cleverist' child Brooke Bayoude meets the world with her wit and imagination, was the most demanding section to write in Norwegian. In this section, I had to cut a few things that just couldn't be made to make sense; for instance, the whole discussion of the word 'the'. In Norwegian, the definite article is a suffix inflected according to gender and number. Nevertheless, there are places where I believe I have made up for such absences, or at least come up to par. For 'cleverist' I have used a term that might even have been used in English: 'smartist'. 'Smart' is definitely the Norwegian adjective for an intelligent pupil like Brooke, and it can be turned around to work as an abusive word, just like 'clever' is here. I also like that 'artist' forms part of the word.

Finally, a joke: 'Josie Lee went to get her a Valium. What do you give an elephant who is cracking up? Trunkquillizers' (Smith, 2011, p. 317); 'Josie Lee gikk og hentet en pille til henne. Hva gir man en hval som får nervesammenbrudd? Hvalium' (Smith/Alfsen, 2012, p. 256) ('Josie Lee went to get her a pill. What do you give to a whale who is cracking up? Whalium').

Smith's love of words and her playful use of them are obvious and distinguishing qualities in her books. Not just words either – even grammatical structures and uses harbour truths about ways to be in the world. Spoken and written language is a human thing, and humanity is what is discovered in Smith's poetic exploration of it. Let others pursue this in analytical depth. My wish has been simply to give you a practical idea of the kind of local sticks and stones one can lay hands on in trying to play Smith's kind of music in another language.

Gillian Beer Interviews Ali Smith

Cambridge, 8 June 2012

GB: So here we are, Ali Smith and Gillian Beer, and it's just a chance to have some conversation. That's how we see this. One thing I was wanting to ask you about, because I've read a lot of the short stories and the novels but I've not read the play: I wondered whether there was a phase in your life when you were writing poetry and whether you might just start us off by talking about those other genres.

AS: Sure, it's wise of you, because that's exactly right. I think most people do start with poetry in an adolescent way, although I probably started as a child as I had a facility for rhyme. At school we were asked to make some stuff up, and I did it, and it was easy, so I did. I thought of myself as a poet through my teens, as we self-define at 17 – I was a poet. I was pretty dreadful. And I remember, there was a series of creative-writing fellows at Aberdeen University, where I was, to whom I showed my poems, William McIlvanney, Bernard MacLaverty, and then latterly, Iain Crichton Smith, who was there in the year after I left. A friend of mine said 'send Iain some of your poems, because he'll be great'. And he wrote back and said, 'you shouldn't be writing poems, you should be writing prose'. I sent him a story and several poems, and he said, 'no, you're a prose writer'. And I thought, no I'm not. I'm a tragic poet. Meanwhile, I came to Cambridge and then started writing plays. While we were here, I met my partner, Sarah, and we formed our own company. So my, I suppose you'd call it, apprenticeship, is all poetry and drama, and I avoided prose, if you like.

GB: I find that interesting, because, of course, puns and dialogue, those are the things that give a very peculiar zest to your work. You are so adept at seeing the word within the word, which means something completely different from what the outer shell of the word means, for instance. And I can see how you had that practice with rhyme, because rhyme is never perfect, it's always just . . .

AS: I love that. I know, it's true.

GB: It's trying to be perfect, but if it's perfect it's not a rhyme. What do they call it in French, *'rime tres royal'* I believe, which is where you say 'zest' and then you say 'zest' again, and that's a rhyme.

AS: Is it?

GB: Apparently.

AS: The French have made an excuse for getting away with real rhyme. We don't have it. We flounder about in the imperfect shallows.

GB: Yes, rhyme trains us in doubling, and also dialogue is everywhere in your work.

AS: Yes. I think everything is voice. I don't think anything exists without voice. The first thing that anything written does is go to voice. And to think that prose doesn't have that voice, even if it is in the third-person voice, is just not using our ears, because everything has voice.

GB: But when you say everything has voice, you're not thinking of a monologue. Or are you thinking about the special rhythms that we discover in ourselves as we write, you know?

AS: Or as we think, or as we walk about. We are constantly, I think, as human beings, narrating things to ourselves, even though we don't actually understand or hear that as specific voice. Everything does have voice, a structure has voice, a set of words that's written down, no matter what person has said it, has a voice. I don't mean style, I mean there's a voice. I mean that at every point there's a calibration of voice happening, and what's interesting to me really is what the calibration is, where it's coming from, who's got the authority to have the voice. Is there authority? Are we making up authority? Do we make the voice up or does the voice impinge on us? It's never a monologue. Even a monologue is never a monologue. It always implies.

GB: Because even a single sentence always has a number of voices in it: the wayward, the conformist, the one who is seeking the end of the sentence, and then the surprise. That always seems to me extraordinary, how difficult it is to foresee even the most simple sentence that another person is going to utter. We all think we know those phatic sayings, and so on, but you're all the time surprised by the way a sentence ends.

AS: I know. I love that moment where something will swerve off. Where we thought we understood what the person was saying, but we don't. Or even if we hear the words we expected, actually something else happened. So someone said to us what we expected them to say, but actually it will mean the opposite. There's a lovely thing that Hitchcock says about – I think he's a great understander of voice actually. Even in silent film he's a great understander of voice. But when he moves into sound he really understands how we use language, so he says, if a girl says, I'm so happy, she has to be crying. You have to see a conflict, you know, you have to recognize a conflict in almost everything. A conflict of possibilities. Or a meeting of possibilities.

GB: Yes, congruence and incongruence lying very, very close alongside each other. Yes, and film has been very important to you hasn't it?

AS: I think probably, well in our time it has been the most immediate way of telling stories. By immediate I mean sensory immediacy as well as structural immediacy. It goes direct into the brain through the eyes. It's communal at the same time as very, very individual as an experience. And for the last hundred years it's how we've been telling . . . pre-dating film in fact, film was a mode that Thomas Hardy was using. He understood all about the long shot, and the close-up, and the pan . . .

GB: The person coming over the hill.

AS: Hardy was prescient about form, and that was the narrative form the next century took.

GB: I was thinking about touch then. Because obviously film uses the haptic, the way the eye becomes touch, and yet, at the same time in film there's always the impossibility of touch. Whereas in the theatre you have at least by proxy the sense that you are close in . . .

AS: That you are really there, because every breath has also been breathed by the people on stage. Which is why I think film gets closer to dream, because we are in a state which is a removed state even though we are completely present, so that's why in a way the best cineastes understand that: that we shift into a new element when we shift into film. But yes, the difference in being in the theatre is something to do with life, something to do with actual breathing people, spontaneity . . . spontanuity . . . that was a word someone made up by mistake and told me about last week – I love the word – spontanuity, continuous spontanuity. It suggests the word continuity.

GB: Yes. Ha! Making it new, all the time.

AS: Ha ha ha.

GB: You quote, in your new lecture essays, from Woolf, where she says . . . I can't get it exactly, but it was something like 'you see so much when you are not there, or when you are not present in the scene'. She's thinking there it seems about cinema, and a feeling of absence.

AS: Really fantastically clear about that, Woolf, about the danger in it, and the way in which we can see something and not have to take it on board, because we know that there's a distance between us and it. She's looking at photographs and at film, and she identifies the space we can take with still photography, but with film I think she does think it's like a dream, she does think it's like, well, I wasn't there. It does reinforce both the 'thereness' and the 'not thereness'.

GB: Because in dream, the dreamer is there, is *It*.

AS: Is producing it, but not producing it, you know, has no control over it. Or do we have control over our dreams? I remember wondering as a child whether we did have control over our dreams, and I wonder now . . . I was thinking about this this morning because I knew we were going to be speaking, and I was thinking about Angela Carter and I was thinking about the way she would present a structure with which you could do what you liked with the end, and that was structurally the most obvious thing she did.

GB: Yes.

AS: And I was thinking about how that didn't reach me first through Carter. It reached me first through Liz Lochhead. When I was about 18 maybe, I'd read her book called *The Grimm Sisters*, which was a retelling mode of that time, living through that time. And I wonder, can we at some point in a dream say, I'm not liking this dream or I want to change this dream, or there's an exit door or something.

GB: Apparently there's a fashion for lucid dreaming . . .

AS: What's that?

GB: Apparently it is the kind of dream you were just describing where you go into the dream and then you shape it or swerve it. Now how people can do this I've no idea, and I suspect there's a lot of self-delusion involved. Because really, the one thing that dreaming does do for you is that when you get to the intolerable moment, you wake up.

AS: Exactly.

GB: I mean like the end of *Alice's Adventures in Wonderland*, or the end of *Through the Looking Glass*. There comes the moment when 'you are all just a pack of cards', or the queen disappears into the soup . . .

AS: It's a matter of trusting our subconscious, rather than messing with our subconscious.

GB: Yes.

AS: You let that happen. You let it go to the point at which you will wake yourself up.

GB: Yes. I mean you never actually die in a dream, do you?

AS: No, because you can't.

GB: No. So when it gets to that point where all the malign forces are surrounding you, you say, hold on, none of this, enough of this, and you're awake.

AS: So that's the real lucid dreaming.

GB: Ha, ha, ha.

AS: Ha. Real lucid dreaming is letting it all go. Allowing it to take the form it takes.

GB: Yes.

AS: I prefer that.

GB: But dreaming is very important in your work, and it's not divorced from ordinary life, it's not made to be a little symbolic statement.

AS: No, I don't know. I have no idea . . .

GB: That's very striking to me. That it's in no way an allegory of the situation. It's, as it were, a deviant form of consciousness, I suppose you might call it more closely.

AS: Oh, I like that very much, a deviant form of consciousness.

GB: Yes. And I suppose it's related to the other great theme: that there's always another story. That comes up again and again in what you are doing, and it's related to the question of authority: where we place authority, whether there has to be authority, or whether there can be a kind of neutralized zone in which all stories are, if not current, all there. They're all potential.

AS: Yes. Though some are more equal than others. Ha!

GB: Ha, ha. Yes. Some you choose to tell, some you choose not to.

AS: Some are more heard than the others, more conscious than others.

GB: Do you listen to people when you are on buses or trains? Do you have the habit . . .?

AS: No, not really. Yes and no. I mean, it's not like Mansfield who would have her notebook, sitting behind the bushes at the spa in Germany, and write down the things that people were saying. I actually think it's more subconscious than that . . . that what we do hear, what happens or strikes us around us, goes in and then ferments and something comes of it later. Much less conscious than that but it is about allowing yourself to be open to whatever is around you . . . not just the person who is speaking but the person who is not speaking as well, or the fact that the bottle is rolling around on the bus floor.

GB: You get that, of course, brilliantly, and in a very comic way, in the dinner party scene in *There but for the*, because there is one person who remains almost entirely silent throughout. And then of course you . . . me, as reader, later realizes that that silence was actually a signal of his goodness. And he escapes, he is elsewhere later in the book.

AS: Oh, I'm glad you see that. Most people think that character doesn't even exist or isn't drawn properly or something. He's very important . . . it is very important that he keeps his distance. He's a quiet force. When he does speak, he speaks twice, I think . . . just a signal, a little social signal. That was an interesting scene to try to write. I had to do it visually actually. I had to make a map of where all the people were all sitting. But the simple act of making a visual map, of all of those people around a table, allowed the whole scene to happen, because in position everything sparked off everything else. I don't know if you were there . . . I spoke about this at one of the talks, maybe in Cambridge, I can't remember now . . . I haven't spoken much about this book, actually. It's still quite an unarticulated book for me, but I remember saying . . . One of the reasons I wrote that scene was because I read Penelope Fitzgerald talking about Lawrence, and somewhere she says, Lawrence is good with more than three people in a room. Not very many writers can do more than three people in a conversation. And I remember thinking, well, I've got this dinner party, but I wonder if I can do it. I wonder how to do it, I wonder how to keep nine people all in a rhythm, or a place, and so the visual mapping out of it was what allowed that scene to happen. Because immediately the kind of laser-crossovers of all of the things that were said sparked the next thing and the next thing . . .

GB: Yes, and the person who can't quite hear at the other end of the table.

AS: Yes.

GB: Yes. And of course you use the device of the uninvited guest as well.

AS: Yes. I love it. It's a very good strong old story.

GB: Yes. And you use it several times in your work, don't you?

AS: Yeah, I have to stop.

GB: Amber of course . . .

AS: How *can* I stop? It's just a prevalent pressure at the moment, as a narrative pressure, and it's in the news, and we're ignoring it. As our countries and our world becomes smaller, and yet we're bordered, everything is about the stranger. So if we don't play attention to what the story of the stranger means, and if we forget the goodness of the stranger, the way in which inordinate hospitality was signalled as crucial to survival, never mind to immortality, and also simply to obvious benign-ness. If we don't pay attention to the things that happen when something enters our world from outside, and if every dominant narrative tells us to dislike it, then I don't know how we'll manage to stay human.

GB: Another thing that was in my mind when you were describing the dinner party was how important houses and rooms are in your work. Not necessarily where rooms lie in the house but a sense of . . . not just the shell but the being . . .

AS: The being of place . . .

GB: Yes, of place. And I know you've said more than once that you don't think of your work as autobiographical, but I was wondering how . . . when you think of a house, whether there is a house from your own early life that comes to your head?

AS: No . . . a really good, wonderful thing happens when you sit down to try to write something, which is that place produces itself. And I feel like I have lived in all of those houses I wrote about, even though they don't exist, none of them exists. But when a voice comes with a story, that's the imagination, it usually brings with it a place, a place that it's been, and a place that it is, and even sometimes a place that it's going to be. It's a matter of listening properly and seeing what the atmosphere around the voice is, because that dictates the shell, if you like, that dictates the structure from which the voice came and where it will go. So I have in my head a lot of clear places that just don't exist, and it's a real relief sometimes at the end of a novel to get out of these places, because they really are as material as the houses we live in, and every voice comes accompanied by a materialist backflow of stuff. It's clearing through that stuff to get to the voice and also to show the shell as the real habitat it is. That's really interesting, I'd never thought of that. You know, for instance, when I was writing *Artful*, I know exactly where those people live. I know what this room looks like, it's upstairs, and I know what the other room looks like, where the window is, where that window is, what the study is like, what the living room . . . how the stairs work, where the kitchen is. It's not a real place; those characters, also not real, came with their own house. Maybe we do . . . like snails . . . It's interesting, we are talking a lot about shells – that's our protection; the material world is our protection. Maybe we walk about all the time with our houses on our backs.

GB: Yes. But of course the reader reinvents that house, so the house survives the reading of your books. All those houses for me are quite dramatically there, but independent of your story to some degree. You set out the architectonics of the house, but I'm sure I import other known or unknown houses, as readers always do. We all remake the book as we bring in our own landscapes.

AS: As long as the roof holds, we're fine.

GB: Yes.

AS: As long as the structure is properly made. I do think that everything written is about the holding of structure, the force of form. The form can hold anything. As long as, as readers, we're not being rained on or blown away in the telling, doesn't matter what happens, probably the story will hold. We can do anything in fact, there can be any weather – within the structure.

GB: In other words, your work is so lateral. The way the stories work, the connections, the sudden insights, the comedy, so much is unforeseeable.

AS: Oh good.

GB: So it's always fascinating to me that form matters so much in the work.

AS: Yeah, that really matters. Form gives you the space to do anything and everything, within the structure, within the form . . . that's structure not stricture. We can experience . . . we are talking about dream again . . . we can actually go to that place, and be alright or survive or understand it, or come back with a new vision of it or of ourselves in communication or in conflict with it.

GB: Yes. One of the early stories that I really love, and that I've gone on living with ever since I read it in *Free Love*, is the one near the end, 'The Unthinkable Happens to People Every Day'. It's a story that is very beautifully self-circling. Things happen towards the end and you realize in retrospect that they're there because of something that happened unnoticed at the beginning. That word 'unthinkable', has so much menace, and indeed, the whole story begins with awful things being told on daytime television. So your whole mind is set towards some appalling outcome as this man sets off in his car, and then he encounters this child by the loch, and he walks into the loch, and he gets soaking wet, and he comes out again. And then the child says, well come up on our roof, and he does, and then her mother comes out, and . . . Ah yes, so you've been up on our roof. And it's the most blissful story because all those anxieties are absorbed. All the reader's anxieties and expectations . . . the unimaginable, the unthinkable, the unsayable – all those things that in fact we do think, imagine and say, are lurking in the story, but then they're exonerated. And it's a story without sentimentality, that's what's so curious; because on the face of it, if you describe what happens . . . you think how does she do that without just getting whimsical? Is it one that you remember well, that story? I mean, you've written so many by now.

AS: I remember where the title came from. It's an early one, I didn't write it in Edinburgh, but I was still living in Edinburgh, and I was down in the bowels of the modern art gallery, in the cafe, and someone had a newspaper, and the word 'unthinkable' was in a headline on the newspaper. And I remember thinking, the unthinkable happens all the time, in every single newspaper, everyday. Then I thought that's an interesting passage, from the unthinkable to everyday. So I think that story comes directly from its own title, and also from the fact that when I'd come down to England, when I was living here again, presumably its seed was North. So there's something of home and away in it.

GB: Yes.

AS: The thing about sentimentality . . . it's a bit like something unedited. We simply have to pare things down, and they will reveal themselves more clearly. With the baggage gone we can really see what something is. So, sentimentality invites melodrama, because there is so much thought and baggage around it. All we have to do is pare it down. It's really craft based . . . it's just all about by which means I might break into the right place. It's really practical; you just make it as tight as possible.

GB: When you say you edit, do you cut a lot when you revise? Or do you pare down the sentences?

AS: I'm always editing. A sentence gets written and then gets edited, and then another sentence comes from that edit. And then another sentence comes, and then you look at all three together, and then you know what else to take out. But that also tells you which way to go, so I don't think there's anything in it beyond allowing your instinct to do the thing and then editing it back. It's really practical, and I think that does avoid all the '-alities', all the '-alities', the ways in which the things fix themselves into form, in a way which makes them smaller. If we keep it open and clean, then it's freed up as a sentence, and rhythmic. Because rhythm is not sentimental; rhythm is basic to our hearts; rhythm is a way in which we can make things so much better without sentiment. It goes directly to the source of breathing . . .

GB: Yes. That's what I was wondering about, because when you said 'editing', I remember thinking that in fact your sentences have this wonderful flow of the justified and the unexpected. So I don't feel they are just wandering off, I feel, ah yes, I see how it got from here to there, and yet I didn't foresee that. And of course that's partly why they are so enticing to a reader, because it's a story you don't know already.

AS: Yes, but it does ask a fair faith or a trust from a reader. It does ask you to come along down a road which you might not otherwise accept. And I know I'm doing that sometimes, and I can't not.

GB: No.

AS: That's just the way it is, and I'm lucky if my readers come down the road if they don't trust it. It's about trust.

GB: Yes, and so much of it is about love, as well. And so often there are two people who are in the story, as it were behind the story, who are half telling, half generating the story, and the story is not about them necessarily. The very disquieting one, called 'No exit', is about somebody in the cinema and – it's very funny as well – somebody else walks out of a door marked 'emergency exit', and the teller of the story knows that it's blocked when this person gets to the bottom, and moreover that she won't be able to come back up. And then the events go from there: so there's all the guilt of 'what should I do, oh bother, I haven't actually done it, I meant to tell them as I left the cinema, but it hasn't happened, but I'm sure she'll be alright', and so on. All those things that we all do, all the time: this question of how far you are responsible for somebody you don't know, who's just alongside you. But then the story turns gradually into a critique of a past love affair that's not quite past, and the regeneration of the relationship. Now, for me it was intriguing too, because I thought I knew this cinema. Indeed to me it was the Picture House in Cambridge. And then I was thinking, 'oh dear, have they really not got all their exit mechanisms open'?

AS: Ha!

GB: Which is a wonderful example of how the reader absolutely populates the work.

AS: Well, yeah. But in a way the story, generating story, includes the reader at all points, because the reader will generate his or her own story, as he or she reads alongside, so exactly that. So I suppose one of the things that's most important but almost impossible to do, because you can't actually assure yourself that you are doing it, is to leave room for the reader. And in the way that placing your story alongside the story will do that, because it allows for all sorts of other stories to propagate from the told narrative. It's like a narrative free-for-all, which at the same time will hold you steady. It's not the Cambridge Picture House; it's a completely made up place, but it's real, so . . .

GB: I'm sure the Picture House is very legal, in every way . . .

AS: Just don't go through that door, in Screen One, on the left . . . that just leads down to a concrete door under the bar.

GB: Ha! Yes, and the telephone comes in, and the way they are talking to each other in the night, these two who have been lovers. I like that: all these different modes of communication that you use, and the way the stories are very free, not time-free, no, very much linked into what's current. But also not a bit worried about being in the past as well.

AS: I think the exciting thing about all the new ways that we have to communicate, all of them, there are new ways every day . . . they have 140 characters or they have email shape or they take text shape, and whatever shape the future will take, we don't know . . . but stories, they hold them all, and that's exciting. I remember seeing Laurie Anderson, the New York artist and performer, and someone said to her, as they watched her using all of these electric machines, mysterious looking, almost like engineering structures around her, which she would press to make a certain kind of noise . . . someone said to her, 'Why do you have all of this technical machinery around you?' And she held up a pencil and said, 'It's exactly the same as this.' And she was right; they are just, all the same, modes of communication, and story in itself will always be old, in the way that we need stratification, so that all of the stuff on the surface will always stratify through story regardless, and then . . . I'm reading on a grant body, not a grant body, but a prize that gets given out every year, and it's been really interesting to me to watch the ways in which over the last ten years people will have been including technology, and it's always tragic; there's always someone lying on the side of the road holding a mobile phone in their hands, and they're dead, but they're holding their phone. That's what happens, you know in the end we have to understand the metaphysical quality, and all that will happen is that story will keep on producing itself no matter what we think we are left with or we are stuck with.

GB: Yes, and the stories multiply. Your work is very rich in the presence of other literary voices, and very freely so. You don't feel that you are reaching for them; they are simply there, as part of your daily being. A couple of people always strike me, and particularly one, Edwin Morgan, and I wonder if you'd like to talk briefly about him?

AS: See a great smile is on my face just at his name, Edwin Morgan. He's a writer who I don't think I would exist without actually. A Scottish poet and translator and playwright. Over the years it's become more and more apparent to me that Morgan is the quiet hub at the centre of all of the aesthetic transformations which happened in Scotland, he changed things and made things possible . . . he was about art and politics and an intellectual understanding and an openness of nature. His poems are like . . . well, they're like whole universes; they just give you the world, and then they give you the space round the world, and then they give you the space round the space round the world. It's all about a kind of open resonance with Morgan, again someone through whom all the voices pass, all the literary voices pass, and his work is so playful, genuine, satisfying . . .

GB: Material.

AS: Yes, really material.

GB: I love the one where he makes up shapes to be the poem.

AS: Yes, so he's a concrete poet, and he's a sonneteer. There's a book of collected translations by Edwin Morgan, and you cannot believe the number of people whose works he translates into English and Scots too. God it's the most glorious book. And also the sense of creativity, of open creativity . . . the basis of creativity being playfulness and curios-ity, that thing which Koestler says that inhabits all living beings, which is curiosity and playfulness, you know, at that point of coming alive, you go, 'What's that? What is it?' Anyway, I once saw Morgan read . . . I saw him read several times, but the last time I saw him read was at the Edinburgh festival, and he was quite ill at this point, and he read quietly from his most recent work, which was about Polari or gay speak in Glasgow, and he took the top off the tent with energy, and the whole kind of sense of something being freed . . . Morgan's about that. He's about the way that things come into connection with each other, the planets pass each other in the galaxy and something happens between them, and he does that on both a planetary level and right down to the detailed wordplay level. Everything he does just touches that live electricity. I can't tell you how freeing he is to have read or to read. And it's that playfulness, that openness, that selflessness . . . there's a great selflessness at the centre of Morgan's work, and nobody knows who Morgan is in England, almost nobody's heard of him.

GB: Really?

AS: Yes. Very few people have heard of Morgan down here. Partly, it's because he was a very modest man, and he stayed up in Scotland; he carried on his work very quietly, you know, Morgan removed himself. The self-removal is the source of creativity, and the sense in which he let something pass through to take it on first . . . his self-removal made space for his work to be so great, actually, I think.

GB: Yes. And there's one of his poems which I think you actually sent me as a Christmas card one time.

AS: 'A Chihuahua'.

GB: Yes. And then there's another one called 'Sunset' which I have on my computer, on my desktop, as the poem to have as you age. It's a beautiful poem, and again it has this mixture of quietude and attention and pure unexpectedness. And that's the other side of curiosity, isn't it? That when you are curious sometimes you find the humdrum and sometimes you find things that are both humdrum and totally unexpected. That's what he can get.

AS: Yes, in everything he does. Again, really late in his work he wrote a collection of poems all taking the same form, a series called *Love and a Life*, and they are so beautiful. They're autobiographical, and in one of them towards the end, he says, he quotes Dante, Dante was sure the stars were rolled out by love. And in a way that's it . . . he goes to the source, and he goes to the source openly, and the source then passes through him openly to everybody and everything else. And there's a kind of looking at the world in its darkness, and it doesn't dispel the dark, but it allows you to see where you are.

GB: Yes.

AS: He's glorious, Morgan. He rhymes 'hum-ba-ba' with 'rum-ba-ba'. And he rewrites Gilgamesh and he makes a new beautiful elegy of the elegy which has already been translated and translated and translated. And he knows that it passes through us, forever, and again, I think that's one of the most important things we can know. It isn't us, but it passes through us, and it passes to the next and the next and the next, and it's an inheritance which we have to hand on openly.

GB: So it's the translation in that sense that becomes very important.

AS: Really important.

GB: And in your new work, in *Artful*, I notice that when you are quoting a poet you also tell us who is the translator, and that that person is co-creating the poem.

AS: And interestingly it makes it an untranslatable book, to have done that. Because I'm quoting from English all the time in the book. So my Norwegian translator, whom I love, read *Artful* and said, you know, I can't do this, impossible, because you are always referencing the

English translation, which would mean we would have to interlay all of the translations, an interesting problem . . .

GB: Yes, that is an intriguing problem. I never thought of that.

AS: Me neither, because I thought it was pretty straight forward, but no, because translations will always be themselves at the same time as being the sort of material. Again, that's a dialogue. Oh, I think one of the best things ever about writing any book has been being translated. Ovid uses 'translated' for 'changed': he was translated into a bird; she was translated into a tree . . . in English, obviously.

GB: Yes, *Metamorphoses*, yes, absolutely. It's always intrigued me because I've recently been working on Lewis Carroll, how Carroll's works have been endlessly translated. On the face of it they look very difficult to translate because they are full of wordplay, pun and so on, and yet translators love them. They're all over the world, in I don't know how many languages . . . almost every Indian language apparently. But what do you experience when you are translated, because you must be translated now into some languages you don't speak?

AS: Lots of languages I don't speak. I always know whether the translator is good from the questions that she or he usually asks. Because if they will be asking questions about whether or not it's possible to change a metaphor, I know it's going to be good, because they are going to the source of the thing which makes the change happen, rather than asking, 'Are the boots on page fifteen knee-length boots or ankle boots?' . . . there are different words for differing boots in different languages. So, there is a material level and then there is a metaphoric level. And if they are saying, 'I can't translate "falling down a well" with the notion of wellness and health, because we don't have that, but I can translate it into something about fish, for we have a salmon, which is the word "souk", which is also the word "sick", so maybe we can just change the element', which is one of the things that happened in the Norwegian translations. And then you know that your translator is making the book in the language absolutely as the language should be doing it. Translators go to the source of the point at which language itself translates, metaphor.

GB: And do you translate yourself? Do you translate other people?

AS: No, never have. Ah, no, only at the very end of *Artful*, with that very little piece of very simple Greek.

GB: Yes, because one of the jokes at the end of *Artful* is that the nonsense words that are persistently occurring turn out to be Greek: 'it's all Greek to me'.

AS: Yes.

GB: And I was delighted by that. But I also felt a slight disappointment, because I felt, is there no place for meaninglessness?

AS: Ha, ha, ha! Yes, but the thing about meaninglessness – I suppose this is what *Artful* is doing – the thing about meaninglessness is that it never stays meaninglessness for long, because we will make meaning of it. I mean, we will translate our meaninglessness. We are human beings; it's what we do. The character in *Artful* is . . . it's a great liberation for him or her to think there's no meaning in the words. But even seeming meaninglessness is meaningful. In this case, the slippage from 'nonsense' to language, is particularly meaningful, on a much wider scale, a European scale.

GB: Yes. You write a lot about memory, and through memory, and with memory, but you're also very interested in how much we forget – and how we forget. And that seems to me valuable, because recently there's been almost a terrorizing of us through memory, also a kind of sanctification of memory, as though that is the one thing we must do. And I just wondered if you could talk a bit about it?

AS: It's like we are our own archive. We are.

GB: Yes.

AS: In the overflow of information which is around us all of the time, there is a fixing of information which has happened over the last hundred years. I can almost see, I have a vision in my head of crowds and crowds and crowds of our ancestors looking at us as if we are mad. Do we not know how to forget? Do we not know how important it is not to remember? Do we not know how important it is to let things go? Again there's a kind of fixing of ourselves in memory. Memory is really interesting, because we will forget what we need to forget. So going back and constantly trying to find out everything about ourselves is again a kind of fixing of ourselves. I was talking to a psychologist at St Andrews University about this when I was up there in November. He's studying dementia, and he's very interested in the ways in which we *never* have no memory. Even someone at the most miserable point of dementia still has memory, because there is something, there is always something, there is always something being remembered. Memory in a way produces us, fixes us. But we have to allow for what we have forgotten, because memory is also what we have forgotten, memory holds them both. It's like what we were just saying about the relationship between meaningless and meaningful. We have to allow for some things to be the spaces that we left, rather than the spaces that we inhabit.

GB: Yes, so we don't always have to occupy everything.

AS: No, that's right. Like the Edwin Morgan poem that's quoted in *Artful*. He says, 'Hoards, posterities, judges vainly cram the space my love and I left yesterday.' It's right, you know, that space is much more . . . He's playing on Shakespeare's 'Not marble nor the gilded monuments' sonnet. And you know, he's quite right, all the things that are left in stone can never fill the space we left. That's all we need to know is that we left the space and we leave the space.

GB: Hardy's wonderful about that as well.

AS: Yes, absolutely. There's always trouble when characters try to fix identity in Hardy.

GB: And the whole question of fixed identities: in a lot of your work, there is this . . . how to put it . . . I was going to say a slack of identity but that sounds offensive. But you see what I mean, that it's not all tightened up and held through tension. There's room for the softening of the rope.

AS: Ah, I like that. To be fluid, not to be fixed . . . it's muscular actually, it's about not stressing ourselves to such an extent that we can't move. Because we need to move, we need to change, and this last century, as far as I can see, it's been a century of self-recording which negates the living self. What, what, what are you doing trying to see what you look like at every point? You're not even seeing what you are seeing anymore, because you are only seeing the thing which you took the picture of, or you were taking a film of. You know, there's a removal of something stratified and crucial and only seeing the surface that can then present what happened.

GB: Yes.

AS: Because the space is so much bigger.

GB: I quite agree with that. I think, out of inertia perhaps more than opinion, I never take a camera with me when I travel because I find that it reifies what's happened. I remember certain things, bits around that picture, but I forget other things that I don't forget if I've just got my own thoughts and senses as a response.

AS: Yes, if we are present. If we are actually present.

GB: Yes. And of course it relates to desire and love as well. Gender is so malleable, and . . .

AS: And yet we pretend it isn't. And everything in a structured, very capitalist world tells us the things we should be and the things we should be buying and the things we should be being and the ways we should be living, but we are fluid creatures, and so I think we . . . ach but there's a great safety in fixity, a great safety in fixity. And in a way it's not safe to *not* fix your approach. But look at how many cars have Sat Navs telling them to go the wrong way.

GB: And so you loyally go through the ford, or don't get through the ford.

AS: I know. I love how there's a choice of voices on Sat Navs. You can be told by who you want to be told by, a man or a woman or a strict sounding man or a strict sounding woman or a regional accent, and it's a machine.

GB: It's a machine. Yes, but it's true, I have to confess that I do say, 'Oh that woman is telling me so and so.'

AS: Well, in a machine world we actually do need the human.

GB: Yes. And I feel on the whole grateful to her, though sometimes irritated.

AS: Yes, 'You turn, you turn, you turn.'

GB: Well now, are there things we haven't talked about that you think we might?

AS: What? For me to say? I can't say . . . I almost can't think about it. I almost . . . in fact I choose not to.

GB: No, that's fine. And I've been here just to provoke some thoughts.

AS: I'll say what I think about that. Not you provoking thought, which has been to me really eye-opening and exciting, to talk like this. We've covered some ground I just didn't know or wouldn't have seen, things nobody's ever asked me about before. It's very exciting. And I do think that self-consciousness gets in the way of the kind of writing output, the act of making a book or a story or a piece, allowing it to be itself. The more I think about what I do, the less I'll be able to do it on its terms. And there is something about an unfixing in that.

GB: Yes, and you always use multiple voices, and of course people have commented a lot about the way you use children.

AS: I think that's really interesting. I think that's a bit like saying Jane Austen writes on a tiny piece of ivory. I've no notion why people are drawn to the children. I think it just means that we are in a time that is drawn to children or in which people want to be nostalgic about their child selves. So they get drawn to the place where they think nostalgia or safety will reside in – the children.

GB: Yes, though I think, on the whole, when writers write about children they don't write about children, they write about being an adult remembering being a child.

AS: They think they are writing children, but actually . . .

GB: Yes, and they don't give the child its own voice. And, I mean, of course you're writing as an adult writing to other adults, and sometimes through the voice of a child. But the children in your books do have a sort of swerve of knowledge in a way that isn't always accountable, and that doesn't sound like your orthodox child being written by an adult, and I do think it is . . . (though I can understand why you are cautious about people spending too much time thinking about them) . . . I do think it is unusual.

AS: I know that I think that that child state is a state of moral understanding, where you really are discriminating the rights and wrongs, the goods from the bads, and you are also encountering grey in-between, and trying to work out where you are, you know, because as information comes to you, you siphon it so much more clearly than we do when we come to the teenage point where things begin to codify, and then into adulthood, where things begin to narrativize. Where adults really do, we do tell ourselves those fixed stories about ourselves because it's the only way that we can stay safe with the sense of identity. So we do tend to go, 'Well, this is the person that I am, and this is what made me the person that I am.' There's always, always a sense of third-person narrative about adults. So when I was writing *The Accidental*, the kids were written in the present tense, because they're in the present tense, and the adults were written in the past, because in the present they're already experiencing the past, right now they're experiencing the past, immediacy has already written itself into the past. With kids it just seems to me we are closer to the skin. You have not developed that hide or that thicker skin.

GB: Yes, and the categories you are using are not identical with the ones that adults use.

AS: Yes, exactly.

GB: Yes. Shall we stop there?

AS: Yes, that's perfect.

Notes

Chapter 1

1   Holly Prescott (2011) also comments on Pile's relevance to Smith's work, particularly *Hotel World*. See pp. 6–7. More generally, Prescott identifies the necessity of reading space in contemporary fiction, by Smith, Iain Sinclair, Rachel Lichtenstein, Monica Ali and Nicholas Royle, as an agent of its own. She writes, 'Whenever urban space is envisioned as provoking profound anxiety in the human subject due to its ability to confound that subject, so can urban space be said to achieve an agency of its own' (Prescott, 2011, p. 14). My reading of Smith's short stories asserts a similar idea of agency as non-human and spatial and in this sense is indebted to Prescott for inspiration. However, I take a more positive position than she does regarding the relationship between human potential and space in Smith's short stories, seeing space here as affirmative as well as traumatic, capable of enabling a more vibrant and meaningful human experience. My emphasis on the philosophy of Deleuze and Guattari, absent from Prescott's reading, is central to this.

2   Prescott also comments on this subject-centred dimension of de Certeau's theory, highlighting how de Certeau argues 'that "places" become "spaces" through their being brought to life through human actualisation, such that "the street geometrically defined by urban planning is transformed into a space by walkers"' (Prescott, 2011, p. 2). For Prescott, this 'bias towards intentional human agency' (p. 3) obstructs a proper appreciation of space in contemporary literature in so far as it discounts space's own capacity to 'obfuscate, displace or censor meaning and motivation within urban space' (p. 7) and in this way direct the progression of the narrative. I make a similar argument here, while again focusing on space's enabling and empowering potential in Smith's short stories, rather than on its constricting or traumatic dimensions.

Chapter 2

1   The mentions in *A Room of One's Own* of 'Sir Chartres Biron', 'Sir William Joynson Hicks' and 'Sir Archibald Bodkin' (Woolf, 1929, pp. 123, 129–30, 168), all of whom played key roles in the prosecution of Radclyffe Hall's 1928 Sapphic novel, *The Well of Loneliness*, are also significant in this context: Sir Chartres Biron was the presiding magistrate at the trial; Sir William Joynson Hicks, the Home Secretary; Sir Archibald Bodkin, the Director of Public Prosecutions.

2   The argument in favour of this, Gulliver notes, is 'that since Words are only Names for Things, it would be more convenient for all Men to carry about them, such Things as were necessary to express the particular Business they have to discourse on' – an expediency which, Gulliver reports, 'would serve as an Universal Language to be understood by all civilized Nations' and have the result that the meaning of the objects or 'their Uses might easily be comprehended' (Swift, 2005, p. 173). The Lagado Professors' experiment is of course doomed to failure: anyone who follows it in practice is literally weighed down by the number of things they must carry with them for anything but the most simple of conversations.

Chapter 3

1   I wish to thank SunHee Gertz and the editors of this collection for their generous and invaluable feedback on earlier drafts of this chapter.

2   Monica Germanà has underscored the pervasiveness of ghost motifs in Scottish women's writing and has traced a thematic link from contemporary Scottish writers, including Ali Smith, to early Scottish ballads and folk tales. I hope that the present chapter will expand on some of her insights, especially the observation that spectres enable 'ontological inversions' and constitute a mode of subaltern critique (Germanà, 2009, p. 2).

3   It is important to underscore that Derrida contextualizes his discussion of spectrality within a harrowing account of the salient features of globalization, including unemployment, the disenfranchisement of homeless citizens, a 'ruthless economic war', the aggravation of foreign debt, the arms industry and spread of nuclear weapons, ethnic wars, and the rise of 'phantom-states' and drug cartels (Derrida, 1994, pp. 100–7). My contention here is that Smith's fictions self-consciously deploy the figure of spectrality as an intervention in this guise of the 'global'.

4   One may see in this reference to the 'imaginary order' depicted in the photograph an allusion to Benedict Anderson's *Imagined Communities* (1983). In a later work, *The Spectre of Comparisons* (1998), Anderson develops a notion of spectrality that resonates with Eve's experience of 'secondariness' upon looking at the photograph: the sense that the image is only a spectral copy of some primordial experience. He begins *Spectre of Comparisons* with a passage from *Noli Me Tangere*, a nationalist novel by the Filipino writer Jose Rizal, that describes the return of the protagonist to colonial Manila after time away in Europe: the hero gazes upon a botanical garden, only to be struck by the shadowy image of similar gardens he gazed upon in European cities. Anderson describes 'a kind of vertigo' emerging from this comparison, and it is this sense of estrangement from the bourgeois image, elicited by a lingering awareness of what has been disavowed, that I wish to call to mind in my reading of *The Accidental* (Anderson, 1998, p. 2).

5   With these terms, plenitude and absence, I intend to allude to Derrida's concept of the 'supplement.' Derrida describes the supplement as a 'subaltern instance': 'As substitute, it is not simply added to the positivity of presence, it produces no relief, its place is assigned in the structure by the mark of emptiness' (1997, p. 144).

6   This concept is most frequently associated with Adorno's aphoristic work, *Minima Moralia* (2006). See also Jameson (2007, p. 86) and Richter (2007, p. 153).

7   Although a full treatment of Smith's short stories lies beyond the scope of this chapter (see Chapter One in this book), it is worth emphasizing the predominance of the theme of spectral intrusion. For example, in her first collection of short stories, *Free Love*, an earnest book collector who suddenly decides to tear the pages out of books as she reads them functions much as Amber does in *The Accidental*, insofar as she reduces whole 'canonised' narratives into fertile fragments: 'pages flutter across motorways or farmland, pages break apart, dissolve in rivers or seas' (Smith, 1997, p. 29). In 'The Third Person', the narrator is figured as an agent of spectral disruption; stories are begun and discarded by the 'third person,' figured as a 'presentiment of God' and a 'revitalization of the dead' (*The First Person and Other Stories*, 2008: pp. 68–9). In 'Being Quick' (*The Whole Story and Other Stories*, 2003), the spectre of death appears quite literally in human form to a young woman returning home to her lover. The woman's subsequent breakdown, reminiscent of Lise's in *Hotel World*, and recuperation enabled by the deep empathic response of her lover attests once again to Smith's interest in love as a response to the arrival of something 'wholly' other.

8   The notion of time being 'out of joint' recalls Derrida's well-known evocation of *Hamlet* in *Specters of Marx* (see 1994, esp. p. 20).

Chapter 4

1 Brooke sings the song as follows: 'I know where I'm going/And I know who's going with me/I know who I love/And the deer know who I'll marry' (2011, p. 339). One interpretation of the 'dear' in the original is as a euphemism for the devil.

2 The full implied phrase is attributed to the evangelical preacher John Bradford in the sixteenth century, and is widely used to indicate a fate that could have been one's own, but from which one was protected. The novel hints constantly at the complete phrase. The word 'grace' first appears on page 58, and starts to recur with some frequency as a name from page 230. The words 'god', 'go' and 'I' are present throughout the text, but are particularly dense and suggestive on pages 239–40. 'I' is often rendered as a pun on the word 'eye': e.g. 'Was God in the eye of that rabbit? Well you can just go and get lost' (Smith, 2011, p. 240).

3 The wording here comes from Derrida's 'The Law of Genre' (1992, p. 228) but the figure of an inside which is bigger than the outside, or located outside the outside, repeats throughout Derrida's work, especially in the early writings.

4 The phrase 'grammatical forms' is potentially misleading here because the imperfective and the perfective are not always captured in tense forms (see Downing and Locke, 2006, p. 370). The perfective aspect sees a situation as a complete whole where the imperfective views the situation from an internal stage as ongoing and incomplete.

5 We might think here of the title of one of Smith's story collections, *The Whole Story and Other Stories* (2004), which promises an impossible combination of the viewpoint of completion with that of continuation and becoming.

6 The homophony of 'will be' and Wilby is the basis of many puns in the novel, particularly in the 'future conditional' section devoted to Lise's narrative: e.g. 'Lise will be unable to recall' (Smith, 2001, p. 111); 'In six months Lise will be unable to remember' (Smith, 2001, p. 114). There is an echo here of Muriel Spark's Lise in *The Driver's Seat*, a proleptic novel that offers repeated flashes of Lise, its protagonist's future: 'She will be found tomorrow morning dead from multiple stab wounds' (1974, p. 25).

7 The 'future anterior' tends not to be used in English, but predominates particularly in French grammar. The phrase is also adopted in French and German philosophy to describe the structure of temporal becoming in general, as well as the temporality of writing. For a full discussion, see Mark Currie (2013), *The Unexpected: Narrative Temporality and the Philosophy of Surprise* (Edinburgh: Edinburgh University Press).

8 The blunt perfective 'Dead' is the word that nobody will say, as Clare notes, preferring the periphrasis 'passed away'.

9 The terminology changes throughout Derrida. These terms come from 'Typewriter Ribbon', but elsewhere there is the future anterior and the messianic, or in the early critiques of phenomenology, structure and genesis.

10 These are the words that both open and close the novel, and it is striking that reviewers so often described this book as one that you have to begin again as soon as you reach its end. *There but for the* and *Hotel World* both conclude with several blank pages, so that the endings reproduce the blankness through which incompletion is signified while the novels are in progress.

11 'Litter-ature! Litter is even brighter than, more powerful than, more enduring than art, and "if you want permanence", Edwin Morgan says in this 1987 poem, it'll last' (Smith, 2012, p. 70).

Chapter 5

1 Here and throughout – unless otherwise indicated – I'm using the noted 1567 Arthur Golding translation of Ovid's *Metamorphoses*, the sprightliness of which makes it a good match for Smith's own text.

2   NB Irving Massey's take on metamorphosis as: 'a critique of language (as is evident from the animal or other nonhuman forms that it often employs), [. . .] a critique from beyond the point where language has been forced on one. It is set up on the other side of language – after one has gone mad through preoccupation with language, taking it so seriously that it has become a physical thing again' (Massey, 1976, p. 1).

3   Puck is referred to throughout *A Midsummer Night's Dream* as 'boy' – which is a gender indeterminate position within renaissance theatre, and the role would have been played by 'boy players' who also, for the most part, played female roles. He is also a facilitator, of course, of various erotic couplings, arguably spreading romantic chaos in his wake. I'm grateful to Katherine Graham for alerting me to the 'Robin Goodfellow'/Puck connection.

4   Canongate website says of the series: 'The Myths series gathers the world's finest contemporary writers for a modern look at our most enduring myths', and: 'Myths are universal and timeless stories that reflect and shape our lives – they explore our desires, our fears, our longings, and provide narratives that remind us what it means to be human.' See www.themyths.co.uk/.

5   I'm grateful to Fiona Tolan for a discussion of this point about the significance of feminist politics within Smith's work, following a presentation of an earlier version of this chapter at the 'What Happens Now? 21st Century Writing in English' conference at the University of Lincoln, 16–18 July 2012.

Chapter 7

1   For a somewhat different view of how the temporality of 'death in life' operates in *Hotel World* within the context of Derrida's conceptualizations of the gift and exchange, see Bennett (2012, pp. 78–82).

2   The term 'hauntology' is, of course, that of Derrida, who deploys it in *Spectres of Marx* to indicate, among many other things, the presence of the past in the present as a condition of being. Derrida's conception of the uncanny in *Spectres* resonates with that of the stranger Kristeva: for him, the uncanny is 'a stranger who is already found within (*das Heimliche-Unheimliche*), more intimate with one than oneself, the absolute proximity of a stranger whose power is singular *and* anonymous (*es spukt*), an unnamable and *neutral* power, that is, undecidable, neither active nor passive, an identity that, *without doing anything*, invisibly occupies places belonging finally neither to us nor to it' (1993, 172).

3   I am relying on Miller for the definition of this trope that rhetorically 'ascribes a name, a face, a voice to the absent, the inanimate, or the dead' (Miller, 1990, p. 4). In his reflection on Ovid's *Metamorphosis*, Miller suggests that the trope of prosopopoeia can be viewed doubly as the 'trope of mourning' and 'reanimation' (Miller, 1990, p. 4); I will suggest later how Alhambra embodies this duality as the recording, historicizing angel of annihilation and rebirth of identity the principal characters of the novel experience as the consequence of their encounter with the stranger, Amber. The 'regenerative' potential of metamorphic transformations is, of course, explored fully by Smith's rewriting of Ovid's text in *Girl meets boy* (2007).

4   For a quite different, and very compelling reading of 'contingency' in *The Accidental* as contributing to the novel's investigation of the relationship between private trauma and public event (in the novel, the implicit references to the Iraq War) see Horton (2012).

5   One of the novel's epigraphs – that from John Berger's essay 'a Man with Tousled Hair' – illuminates the sense of 'public' knowledge that Amber embodies: 'Between the experience of living a normal life at this moment on the planet and the public narratives being offered to give a sense to that life, the empty space, the gap, is enormous' (Berger, 2001, p. 176). To the Smarts, Amber's visitation reveals, in multiple ways, the 'empty space', or the 'space that wrecks the abode' of domesticity, and its foundation upon the public lie of normality.

References

Works Cited by Contributors

Introduction: *Monica Germanà* and *Emily Horton*

Clarke, A. (2011), 'There but for the by Ali Smith – Review'. *The Guardian*, 1 June. Available at: www.guardian.co.uk/books/2011/jun/01/ali-smith-there-but-for-the-review.

Denes, M. (2003), 'A Babel of Voices'. *The Guardian*, 19 April. Available at: www.guardian.co.uk/books/2003/apr/19/fiction.shopping.

Eshelman, R. (2004/2005), 'Checking Out of the Epoch: Performatism in Olga Tokarczuk's "The Hotel Capital" vs. Late Postmodernism in Ali Smith's *Hotel World* (with remarks on Arundhati Roy's *The God of Small Things* and Miloš Urban's *Sevenchurch*), *Anthropoetics* 10 (2).

Gapper, F. (2003), 'Ali Smith', *Mslexia* 18, July/August/September. Available at: www.mslexia.co.uk/magazine/interviews/interview_18.php.

Germanà, M. (2010), *Scottish Women's Gothic and Fantastic Writing*. Edinburgh: Edinburgh University Press.

Gonda, C. (1995), 'Mapping Scottish/Lesbian/Writing', in *Gendering the Nation: Studies in Modern Scottish Literature*, Christopher Whyte (ed.). Edinburgh: Edinburgh University Press, 1–24.

Higginbotham, E. (2012), 'A Rare Conversation with Ali Smith'. *Cambridge News*, 16 February. Available at: www.cambridge-news.co.uk/Whats-on-leisure/Books/Interview-Archive/A-rare-conversation-with-Ali-Smith-16022012.htm.

Marr, A. (2012), 'Start the Week: Modernism with Ali Smith and Kevin Jackson'. *BBC Radio Four*, 22 October.

Myerson, J. (2012), 'Artful by Ali Smith – Review'. *The Observer*, 18 November. Available at: www.guardian.co.uk/books/2012/nov/18/artful-ali-smith-review.

Sankovich, N. (2011), 'There but for the by Ali Smith: A Close Look at Where We Are Now'. *Huffington Post*, 15 September.

Smith, A. (1995), *Free Love and Other Stories*. London: Virago.

—(1997), *Like*. London: Virago. Repr. 1998.

—(1999), *Other Stories and Other Stories*. London: Penguin. Repr. 2004.

—(2001), *Hotel World*. London: Hamish Hamilton.

—(2005), *The Accidental*. London: Hamish Hamilton.

—(2006), *The Seer*. London: Faber.

—(2007a), 'So Many Afterlives from One Short Life', *The Telegraph*, 7 April.

—(2007b), *Girl meets boy*. Edinburgh: Canongate.

—(2011), *There but for the*. London: Hamish Hamilton.

—(2012), *Artful*. London: Penguin.

Smith, C. (2007), 'Ali Smith Interviewed by Caroline Smith', *Brand Literary Magazine*, 1 (Spring), 75–9.

Chapter One: **Contemporary Space and Affective Ethics in Ali Smith's Short Stories,** Emily Horton

Augé, M. (2006 [1995]), *Non-Places: Introduction to an Anthropology of Supermodernity*, J. Howe (trans.). London: Verso.

Barnett, R. S. (2005), *A Space for Agency: Rhetorical Agency, Spatiality, and the Production of Relations in Supermodernity*. Unpublished MA Thesis: North Carolina State University.

Benjamin, W. (1929–1940), *The Arcades Project*, H. Eiland and K. McLaughlin (trans.). London: Belknap Press, (republished 1999).

Braidotti, R. (2006), 'Affirmation versus Vulnerability: On Contemporary Ethical Debates', *Symposium: Canadian Journal of Continental Philosophy* 10 (1), 235–54.

Colebrook, C. (2004), 'The Sense of Space: On the Specificity of Affect in Deleuze and Guattari', *Postmodern Culture* 15 (1), 1–46.

De Certeau, M. (1984), *The Practice of Everyday Life*, S. Rendall (trans.). Berkeley: University of California Press.

Deleuze, G. (1988), *Spinoza: Practical Philosophy*. San Francisco, CA: City Lights Books.

Deleuze, G. and Guattari, F. (1987), *A Thousand Plateaus: Capitalism and Schizophrenia*, B. Massumi (trans.). Minneapolis: University of Minnesota Press.

—(1994), *What Is Philosophy?* London: Verso.

Denes, M. (2003), 'A Babel of Voices'. *The Guardian*, 19 April. Available at: www. guardian.co.uk/books/2003/apr/19/fiction.shopping.

Guattari, F. (1995), *Chaosmosis: An Ethicoaesthetic Paradigm*. J. Pefanis (trans.). Bloomington: Indiana University Press.

Katz, J. (1999), *How Emotions Work*. Chicago, IL: University of Chicago Press.

Marcus, L. (2007), 'Psychoanalytic Training: Freud and the Railways', in *The Railway and Modernity: Time, Space, and the Machine Ensemble*, M. Beaumont and M. Freeman (eds). Bern, Switzerland: Peter Lang, 155–76.

Mansaray, A. (2007), 'Review of *Real Cities: Modernity, Space and the Phantasmagorias of City Life*', by S. Pile. Urban Geography Research Group Book Review Series, 6 June.

Pile, S. (2005), *Real Cities: Modernity, Space and the Phantasmagorias of City Life*. London: Sage.

Prescott, H. (2011), *Rethinking Urban Space in Contemporary British Writing*. Doctoral Thesis: University of Birmingham.

Smith, A. (1995), *Free Love and Other Stories*. London: Virago.

—(1997), *Like*. London: Virago.

—(2004 [1999]), *Other Stories and Other Stories*. London: Penguin.

—(2001), *Hotel World*. London: Hamish Hamilton.

—(2004 [2003]), *The Whole Story and Other Stories*. London: Penguin.

—(2009 [2008]), *The First Person and Other Stories*. London: Penguin.

—(2009), 'The Definite Article'. London: The Royal Parks.

—(2009a), 'The Birdport Prize: Short Story Report', www.bridportprize.org.uk/content/2009-winners [accessed 8 September 2012].

—(2010), 'The Art of Elsewhere'. Edinburgh International Book Festival. Available at: www.edbookfest.co.uk/new-writing/the-art-of-elsewhere.

Smith, D. (2007), 'Deleuze and the Question of Desire: Toward an Immanent Theory of Ethics', *Parrhesia* 2, 66–78.

Thrift, N. (2004), 'Intensities of Feeling: Towards a Spatial Politics of Affect'. *Geografiska Annaler* 86 (1), 57–78.

Chapter Two: Simile and Similarity in Ali Smith's *Like*, Ian Blyth

Boswell, J. (1949), *The Life of Samuel Johnson, LLD*. 2 vols. London: Dent.

Cixous, H. (1986), 'Sorties: Out and Out: Attacks/Ways Out/Forays', in *The Newly Born Woman*, H. Cixous and C. Clément, B. Wing (trans.). Minneapolis: University of Minnesota Press, 63–132.

—(1990), *Reading with Clarice Lispector*, V. A. Conley (ed. and trans.). Minneapolis: University of Minnesota Press.

—(1991), *Readings: The Poetics of Blanchot, Joyce, Kafka, Kleist, Lispector, and Tsvetayeva*, V. A. Conley (ed. and trans.). Minneapolis: University of Minnesota Press.

Eliot, T. S. (1959), *Four Quartets*. London: Faber and Faber.

Hogg, J. (2002 [1824]), *The Private Memoirs and Confessions of a Justified Sinner*, P. D. Garside (ed.). Edinburgh: Edinburgh University Press.

Jordan, J. (1999), 'Dropped Stitches', *London Review of Books* 21 (3) (1 July), 33.

Lispector, C. (1989), *The Stream of Life*, E. Lowe and E. Fitz (trans.). Minneapolis: University of Minnesota Press.

Smith, A. (1997), *Like*. London: Virago.

—(2001), *Hotel World*. London: Hamish Hamilton.

—(2003), 'May', in *The Whole Story and Other Stories*. London: Hamish Hamilton, 53–69.

—(2005), *The Accidental*. London: Hamish Hamilton.

—(2008), 'The Second Person', in *The First Person and Other Stories*. London: Hamish Hamilton, 119–34.

Swift, J. (2005), *Gulliver's Travels*, C. Rawson (ed.). Oxford: Oxford University Press.

Woolf, V. (1929), *A Room of One's Own*. London: Hogarth Press.

—(1931), *The Waves*. London: Hogarth Press.

Yeats, W. B. (1966), *Selected Plays*, A. N. Jeffares (ed.). London: Macmillan.

Chapter Three: **Narrating Remainders: Spectral Presences in Ali Smith's Fictions,** Stephen Levin

Adorno, T. (2006), *Minima Moralia: Reflections from Damaged Life.* London: Verso.

Anderson, B. (1983), *Imagined Communities: Reflections on the Origin and Spread of Nationalism.* London, Verso.

—(1998), *The Spectre of Comparisons: Nationalism, Southeast Asia and the World.* London: Verso.

Augé, M. (2000 [1995]), *Non-Places: Introduction to an Anthropology of Supermodernity.* London and New York: Verso.

Baucom, I. (2001), 'Globalit, Inc.: Or, the Cultural Logic of Global Literary Studies', *PMLA* 116, 158–72.

Benjamin, W. (2003), 'On the Concept of History', in *Walter Benjamin, Selected Writings, Volume 4, 1938–1940,* H. Eiland and M. W. Jennings (eds). Cambridge, MA: Belknap Press of Harvard University Press.

Borradori, G. (2003), *Philosophy in a Time of Terror: Dialogues with Jurgen Habermans and Jacques Derrida.* Chicago, IL: University of Chicago Press.

Derrida, J. (1987), *The Post Card: From Socrates to Freud and Beyond,* A. Bass (trans.). Chicago, IL: University of Chicago Press.

—(1994), *Specters of Marx: The State of the Debt, the Work of Mourning, and the New International,* P. Kamuf (trans.). New York and London: Routledge.

— (1997), *Of Grammatology,* G. C. Spivak (trans.). Baltimore, MD: Johns Hopkins University Press.

Felman, S. and Laub, D. (1992), *Testimony: Crises of Witnessing in Literature, Psychoanalysis, and History.* New York: Routledge.

France, L. (2005), 'Interview with Ali Smith'. *The Observer.* Observer Review section, 21 May, 15.

Freud, S. (1933), *New Introductory Lectures on Psychoanalysis,* Strachey, J. (ed.). Reprint, New York: Norton, 1965.

Germanà, M. (2009), 'Embodying the Spectral Self: The Ghost Motif in Scottish Women's Writing', *The Bottle Imp* 6, 1–2.

Greenblatt, S. (1988), *Shakespearean Negotiations.* Berkeley: University of California Press.

Jameson, F. (2007), *Late Marxism: Adorno, Or the Persistence of the Dialectic.* London: Verso.

—(2008), 'Marx's Purloined Letter', in *Ghostly Demarcations: A Symposium on Jacques Derrida's Specters of Marx,* M. Sprinker (ed.). London: Verso, 26–67.

Marx, K. (1972), *The Marx-Engels Reader,* K. Tucker (ed.). New York: W. W. Norton.

McGuire, M. (2009), *Contemporary Scottish Literature.* New York: Palgrave Macmillan.

Richter, G. (2007), *Thought-Images: Frankfurt School Writers' Reflections from Damaged Life.* Palo Alto: Stanford University Press.

Smith, A. (1998 [1997]), *Free Love and Other Stories.* London: Virago.

—(2001), *Hotel World.* New York: Anchor Books.

—(2003), *The Whole Story and Other Stories*. New York: Anchor.
—(2005), *The Accidental*. New York: Anchor Books.
—(2009 [2008]), *The First Person and Other Stories*. London: Penguin.
Toíbín, C. (ed.) (2001), *The Penguin Book of Irish Fiction*. London: Penguin.

Chapter Four: **Ali Smith and the Philosophy of Grammar,** Mark Currie

Currie, M. (2013), *The Unexpected: Narrative Temporality and the Philosophy of Surprise*. Edinburgh: Edinburgh University Press.
Derrida, J. (1992), 'The Law of Genre', in *Acts of Literature*, D. Attridge (ed). London and New York: Routledge.
—(2002), 'Typewriter Ribbon: Limited Ink (2)', in *Without Alibi*, P. Kamuf (ed. and trans.). Stanford, CA: Stanford University Press.
—(2007) *Psyche: Inventions of the Other*, Vol. 1, P. Kamuf and E. Rottenberg (eds). Stanford, CA: Stanford University Press.
Hardy, T. (1992), *Tess of the D'Urbervilles*. London: Wordsworth.
Hartley, L. P. (2004 [1953]), *The Go-Between*. London and New York: Penguin.
Smith, A. (2001), *Hotel World*. London: Penguin.
—(2005), *The Accidental*. London and New York: Penguin.
—(2011), *There but for the*. London: Hamish Hamilton.
—(2012), *Artful*. London and New York: Hamish Hamilton.
Spark, M. (1974 [1970]), *The Driver's Seat*. Harmondsworth: Penguin.

Chapter Five: **Queer Metamorphoses: *Girl meets boy* and the Futures of Queer Fiction,** Kaye Mitchell

Adcock, F. (1994), 'Iphis and Ianthe', in *After Ovid: New Metamorphoses*, M. Hofmann and J. Lasdun (eds). New York: Farrar, Straus and Giroux, 219–21.
Ahmed, S. (2006), *Queer Phenomenology*. Durham, NC: Duke University Press.
—(2010), *The Promise of Happiness*. Durham, NC: Duke University Press.
Bradford, R. (2007), *The Novel Now*. Oxford: Blackwell.
Butler, J. (1990), *Gender Trouble*. London: Routledge.
—(1991), 'Imitation and Gender Insubordination', in *Inside/Out: Lesbian Theories, Gay Theories*, D. Fuss (ed.). London: Routledge, 13–31.
—(1993), *Bodies That Matter*. London: Routledge.
—(2004), *Undoing Gender*. London: Routledge.
Carter, A. (1979), *The Sadeian Woman*. New York: Pantheon.
Cvetkovich, A. (2003), *An Archive of Feelings*. Durham, NC: Duke University Press.
Davies, S. (2007), 'Girl meets boy, by Ali Smith' [review]. *The Independent*, Friday, 23 November. Available at: www.independent.co.uk/artsentertainment/books/reviews/article3185266.ece.

Dinshaw, C. (2009), 'Temporalities', in *Oxford Twenty-First Century Approaches to Literature: Middle English*, P. Strohm (ed.). Oxford: Oxford University Press, 107–23.

Doan, L. (ed.) (1994), *The Lesbian Postmodern*. New York: Columbia University Press.

Doan, L. and S. Waters (2000), 'Making Up Lost Time: Contemporary Lesbian Writing and the Invention of History', in *Territories of Desire in Queer Culture: Refiguring Contemporary Boundaries*, D. Alderson and L. Anderson (eds). Manchester: Manchester University Press, 12–28.

Feldherr, A. (2002), 'Metamorphosis in the *Metamorphoses*', in *Cambridge Companion to Ovid*, P. Hardie (ed.). Cambridge: Cambridge University Press, 163–79.

Fitzgerald, M. (2008), 'Girl meets boy'. *The Observer*, 28 September.

Freeman, E. (2010), *Time Binds: Queer Temporalities, Queer Histories*. Durham, NC: Duke University Press.

Griffin, G. (1993a), *Heavenly Love? Lesbian Images in Twentieth-Century Women's Writing*. Manchester: Manchester University Press.

—(1993b) (ed.), *Outwrite*. London: Pluto Press.

Gunn, K. (2007), 'Here's to Second Chances'. *The Observer*, 28 October. Available at: www.guardian.co.uk/books/2007/oct/28/fiction.alismith.

Halberstam, J. (2005), *In a Queer Time and Place*. New York: New York University Press.

Hallett, J. P. (1997), 'Female Homoeroticism and the Denial of Roman Reality in Latin Literature', in *Roman Sexualities*, J. P. Hallett and M. B. Skinner (eds). Princeton, NJ: Princeton University Press, 255–73.

Halperin, D. M. (1995), *Saint Foucault*. Oxford: Oxford University Press.

Halperin, D. M. and V. Traub (eds) (2009), *Gay Shame*. Chicago, IL: Chicago University Press.

Hardie, P. (2002), 'Introduction', in *Cambridge Companion to Ovid*, P. Hardie (ed.). Cambridge: Cambridge University Press, 1–10.

Hofmann, M. and Lasdun J. (eds) (2009), *After Ovid: New Metamorphoses*. New York: Farrar, Straus and Giroux.

Jackson, R. (1981), *Fantasy: The Literature of Subversion*. London: Routledge.

Jagose, A. (1996), *Queer Theory: An Introduction*. New York: New York University Press.

Love, H. (2007), *Feeling Backward: Loss and the Politics of Queer History*. Cambridge, MA: Harvard University Press.

Makowski, J. (1996), 'Bisexual Orpheus: Pederasty and Parody in Ovid', *Classical Journal* 92 (1), 25–38.

Massey, I. (1976), *The Gaping Pig: Literature and Metamorphosis*. Berkeley: University of California Press.

McHale, B. (1987), *Postmodernist Fiction*. London: Routledge.

Mitchell, K. (2008), 'Unintelligible Subjects: Making Sense of Gender, Sexuality and Subjectivity after Butler', *Subjectivity* 25, 413–31.

Muñoz, J. E. (2009), *Cruising Utopia*. New York: New York University Press.

Munt, S. R. (ed.) (1992), *New Lesbian Criticism*. Brighton: Harvester Wheatsheaf.

—(1994), *Murder by the Book*. London: Routledge.

—(2007), *Queer Attachments: The Cultural Politics of Shame*. Aldershot: Ashgate.

Nims, J. F. (ed.) (2000), *Ovid's Metamorphoses*, Arthur Golding (trans. 1567). Philadelphia, PA: Paul Dry Books.

Osborne, P. and L. Segal (1994), 'Gender as Performance: An Interview with Judith Butler', *Radical Philosophy* 67, 32–9.

Palmer, P. (1993), *Contemporary Lesbian Writing*. Open University Press.

—(1999), *Lesbian Gothic*. London: Continuum.

Pintabone, D. (2002), 'Ovid's Iphis and Ianthe: When Girls Won't Be Girls', in *Among Women*, N. Sorkin Rabinowitz and L. Auanger (eds). Austin: University of Texas Press, 256–85.

Robinson, D. M. (2006), *Closeted Writing and Lesbian and Gay Literature*. Aldershot: Ashgate.

Roof, J. (1991), *A Lure of Knowledge: Lesbian Sexuality and Theory*. New York: Columbia University Press.

Sedgwick, E. Kosofsky. (1994), *Tendencies*. London: Routledge.

Smith, A. (2007), *Girl meets boy*. Edinburgh: Canongate.

Taylor, C. (2007), 'A Change for the Better'. *The Independent*, 28 October. Available at: www.independent.co.uk/arts-entertainment/books/reviews/girl-meets-boy-by-ali-smith-397883.html.

Traub, V. (2002), *The Renaissance of Lesbianism in Early Modern England*. Cambridge: Cambridge University Press.

Walker Bynum, C. (2005), *Metamorphosis and Identity*. New York: Zone Books.

Warner, M. (2002), *Fantastic Metamorphoses, Other Worlds*. Oxford: Oxford University Press.

Wiegman, R. (1994), 'Introduction: Mapping the Lesbian Postmodern', in *The Lesbian Postmodern*, L. Doan (ed.). New York: Columbia University Press, 1–20.

Chapter Six: **Narrating Intrusion: Deceptive Storytelling and Frustrated Desires in *The Accidental* and *There but for the*,** Ulrike Tancke

Churchwell, S. (2011), '*There but for the*, by Ali Smith – Review.' *The Observer*, 5 June. Available at: www.guardian.co.uk/books/2011/jun/05/there-but-for-the-review/print.

Germanà, M. (2010), *Scottish Women's Gothic and Fantastic Writing: Fiction Since 1978*. Edinburgh: Edinburgh University Press.

Gray, J. (2002), *Straw Dogs: Thoughts on Humans and Other Animals*. London: Granta.

Hesford, W. S. (2006), 'Staging Terror', *TDR: The Drama Review* 50 (3), 29–41.

Müller-Wood, A. and J. Carter Wood (2010), 'How Is Culture Biological? Violence: Real and Imagined', *Politics and Culture: Symposium on the Question 'How Is Culture Biological?' – Six Essays and Discussions*. 29 April. Available at: www.politicsandculture.org/2010/04/29/ symposium-on-the-question-how-is-culture-

biological-six-essays-with-discussions-essay-2-by-anja-mueller-wood-and-
john-carter-wood-how-is-culture-biological-violence-real-and-imagined/.

Pols, E. (1992), *Radical Realism: Direct Knowing in Science and Philosophy*. Ithaca
and London: Cornell University Press.

Siegel, L. (2005), 'The Imagination of Disaster'. *The Nation*, 24 March. Available
at: www.the nation.com/article/imagination-disaster.

Smith, A. (2006 [2005]), *The Accidental*. London: Penguin.

—(2011), *There but for the*. London: Hamish Hamilton.

Tew, P. (2007), *The Contemporary British Novel*, 2nd edn. London: Continuum.

Weiss, G. (1999), 'The Abject Borders of the Body Image', in *Perspectives on
Embodiment: The Intersections of Nature and Culture*, G. Weiss and H. F. Haber
(eds). New York and London: Routledge, 41–59.

Whitehead, A. (2004), *Trauma Fiction*. Edinburgh: Edinburgh University Press.

Chapter Seven: 'The Space That Wrecks Our Abode': The Stranger in Ali Smith's *Hotel World* and *The Accidental*, Patrick O'Donnell

Agamben, G. (1993), *Infancy and History: Essays on the Destruction of Experience*,
L. Heron (trans.). New York: Verso.

Appiah, A. (2006), *Cosmopolitanism: Ethics in a World of Strangers*. New York:
W. W. Norton.

Bennett, A. (2012), *Afterlife and Narrative in Contemporary Fiction*. New York:
Palgrave Macmillan.

Berger, J. (2001), *The Shape of a Pocket*. New York: Vintage.

Derrida, J. (2004 [1993]), *Spectres of Marx: The State of Debt, the Work of Mourning,
& the New International*, P. Kamuf (trans.). New York: Routledge.

Horton, E. (2012), '"Everything You Ever Dreamed": Post-9/11 Trauma and
Fantasy in Ali Smith's *The Accidental*', *MFS: Modern Fiction Studies*, 58 (3),
637–54.

Jencks, C. (1997), *The Architecture of the Jumping Universe*, rev. edn. Chichester,
West Sussex: John Wiley & Sons.

Kristeva, J. (1994), *Strangers to Ourselves*, Leon S. Roudiez (trans.). New York:
Columbia University Press.

Miller, J. H. (1990), *Versions of Pygmalion*. Cambridge, MA: Harvard University
Press.

Smith, A. (2002 [2001]), *Hotel World*. New York: Random House.

—(2007 [2005]), *The Accidental*. New York: Random House.

Chapter Eight: Idiosyncrasy and Currency: Ali Smith and the Contemporary Canon, Dominic Head

Bergonzi, B. (1990), *Exploding English: Criticism, Theory, Culture*. Oxford:
Clarendon Press.

Birne, E. (2005), 'The Day Starts Now', *London Review of Books* 27 (12) (23 June), 30–1. Available at: www.lrb.co.uk/v27/n12/eleanor-birne/the-day-starts-now.

Churchwell, S. (2011), *'There but for the*, by Ali Smith – Review'. *The Observer*, 5 June. Available at: www.guardian.co.uk/books/2011/jun/05/there-but-for-the-review/print.

Foden, G. (2001), 'Check in, Drop Out'. *The Guardian*, 14 April. Available at: www.guardian.co.uk/books/2001/apr/14/fiction.alismith/print.

Gapper, F. (2003), 'Ali Smith', *Mslexia* 18, July/August/September. Available at: www.mslexia.co.uk/magazine/interviews/interview_18.php.

Hughes-Hallett, L. (2005), 'Angel in the Architecture'. *The Sunday Times*, 'Culture', 22 May, 53.

McEwan, I. (1997), *Enduring Love*. London: Jonathan Cape.

—(2005), *Saturday*. London: Jonathan Cape.

McGrath, C. (2011), 'After Hiding, He Becomes a Celebrity'. *The New York Times*, 18 October. Available at: www.nytimes.com/2011/10/19/books/there-but-for-the-by-ali-smith-review.html?_r=1&pagewanted=print.

Murdoch, I. (1990 [1961]), 'Against Dryness: A Polemical Sketch', in *The Novel Today: Contemporary Writers on Modern Fiction*, Malcolm Bradbury (ed.). London: Fontana, 15–24.

Ratcliffe, S. (2005), 'Life in Sonnet Form'. *Times Literary Supplement*, 5329, 20 May, 19–20.

Smith, A. (2001), 'Creative Writing Workshy', in *The Creative Writing Coursebook*, J. Bell and P. Magrs (eds). London: Macmillan, 24–8.

—(2002 [2001]), *Hotel World*. London: Penguin.

—(2005), *The Accidental*. London: Hamish Hamilton.

—(2011), *There but for the*. London: Hamish Hamilton.

Tait, T. (2012), 'The Absolute End', *London Review of Books*, 34 (2), 26 January, 32–3.

Upchurch, M. (2002), 'The Ghost in the Minibar'. *The New York Times*, 3 February. Available at: www.nytimes.com/2002/02/03/books/the-ghost-in-the-minibar.html.

Chapter Nine: 'The Uncanny Can Happen': Desire and Belief in *The Seer*, Monica Germanà

Ahmed, S. (2004), *The Cultural Politics of Emotion*. Edinburgh: Edinburgh University Press.

Augé, M. (1995 [1992]), *Non-Places: Introduction to an Anthropology of Supermodernity*, J. Howe (trans.). London: Verso.

Azari, E. (2008), *Lacan and the Destiny of Literature*. London: Continuum.

Belsey, C. (1994), *Desire: Love Stories in Western Culture*. Oxford: Blackwell.

Berger, J. (2008 [1972]), *Ways of Seeing*. London: Penguin.

Bersani, L. (1984), *A Future for Astyanax*. New York: Columbia University Press.

Goodheart, E. (1991), *Desire and Its Discontents*. New York: Columbia University Press.

Holdsworth, N. (2003), 'Travelling across Borders: Re-Imagining the Nation and Nationalism in Contemporary Scottish Theatre', *Contemporary Theatre Review* 13 (2), 25–39.

Irvine, W. B. (2006), *On Desire: Why We Want What We Want*. Oxford: Oxford University Press.

Kristeva, J. (2000), *The Sense and Non-Sense of Revolt: The Powers and Limits of Psychoanalysis*, Vol. I, J. Herman (trans.). New York: Columbia University Press.

Lacan, J. (1977), 'The Direction of the Treatment and the Principles of Its Power', *Écrits: A Selection*, A. Sheridan (trans.). London: Routledge, 226–80.

Lucretius (60 BC), *On the Nature of the Universe*, R. Melville (trans.). Oxford: Oxford University Press. Repr. 1997.

Matthews, G. (2012), *Ethics and Desire in the Wake of Postmodernism: Contemporary Satire*. London: Continuum.

Smith, A. (1995), *Free Love and Other Stories*. London: Virago.

—(1998 [1997]), *Like*. London: Virago.

—(2006), *The Seer*. London: Faber.

Various Artists (2007), *Ballads of The Book*. Chemikal Underground Records.

Wright, E. (1999), *Speaking Desires Can Be Dangerous: The Poetics of the Unconscious*. Cambridge: Polity.

Afterword: Sidekick Doubling the Tune: Writing Ali Smith in Norwegian, Merete Alfsen

Smith, A. (2001), *Hotel World*. London: Hamish Hamilton.

—(2004), *Hotell Verden (Hotel World)*. M. Alfsen (trans.). Oslo: M. Pax Forlag A/S.

—(2005), *The Accidental*. London: Hamish Hamilton.

—(2005), *Hele historien og andre historier (The Whole Story and Other Stories)*, M. Alfsen (trans.). Oslo: Pax Forlag A/S.

—(2006), *Levende bilder (The Accidental)*, M. Alfsen (trans.). Oslo: Pax Forlag A/S.

—(2007), *Girl meets boy*. Edinburgh: Canongate.

—(2007), *Like*, M. Alfsen (trans.). Oslo: Pax Forlag A/S.

—(2008), *The First Person and Other Stories*. London: Penguin.

—(2009a), *Første person og andre historier (The First Person and Other Stories)*, M. Alfsen (trans.). Oslo: Forlaget Oktober.

—(2009b), *Jente møter gutt (Girl meets boy)*, M. Alfsen (trans.). Oslo: Cappelen Damm.

—(2011), *There but for the*. London: Hamish Hamilton.

—(2012), *På stedet mil (There but for the)*, M. Alfsen (trans.). Forlaget Oktober, Oslo.

Further Reading

Works by Ali Smith

Novels
(1997), *Like*. London: Virago.

(2001), *Hotel World*. London: Hamish Hamilton.
(2005), *The Accidental*. London: Hamish Hamilton.
(2007), *Girl meets boy*. Edinburgh: Canongate.
(2011), *There but for the*. London: Hamish Hamilton.

Short Stories

(1995), *Free Love and Other Stories*. London: Virago.
(1999), *Other Stories and Other Stories*. London: Penguin.
(2003), *The Whole Story and Other Stories*. London: Penguin.
(2008), *The First Person and Other Stories*. London: Penguin.
(2008), 'Do You Call That a Christmas Present?', *The Independent*, 21 December. Available at: www.independent.co.uk/arts-entertainment/books/features/ali-smith-do-you-call-that-a-christmas-present-1203321.html.
(2009), 'The Definite Article'. London: The Royal Parks.
(2010), 'The Art of Elsewhere'. Edinburgh International Book Festival, 2010. Available at: www.edbookfest.co.uk/new-writing/the-art-of-elsewhere.

Plays

(2000), 'Trace of Arc', *Mythic Women/Real Women: Plays and Performance Pieces by Women*, L. Goodman (ed.). London: Faber.
(2005), *Just*. London: N T Connections.
(2006), *The Seer*. London: Faber.

Other

(2012), *Artful*. London: Penguin.

Editing

(2000), *Brilliant Careers: The Virago Book of 20th Century Fiction*, A. Smith, S. Wood and K. Boddy (eds). London: Virago.
(2002), *Pretext*, Vol. 5, A. Smith and J. Bell (eds). London: Pen and Inc. Press.
(2005), *New Writing 13*, A. Smith and T. Litt (eds). London: Picador, 18 March.
(2006), *The Book Lover*. London: Constable and Robinson Ltd. Repr. NY: Anchor Books, 2008.
(2009), *Let's Call the Whole Thing Off: Love Quarrels from Anton Chekov to ZZ Packer*, K. Boddy, A. Smith and S. Wood (eds). London: Penguin.

Contributor

(1998), *Wild Ways: New Stories About Women on the Road*, Margo Daly and Jill Dawson (eds). London: Sceptre.
(2002), *Matter*, Issue No. 2, A. Smith, J. Galloway, E. A. Markham, M. Faber, L. Money and E. Pedder (eds). London: Ink.
(2003), *Word Jig: New Fiction from Scotland*, M. Faber, A. Smith, A. Greig and M. Carter (eds). New York: Hanging Loose Press.
(2005), *The Mechanics Institute Review 5*, A. Smith, T. Litt, S. Salway and P. Williamson (eds). London: MA Creative Writing.

(2012), *Here,* A. Warner, A. L. Kennedy, A. Gray, Y. Li, A. Smith, W McIllvanney, T. Breslin, A. Fine, M. Syjuco, D. Gilori, K. Campbell and J. Teagle (eds). London: Elsewhere.

(2012), *Road Stories,* M. Morris and D. Robson (eds). London: Faber and Faber.

Introductions and Forwards

(2005), *The Brighton Book,* J. Winterson, A. Smith, N. Lawson, et al. Brighton: Myriad Editions.

(2005), *The Hearing Trumpet,* by L. Carrington. London: Penguin Classics.

(2007), *The Collected Stories of Katherine Mansfield,* by K. Mansfield. London: Penguin.

(2007), *Essays on the Art of A. Carter.* Rev. and updated edn, L. Sage (ed.). London: Virago.

(2007), *Fair Play,* by T. Jansson, T. Teal (trans.). London: Sort of Books.

(2007), *Sunset Song: Scots Quair Series,* Book 1, by L. Grassic Gibbon. London: Penguin.

(2009), *The Comforters,* by M. Spark. London: Virago.

(2009), *A State of Change,* by P. Gilliatt. London: Capuchin Classics.

(2009), *The True Deceiver,* by T. Jansson, T. Teal (trans.). London: Sort of Books.

(2011), *Travelling Light,* by T. Jansson, Thomas Teal (trans.). London: Sort of Books.

(2012), *Wise Children,* by A. Carter. London: Vintage Digital.

(2012), *Margaret Tate: Poems, Stories and Writings,* Sarah Neely (ed.). Manchester: Fyfield Books.

(2012), *Member of the Wedding,* by Carson McCullers. London: Penguin.

Selected Journalism and Other Writing

(1995), 'And Woman Created Woman: Carswell, Shepherd and Muir and the Self-Made Woman'. *Gendering the Nation: Studies in Modern Scottish Literature,* Christopher Whyte (ed.). Edinburgh: Edinburgh University Press, 25–47.

(2009), 'Why Interview Writers? – Ali Smith', *The Scottish Review of Books* 5 (2). Available at: www.scottishreviewofbooks.org/index.php/back-issues/volume-five/volume-five-issue-two/21-why-interview-writers-ali-smith.

(2011), *Loosed in Translation: A Talk on Sebald and Translation.* London: British Centre for Literary Translation, 31 January.

(2011), 'Once upon a Life: Ali Smith'. *The Observer,* 29 May. Available at: www.guardian.co.uk/lifeandstyle/2011/may/29/once-upon-life-ali-smith.

(2012), 'Ali Smith: Style vs. Content?'. *The Guardian,* 18 August. Available at: www.guardian.co.uk/books/2012/aug/18/ali-smith-novelists-approach-art.

(2012), *The Manchester Sermon: Rebegot.* Manchester Literature Festival, 18 October.

Critical Material

Books

Gerbe, K. (2007), *Narrative Techniques in Ali Smith's Like*. Norderstedt, Germany: GRIN Verlag.

Ross, K. (2003), *Ali Smith's 'Hotel World'*. Edinburgh: Read Around Books (Scottish Arts Council).

Book Chapters

Germanà, M. (2010), 'Witches, Demon Lovers and Female Monsters' and 'Ghosts: Dissolving the Boundaries', in M. Germanà, *Scottish Women's Gothic and Fantastic Writing*. Edinburgh: Edinburgh University Press, 60–97 and 134–72.

—(2012), 'Contemporary Fiction', in *The Edinburgh Companion to Scottish Women's Writing*. G. Norquay (ed.). Edinburgh: Edinburgh University Press, 152–62.

Gifford, D. (1997), ' Contemporary Fiction I', in *A History of Scottish Women's Writing*, D. Gifford and D. McMillan (eds). Edinburgh: Edinburgh University Press, 588–9.

Gonda, C. (1995), 'Mapping Scottish/Lesbian/Writing', in *Gendering the Nation: Studies in Modern Scottish Literature*, Christopher Whyte (ed.). Edinburgh: Edinburgh University Press, 1–24.

Horton, E. (2013), 'A Voice without a Name: Gothic Homelessness in Ali Smith's *Hotel World* and Trezza Azzopardi's *Remember Me*', in *Twenty-First Century Fiction: What Happens Now*, Siân Adiseshiah and Rupert Hildyard (eds). London: Palgrave MacMillan, 132–146.

McCulloch, F. (2012), 'Remember You Must Live. Remember You Most Love. Reminder You Must Leave: Passing through Ali Smith's *Hotel World*', in *Cosmopolitanism in Contemporary British Fiction: Imagined Identities*, F. McCulloch (ed.). London: Palgrave MacMillan, 164–84.

Sánchez García, C. (2012), 'Coming to Terms with Postmodern Artificiality', in *Women's Short Fiction from Virginia Woolf to Ali Smith*, L. Lojo Rodríguez (ed.). Oxford: Peter Lang, 111–24.

Tew, P. (2007), 'Traumatological Families: Nadeem Aslam, Ali Smith and Toby Litt', in *The Contemporary British Novel*, 2nd edn, P. Tew (ed.). London: Continuum, 207–15.

Williams, K. (2006), '"A Different Kind of Natural": The Fiction of Jackie Kay and Ali Smith', in *Ethically Speaking: Voice and Values in Modern Scottish Writing*, J. McGonigal and K. Stirling (eds). New York: Rodopi, 157–78.

Young, T. (forthcoming, 2013), 'You-niversal Love: Intimacy and the second person in Ali Smith's short fiction', in *21st-Century British Writing*, A. Venezia and B. Leggett (eds). Canterbury: Gylphi.

Journal Articles

Bailey, J. (2010), '"What a Story It Could Be": Identity and Narrative Strategy in Ali Smith's *Like*'. *Forum* 11. Available at: www.forumjournal.org/site/issue/11/james-bailey. Accessed 13 March 2013.

Doloughan, F. (2010), 'Bottling the Imagination: Writing as Metamorphosis in Ali Smith's *Girl meets boy*', *New Writing: The International Journal for the Practice and Theory of Creative Writing* 7 (3), 241–51.

Eshelman, R. (Fall 2004 / Winter 2005), 'Checking Out of the Epoch: Performatism in Olga Tokarczuk's "The Hotel Capital" vs. Late Postmodernism in Ali Smith's *Hotel World* (With Remarks on Arundhati Roy's *The God of Small Things* and Miloš Urban's *Sevenchurch)*', *Anthropoetics* 10 (2). Available at: www.anthropoetics.ucla.edu/ap1002/transhotel.htm. Accessed 13 March 2013.

Germanà, M. (2003), '"Une Petite Mort": Death, Love and Liminality in the Fiction of Ali Smith', *Ecloga Online Journal* 3 (Autumn). Available at: www.strath.ac.uk/ecloga/archive/2003/ecloga2003contents/. Accessed 13 March 2013.

—(2009), 'Embodying the Spectral Self: The Ghost Motif in Scottish Women's Writing', *The Bottle Imp* 6, 1–2. Available at: www.arts.gla.ac.uk/ScotLit/ASLS/SWE/TBI/TBIIssue6/Germana.html. Accessed 13 March 2013.

Horton, E. (2012), '"Everything You Ever Dreamed": Post-9/11 Trauma and Fantasy in Ali Smith's *The Accidental*'. *MFS: Modern Fiction Studies* 58 (3), 637–54.

López Sánchez, G. (2010), '"Mind the Gap": Powers of Horror and Trauma in Ali Smith's *Hotel World*', *Atlantis: Journal of the Spanish Association of Anglo-American Studies*, 32 (2) (December), 43–56.

Ryle, M. (2009), 'Neo-Pastoral Eco-didactics: Ali Smith's *The Accidental*', *Green Letters: Studies in Eco-Criticism* 10, 8–18.

Smith, E. E. (2010), '"A Democracy of Voice"? Narrating Community in Ali Smith's *Hotel World*', *Contemporary Women's Writing* 4 (2), 81–99.

Reviews

Free Love and Other Stories

Biswell, A. (1995), 'Mr Self and Ms Ms'. *The Times Literary Supplement*, 3 November.

Gifford, D. (1995), 'Inventing Solace and Despair', *Books in Scotland* 55 (Autumn).

Like

Gifford, D. (1997), 'Darker Than Realism', *Books in Scotland* 63 (Autumn).

Greenlaw, L. (1997), 'In the Kate Bush Era'. *The Times Literary Supplement*, 4 July.

The Other Stories and Other Stories

Broughton, T. (1999), 'Acts of Human Kindness'. *The Times Literary Supplement*, 5 March.
Jordan, J. (1999), 'Dropped Stitches', *London Review of Books* 21 (3), 1 July.

Brilliant Careers: The Virago Book of 20th Century Fiction

Vaux, A. (2000), 'Reference'. *The Times Literary Supplement*, 17 March.

Hotel World

Boyd Maunsell, J. (2001), 'Rooms with a Sombre View'. *Evening Standard*, 31 October.
Bushby, H. (2001), 'Ali Smith's Painful Prose'. *BBC News Online*. 12 October.
Foden, G. (2001), 'Check in, Drop Out'. *The Guardian*, 14 April.
Hutchings, V. (2001), 'Recalled to Life'. *The New Statesman*, 21 May, p. 57.
Murphy, B. (2002), 'This Ghost Stories Colorful Quintet Grapples With Life and Death'. *The Los Angeles Times*, 8 February.
Scurr, R. (2001), 'A Ghost with Guests'. *The Times Literary Supplement*, 23 March.
Taylor, C. (2002), '*Hotel World* by Ali Smith'. *Salon*, 21 Feb. Available at: www.salon.com/2002/02/21/smith_18/. Accessed 13 March 2013.
Upchurch, M. (2002), 'Ghost in the Minibar'. *The New York Times*, 3 February.

The Whole Story and Other Stories

Allen, B. (2003), 'Gender-Neutral'. *The Atlantic Monthly*, 4 May. Available at: www.theatlantic.com/past/docs/issues/2004/05/allen.htm.
Cusk, R. (2003), 'The Real and the Arch'. *The Guardian*, 26 April.
Kamine, M. (2004), 'Books in Brief: Fiction and Poetry; Man Walks into a Bookstore'. *The New York Times Book Review*, 21 March.
Hedgecock, A. (2003), 'Far from Simple Tales'. *The Spectator*, 3 May.
Hunt, S. (2004), 'Against the Current'. *The Village Voice*, 16 March.
Jensen, L. (2003), 'Storm Warning; Do Whirlwind Openings and Pyrotechnic Prose Amount to Proper Stories?', *The Independent*. 5 July.
Ratcliffe, S. (2003), 'Arboreal Encounters'. *The Times Literary Supplement*, 25 April.

The Accidental

Birne, E. (2005), 'The Day Starts Now'. *London Review of Books* 27 (12), 23 June.
Caldwell, Gael. (2006), 'Perfect Stranger'. *The Boston Globe*, 22 January.
France, L. (2005), 'Life Stories'. *The Observer*, 22 May.
Hughes-Hallett, L. (2005), 'Angel in the Architecture', *The Sunday Times*, 'Culture', 22 May.

Kakutani, M. (2006), 'There Enters a Stranger and a Family Finds It's Prism'. *The New York Times*, 27 January.

Mukherjee, N. (2005), 'Stranger in Paradise'. *Times*, 21 May.

Poole, S. (2005), '*The Accidental* by Ali Smith'. *The Guardian*, 11 June.

Ratcliffe, S. (2005), 'Life in Sonnet Form'. *Times Literary Supplement*, 5329, 20 May.

Tancke, U. (2010), '*The Accidental*'. *The Literary Encyclopedia*. Available at: www.litencyc.com/php/sworks.php?rec=true&UID=23033. Accessed 13 March 2013.

Turrentine, J. (2006), 'When a Stranger Calls'. *Washington Post*, 26 February.

The Reader

Morton, B. (2006), 'Ali's Cave'. *The Scottish Review of Books* 2 (4).

The Seer

McMillan, J. (2006), 'Soaring Insight into Life at the Fringes of Our Culture'. *The Scotsman*, 10 May.

Mansfield, S. (2006), 'Ali Smith Tale of Drama Classes, Homecomings and Unfashionably Happy Endings'. *The Scotsman*, 26 April.

Girl meets boy

Barnacle, H. (2007), *Sunday Times*, 11 November.

Berman, J. (2007), 'A New Day'. *The Los Angeles Times*, 28 October.

Clark, A. (2007), 'And Thanks to the Goddess Isis'. *The Times Literary Supplement*, 9 November.

Cummins, A. (2008), 'The One about the Nymph'. *The Times Literary Supplement*, 3 October.

Davies, S. (2007), '*Girls Meets Boy*, by Ali Smith'. *The Independent*, 23 November.

Fitzgerald, M. (2008), '*Girl meets boy*'. *The Observer*, 28 September.

Guinness, M. (2007), 'Old Wine in New Skins'. *The Spectator*, 3 November.

Gunn, K. (2007), 'Here's to Second Chances'. *The Observer*, 28 October.

Kelly, S. (2007), 'Sex Is a Hit and Myth Affair'. *Scotland on Sunday*, 11 November.

LeGuin, U. (2007), 'Sigmund and the Blind Seer'. *The Guardian*, 8 December.

Massie, A. (2007), 'Ch-Ch-Ch-Changes'. *The Scotsman*, 27 October.

Pia, C. (2007), 'Ali Smith – Review'. *The List* 589, 1 November.

Seymenliyska, E. (2007), 'Hit and Myth'. *The Telegraph*, 20 October.

Taylor, C. (2007), 'a Change for the Better'. *The Independent on Sunday*, 28 October.

Ward, M. (2008), *The San Francisco Chronicle*, 1 January.

The First Person and Other Stories

Ahmed. F. (2008), '"Nimble Goddess" Sells Us Short'. *The Guardian*, 19 October.

Akbar, A. (2008), '*The First Person and Other Stories*, by Ali Smith'. *The Independent*, 12 June.

Cummins, A. (2008), 'Ali Smith's Serial Storytelling'. *The Times Literary Supplement*, 1 October.

Donaldson, B. (2008), 'Ali Smith – *The First Person and Other Stories*', The List, 614, 2 October.

FitzHerbert, C. (2008), 'Review: *The First Person and Other Stories* by Ali Smith'. *The Telegraph*, 27 September.

Guest, K. (2008), '*The First Person and Other Stories*'. *The Independent*, 3 October.

Molyneux, J. (2009), '"The First Person" by Ali Smith'. *The San Francisco Chronicle*, 4 January.

Paterson, H. (2008), '*The First Person and Other Stories* by Ali Smith – Review'. *The Telegraph*, 28 October.

Reynolds, S. (2009), '"The First Person and Other Stories" by Ali Smith'. *The Los Angeles Times*, 4 January.

Riley, T. (2008), '*The First Person and Other Stories*, by Ali Smith'. *The Independent*, 19 October.

Ross, C. (2009), 'An Ear for Speech', *The Guardian*, 13 June.

Russo, M. (2009), 'Unhappy Together'. *The New York Times Sunday Book Review*, 23 January.

Sethi, A. (2008), 'For Love and Language'. *The New Statesman*, 9 October.

Tayler, C. (2008), 'Are Your Books Good in Bed?', *The Guardian*, 2 October.

There but for the

Ajayi, A. (2011), 'Books of the Year'. *The Times Literary Supplement*, 2 December.

Akbar A. (2011), '*There but for the*, by Ali Smith'. *The Independent*, 10 June.

Churchwell, S. (2011), '*There but for the*, by Ali Smith – Review'. *The Observer*, 5 June.

Daniel, L. (2011), '*There but for the* by Ali Smith: Review'. *The Independent*, 24 May.

Donalson, B. (2011), 'Ali Smith – *There but for the*'. *The List* 681, 23 May.

Frank, J. (2011), '*There but for the*, by Ali Smith'. *The San Francisco Chronicle*, 2 October.

Gordon, E. (2011), 'Dinner with Ali Smith'. *The Times Literary Supplement*, 23 August.

Goring, R. (2011), 'Ali Smith: *There but for the*'. *The Herald*, 13 June.

Lezard, N. (2012), '*There but for the* by Ali Smith – Review'. *The Guardian*, 17 July.

McAlpin, H. (2011), 'Book Review: *There but for the*, by Ali Smith'. *The Washington Post*, 24 September.

McGrath, C. (2011), 'After Hiding, He Becomes a Celebrity'. *The New York Times*, 18 October.

Shriver, L. (2011), 'Room with a Loo'. *Financial Times*, 28/29 May.

Tait, T. (2012), 'The Absolute End', *London Review of Books*, 34 (2), 26 January.

Artful

Dolan, C. (2012), 'Ali Smith: *Artful*'. *The Herald*, 26 October.

Hahn, D. (2012), '*Artful*, by Ali Smith: Tempted and Seduced, and Up for More'. *The Independent*, 28 October.

Lee-Potter, E. (2012), 'Book Review: *Artful* by Ali Smith'. *Daily Express*, 16 November.

Myerson, J. (2012), '*Artful* by Ali Smith – Review'. *The Guardian*, 18 November.

Stokes, E. (2012), 'Second Readings'. *Financial Times*, 17 November.

Interviews and Profiles

Bowditch, G. (2001), 'From the Bucket to the Booker'. *The Sunday Times*, 14 October.

Denes, M. (2003), 'A Babel of Voices'. *The Guardian*, 19 April.

Donaldson, B. (2011), 'Interview: Ali Smith – *There but for the*. *The List*, 9 August.

Eltringham, D. (2011), 'Small Talk: Ali Smith'. *Financial Times*, 4 June.

France, L. (2005), 'Life Stories'. Interview with Ali Smith. *The Observer*. Review Section, 21 May.

Gapper, F. (2003), 'Ali Smith'. *Mslexia* 18, July/August/September. Available at www.mslexia.co.uk/magazine/interviews/interview_18.php. Accessed 13 March 2013.

Hall, J. (2012), 'The Art of Conversation: Ali Smith Interviewed'. *The Quietus*, 18 November.

Higginbotham, E. (2012), 'A Rare Conversation with Ali Smith'. *Cambridge News*, 16 February.

Logan, B. (2007), 'It's Not about Money'. *The Guardian*, 29 March.

Mathieson, K. (2006), 'Listening for the Voices', *Northings: Highlands and Islands Arts Journal.*

Mulligan, J. (2005), 'A Cycle of Baroque Violence', The Collected Interviews of Jim Mulligan. Available at: www.jimmulligan.co.uk/interview/ali-smith-just. Accessed 13 March 2013.

Murray, I. (ed.) (2006), *Scottish Writers Talking* 3. Edinburgh: John Donald.

Naughtie, J. (2006), 'Ali Smith'. *BBC Radio 4* Bookclub Podcast, 7 May. Available at: www.bbc.co.uk/programmes/p00f8m41. Accessed 13 March 2013.

Northings (2011), 'Short Story Writer and Novelist Ali Smith'. *Wording the Image*, 21 May. Available at: www.wordingtheimage.blogspot.co.uk/2011/05/short-story-writer-and-novelist-ali.html. Accessed 13 March 2013.

Sandler, H. (2009), 'Ali Smith – I Like Women's Writing!'. *Diva: Lesbian Magazine*, 14 February.

Smith, C. (2007), 'Ali Smith Interviewed by Caroline Smith'. *Brand Literary Magazine*, 1 (Spring).

Thursfield, A. (2003), 'Ali Smith: Critical Perspective', *Contemporary Writers*. London: British Council. Available at: http://literature.britishcouncil.org/ali-smith. Accessed 13 March 2013.

Wilton, C. (2011), 'Ali Smith Interview'. *The New Zealand Listener*, 19 November. Available at: www.listener.co.nz/culture/books/ali-smith-interview/. Accessed 13 March 2013.

Winterson, J. (2003), 'Ali Smith Interview'. *The Times*, 25 April.

Young, T. (forthcoming), 'Interview with Ali Smith'. *Contemporary Women's Writing*, July 2013.

Index

University of Brighton

C21: Centre for Twenty-First Century Writings

Affiliated with Bloomsbury

*Pioneering approaches to and understandings of
twenty-first century writings*

The first decade of the new millennium witnessed a range of exciting developments in contemporary writings in English. From innovations in recognised forms such as the novel, poem, play and short story to developments in digital writings, creative writings and genres. Alongside these developments, the publishing industry also changed, with technological advances giving rise to the dawn of the eBook and corporate sponsorship igniting debates about the usefulness of literary prizes and festivals. As the first Research Centre dedicated to the study of twenty-first century writings, C21 offers a unique research environment that is a hub for wider networks of research in this emerging field.

For more information visit arts.brighton.ac.uk/research/c21

To find out about the Centre journal *C21 Literature: Journal of
21st-Century Writings*
Visit our blog: c21literature.blogspot.co.uk
Follow us on Twitter: @C21Literature @Bloomsburylit